SOUL
BREATHING

Spiritual Light and the
Art of Self-Mastery

Carrie L'Esperance

Bear & Company
Rochester, Vermont • Toronto, Canada

Bear & Company
One Park Street
Rochester, Vermont 05767
www.BearandCompanyBooks.com

Text stock is SFI certified

Bear & Company is a division of Inner Traditions International

Library of Congress Cataloging-in-Publication Data
Names: L'Esperance, Carrie, 1958- author.
Title: Soul breathing : spiritual light and the art of self-mastery / Carrie L'Esperance.
Description: Rochester, Vermont : Bear & Company, 2016. | Includes bibliographical references and index.
Identifiers: LCCN 2015043291 (print) | LCCN 2016009291 (e-book) | ISBN 9781591432494 (pbk.) | ISBN 9781591432500 (e-book)
Subjects: LCSH: Spirituality. | Spiritual life. | Consciousness—Miscellanea.
Classification: LCC BF1999 .L3383 2016 (print) | LCC BF1999 (e-book) | DDC 204—dc23
LC record available at http://lccn.loc.gov/2015043291

Printed and bound in the United States by Lake Book Manufacturing, Inc.
The text stock is SFI certified. The Sustainable Forestry Initiative® program promotes sustainable forest management.

10 9 8 7 6 5 4 3 2 1

Text design by Virginia Scott Bowman and layout by Priscilla Baker
This book was typeset in Garamond Premier Pro with Trajan Pro, Helvetica Neue, and Legacy Sans used as display typefaces

To send correspondence to the author of this book, mail a first-class letter to the author c/o Inner Traditions • Bear & Company, One Park Street, Rochester, VT 05767, and we will forward the communication, or contact the author directly at **carriesoulbreathing@gmail.com**.

For Amanda and Mikaela . . .
and for the youth of the human race
that will inherit the Earth

✴

With Gratitude

We are all forever indebted to the higher realms of Creation and Light as well as the Spiritual forces of good that valiantly and tirelessly serve to sustain, uplift, and enlighten the denser realms of existence regardless of the deep roots of ignorance, manipulation, myth, and superstition that plague sentient, intelligent life. With thanks to all those who contributed to creating this book, especially my friend Jennifer Clarke, and also the talented group of Souls at Inner Traditions • Bear & Company; thank you for giving authors a platform to help teach others.

Sometimes the most real things in the world are the things we can't see.

CHRIS VAN ALLSBURG,
THE POLAR EXPRESS

✳

Author's Note

It is recommended that this book be enjoyed in the quietude of a natural outdoor setting, away from disruptive electromagnetic currents.

CONTENTS

Figure I.1. Author's drawing of black-eyed Susan

INTRODUCTION

*In his life he shuddered, seeing how much inhumanity
there is in man, how much savage brutality lies hidden
under refined, cultured politeness.*

GOGOL, *THE OVERCOAT*

One fine afternoon, at the age of about twelve, I went out into a
wild field behind our family home with a drawing pencil and a piece
of paper. I sat down and quietly proceeded to draw a good rendition
of a black-eyed Susan that poked its colorful head up amidst the tall
grass (see figure I.1). In that eventful moment I had discovered something about myself. I was gifted with a natural proclivity for drawing. This discovery shocked, delighted, and also frightened me. I
questioned from what source this creative ability had arisen—and why?

I began to wonder how to best serve the creative talents that resided
within me and what my responsibilities to the origin of this creativity
would be. Being a reflective and philosophically minded youth, I felt the
deeper inner wisdom and presence of a creative conscious Light within
my very being as a part of me, and there was no separation between *me*
and *it*. Then—as we all do—I grew into the rigors of living and surviving in a competitive material world, exploring and navigating the cultural conventions that are unrelenting and so pervasive in this realm of
existence. During the course of this exploration I remained perennially
attracted to devoting a great deal of my time and thought to balancing
the challenges of the material, mental, and emotional vistas of life while

1

maintaining the original higher awareness of Spiritual Light in my life . . . and this has not been an easy task.

Exploring the various books devoted to religion, I felt that these were not all encompassing—and for me, many of the prevalent religious treatises lacked true spirituality. True spirituality would include treating all sentient life with equality and reverence and honoring the Earth and the environment in which we live. It seemed as though there was no theological book on Earth that answered the perplexing questions or offered a true understanding of that which humanity has termed God.

Sensitive to the chaos in the world, I witnessed the struggle for basic human rights in the heat of July 1967 as I observed, with great concern, the riots in Detroit, Michigan, near to where I lived as a young child. And then America ran headlong into the threat of nuclear war with Russia and the great struggle for peace during the Vietnam War. I observed that society was rife with the denigration of various races of people, as well as irreverence for women and children. In addition to all of this, I observed environmental degradation and that drug and alcohol addiction served as a societal norm for escape.

In my youth I witnessed the lives of inspiring leaders that symbolized hope in America abruptly terminated as President John F. Kennedy, his brother Robert F. Kennedy, and Martin Luther King Jr. were all brutally assassinated one after the other. The troubling fact that a faction of warlike people promoting darkness, destruction, and war were degrading society and extracting too much from the Earth, rather than demonstrating responsible stewardship, haunted my consciousness to the point where I imagined that the floor would give way beneath my childhood bed.

During this period of time, the Detroit area reverberated with the best music in the world. The harmonic sounds of Berry Gordy's Motown music and many others graced the airwaves and served to sooth the Soul. Great music is—and always will be—a cathartic and creative expression for hope and inspiration. The beneficial effect of harmonious music on the human organism is undeniable. It is not the expansive creative function of the mind, but the linear function of the mind and the dispirited, false ego that has polarized and plagued the true evolution of humanity, causing debilitating setbacks in the personal, social, and worldly arenas of life. Soul Breathing offers a comprehensive understanding that will assist humanity in transmuting the polarized thinking of the dispirited ego. The linear functioning of the distorted ego's propensity to dominate and to sacrifice others for its own gain is witnessed in all areas of human endeavor.

As many people remain dedicated to the search for solutions to the numerous challenges in our world, we also see that people are unceasingly influenced to perceive as reality that which is not reality, rather than consulting the inner voice of the Soul Force that resonates with the intuitive stillness of the heart center. It was disappointing to discover along the way that a relatively small percentage of people are genuinely devoted to cultivating the inner voice that sustains and seeds higher Consciousness. Rather than becoming our own authority by cultivating the deeper wisdom of the inner Spiritual Light that guides human Souls, the majority of people have followed the lead of others who seek to manipulate and hypnotize people into being told who they are, what they should believe, what to do, and how to do it.

One day a dear friend, being a photographer, invited me to participate in a short film that he was making. I was to be one of perhaps a dozen or so people to be interviewed and asked one question: how to live? My response to this inquiry was that we must question, or double think, what is presented to us in society and cultivate creative ways of living through personal insight. When the short film was finished, my photographer friend, John Harding, selected his favorite response, which came from a French gentleman who stated, "No one really *knows* how to live!"

This statement provoked in me an alarming question: Why does no one really know how to live? The idea that this concept was an acceptable cultural condition struck me as being disturbing and quite dangerous. After all, have we not inherited thousands of years of philosophical writings and myriad religious treatises? Why has it taken the human family so long to come to an understanding of the axioms that define our existence? Why have so many centuries passed without implementing a true understanding of the essential knowledge that guides real human development?

We are all immersed in a course of lengthy experience, observation, and introspection. We are also agents of evolution that must strive to understand how to live, how to keep the good alive and honor our connection to life as physical, mental, and spiritual beings living on a finite planet. A proper intelligent perspective for this journey will only be possible through cultivating a synergistic relationship between the material and the spiritual realms of existence. There are those in the world who understand the importance of the spiritual unity in life, and there are those who do not honor life and instead practice irreverence regarding the sacred connection to the multidimensionality of life. There is a long-standing tradition of organized religion in the world, and people are encouraged to focus their attentions on separate religious doctrines—yet this does not necessarily lead the individual to a greater understanding of the multidimensional and higher Self. The looming challenges to physical survival and the leprosy of modern technology leave little time for meaningful contemplation regarding authentic spiritual phenomenon and the multidimensional consciousness that offers the possibility that we may come to *know* what we are actually doing.

Humankind vacillates between the mental polarities of consciousness that influence what we think and the inner spiritual Presence that governs what we know. This perceived duality, or separation, results in an undulating and unrelenting graph of upward and downward spirals of existence. The universal struggle between unity and division, or human will and Natural Law, is unnecessary and is harmonized through aligning one's will with one's inner Light—the Spiritual Teacher within. Here duality no longer exists, as all polarities are meant to complement one another. The polarized intellect is capable of comprehending higher frequencies of Light because the center point, or principal Light of Creation, always dwells within the very cells of that which is created.

There is unity in opposites within the higher dimensions of thought. All great forces are dual in nature. The interplay of polarity is actually required to create life. For example, electricity would be impotent without the polarities of positive and negative forces; the material constructs of animal life, vegetation, and mechanics would be ineffectual without their male and female counterparts. The dual nature of fire both purifies and destroys. The twin beams of the atom, protons and electrons, and the spiral structure of DNA are beautiful examples of the wisdom in the unifying principle of polarity that results in Oneness within all diversity to create life.

When we find our true center of Being, what we are really saying is that we have discovered and accepted this unity. The illusion of separatism from this complementary unity engenders chaos, confusion, and conflict. Yet the deeper problem arises with the individual's capacity to discern what faculties assist one in determining truth from fiction, reality from illusion. This requires cultivating a self-evaluation that is not generally supported in systematic and institutional belief systems. The deep insights that trigger the higher understandings of the mind are as varied and unique as personalities are varied and unique. The advanced spiritual masters throughout history have all advocated for the important guardianship of one's own mind. The phenomenon of mind and consciousness is a formidable power directly related to our quality of life.

In the year 1999 I traveled to Delhi, India, with a friend. Our visit resulted in a very touching and powerful experience. I was moved to tears while visiting the humble museum that was lovingly dedicated to the life of the great spiritual leader of India—Mahatma Gandhi, one of the most successful statesmen of our time. Left upon his death as his entire worldly estate were two rice bowls, a spoon, two pairs of sandals, his copy of the Bhagavad Gita, his spectacles, and an old-fashioned turnip watch. Gandhi studied the subject of nonviolence for twenty years before he began his work as a deep student of peace. He recognized the Spiritual Light in all human beings and became a person of high spiritual understanding. He aligned his life with *satyagraha,* or truth force, and practiced the disciplined application of nonviolent resistance to evil. Gandhi's example demonstrates that the true fruits of successful living are not rooted in the material. Rather, the measure of real success is derived from the joy of cultivating spiritual growth and through developing one's mind in proper relationship to the higher Principle that guides us toward a divine pattern of living. Our natural enthusiasm and joy for life is sustained through the Spiritual Light that shines within the mind of the Soul.

It was during a taped interview in 1998, while in Chicago on my first book tour for *The Ancient Cookfire* (the first edition of what is now *The Seasonal Detox Diet*), that I had an epiphany that triggered an expanded understanding of the reality of my life. I realized that my body and my mind functioned as mediums that bridged the world of Spiritual Light with the world of the material human intellect. The work that I was doing seemed to come through me from a higher source, as though both the teacher and the pupil resided within the same individual as one. I seemed to be on a guided mission and a learning process that required a deep trust in this perceived higher Source. It was as though my body and my mind were substructures that received the deeper multidimensional vibratory frequencies of Light that support the evolution of life. This realization served as a catalyst in my quest to further understand and support the ethereal frequencies of Light and the Intelligence of the Soul that guides humankind toward a higher purpose and destiny in life.

As people strive for balance and direction in an unbalanced world, it becomes increasingly important that Soul Breathing not be overlooked, undervalued, or misunderstood. This book offers a convincing body of evidence and wisdom substantiating that the underlying issue of our planetary crisis is an imbalance between understanding how the physical and the spiritual realms of existence work together as one. The information herein represents the culmination of a lifetime dedicated to exploring this inspiration. The purpose of this book is to reveal, share, and acknowledge the deeper spiritual heritage that underlies real human strength. The spiritual heritage of Soul Breathing is supported through many forms of experience, intention, and cultivation. It is this spiritual heritage that we must concentrate upon now . . . more so than ever before.

THE TIMELESS AND
THE SACRED

*The spiritual is not a thing, but the formless force that
manifests its existence through the form of matter.*

I CHING

It is the timeless and the sacred in each of us that compels us to seek
a deeper understanding of the mystery of ourselves. It is from the urge
toward a meaningful direction in life that causes the inquisitive child,
adolescent, and adult to search the libraries for the teachings that will
truly satisfy life's perplexities and unanswered questions.

It is inexplicably felt, it is deeply known; it is not only all around us,
it is within us, although we see it not. It transcends definition, and yet
it is the substance of all spiritual and material experience. The timeless
and the sacred essence of the Spiritual Light within us is the motivating
factor for religion, which varies greatly from one culture to another and
from one land to another. Yet the true intrinsic relationship underlying
all authentic theological practices and devotional rituals is the same. It
honors and represents our bond and our connection with all sentient
life. This connection is alive and present in each moment and lives at the
very center of Intelligence. The evidence of this intelligent Light is manifest in all living things as well as experiences within the deeper movement of our lives. The purpose of this Presence is to align all sentient

beings with the natural currents that move life and to guide each one of us toward a greater purpose within existence. The omnipresent universal Spiritual Light that emanates from life represents a way of communication, recognition, association, and bond with the ephemeral essence of Creation. It is the motivating force that creates life.

The I Ching offers the following fascinating insight: "The intertwinement of matter and spirit is represented by a process of slow organic growth through evolvement of the conscious awareness in a physical body. If there is a purely physical body, there must also be a spiritual body. There cannot be a material body without the energy frequencies that allow for material existence."

There is a large enough body of metaphysical evidence concerning the human family's spiritual legacy that the unseen realms have been proven beyond doubt. The old saying, "What came first—the chicken or the egg?" is a trick question that can only be answered by recognizing that it is not one or the other. Before the chicken or the egg can exist, the whole process of creation must first come into the blueprint of existence through the principle of Mind substance. The chicken then becomes a self-perpetuating entity with the ability to reproduce itself. The very last public statement of the evolutionist Charles Darwin was, "Beyond this which we have built up still remains Principle, which is a mystery to us. There is no effect without a cause and it is impossible to understand the effect without consideration of the cause." Darwin's statement implies that we must eventually come to the understanding that cause must always be the motivating force within effect, for the effect could not propel itself. The underlying meaning of Darwin's statement implies that life does not appear by accident. In esoteric terms, the motivating factor, or cause, that Darwin referred to describes a spiritual essence of Light and power—the ethereal and invisible levels of energy. This is the same concept that Sir Isaac Newton brought forth as the Law of Unification between the celestial and the terrestrial. It was Sir Isaac Newton who discovered that white light divides into the colors of the rainbow when reflected through a crystal prism. All sentient life is imbued with varying qualities of light. The Light of Creation is supercharged with pulsating electrons of feeling awareness or conscious presence that originated in the enigmatic mysteries of Creation.

Electromagnetism produced by electricity creates the magnetic and animating force of the electron—a particle with a negative electrical charge. All of life is imbued with an electric, and therefore magnetic, potential. The omniscient quality of the electron forms the backdrop for creative expression and catalyzes the condensation process of thought into matter. The unique frequency in the atom's nucleus and the electrons vibrating around it determines the form the energy will take on. The higher sciences of Light and Creation employ a step-down process that must be implemented for material worlds to exist and evolve. All sentient life is unified through the spherical domain of the electron. The frequency of the electron permeates the very core of the atom and oscillates between particle and wave shifts that act as the electrochemical model for the expansion of consciousness and matter . . . Consciousness (Spirit) and matter (body) that is mainly composed of Light.

The atom is imbued with the intelligence of the positive electrical charge of the proton and the negative charge of the electron regardless of the fact that it is composed mostly of space. This is because the true essence of space in the atom exists as a multidimensional unit of consciousness, or Mind. Every atom pulsates from the center point of these twin beams of creation. This is the important key to understanding the unifying principle within all diversity. The physical body is a sacred instrument that expresses this Spiritual Unifying Principle as an extension that serves the diversity of life. When we separate ourselves from the reality of this unity, the physical form becomes a limited vehicle that is prone to the illusions of the small, enslaved mind and the false ego.

The Spiritual Light of Unity is a frequency of unlimited permanence, and it is our ultimate connection to an enlarged and expansive quality of Mind, regardless of whether one is alive in a material realm or alive in a spiritual realm. Consciousness is what endures beyond the body. The British biologist Rupert Sheldrake proposed that the morphogenetic field underlying the Universe is consciousness. The invisible spiritual consciousness of the human Soul attempts to gently guide the visible physical form and the personality that is attached to the spiritual essence—yet the material desires and the requirements of survival usually receive more attention, and the subtle wisdom of the Soul is too often left uncultivated and undernourished.

Nevertheless . . . the most important essence of life will always be the timeless and sacred energies of Light that seed life. In the higher realms, the all-prevailing master vibration of Light prevents the aging of the elements. This timeless and sacred Light of the Soul's essence is rooted in the divine origin of Universal Law. The deeper wisdoms and truths are inherent within the human mind and are revealed through experiencing the inner voice of the Soul, or Inner Teacher. This is the experiential awakening of the individual to the higher knowledge that supports life. It is this spiritual heritage of inner Light that inspires the individual to engage in exploring the mysteries of the Self.

In childhood, we are naturally connected to the deeper Presence of the inner voice, and this cherished experience infuses life with meaning and enthusiasm. Children express their inner genius when they are not conditioned with traditions of limitation pressed upon them by cultural status quos and the heedless hegemony of institutions. As the child grows, the child's education is given over to the management of those who influence the greater masses of society and a world that does not acknowledge or nurture the deep inner radiance of the Soul. Eventually, the child may become so smothered by high-handed outside influences that the original spiritual genius of the Soul can barely be distinguished. This bewildering experience is a form of spiritual strangulation that leads to a suppression and estrangement from the natural harmonic laws, as well as an imbalance between the inner and outer realms of existence.

Unless we cultivate a balance between our inner spiritual nature and our outer physical nature, we stumble through life in confusion and without a great deal of meaning, purpose, and direction. Without the ability to understand and express our deeper spiritual reality, physical life becomes a form of bondage that is confining and restrains the creative consciousness from a greater fulfillment of itself.

The human child is a multidimensional being of Light that will ideally grow to become more refined and fruitful with time. Miraculous possibilities abound when a child is properly educated and nurtured. Conversely, the body and mind are prone to excess in many ways, unless there is real guidance in the early and ongoing periods of unfolding. The sensitive child intuitively knows that there is something miraculous residing within the self, and the child begins to understand this . . . but there is still no guarantee that the child will not become entangled by the deep and pervasive roots of ignorance that distort matters that concern the multidimensional realms of existence.

Regardless of the propensity to maintain one's spiritual life through reliance on tradition, myth, and religion, no one can proclaim to know exactly what the enigmas that are termed God, Creation, Spirit, and Soul really are. Perhaps this is because the answer lies right within us as a Mind Principle. The truth is we all can, and we all do, experience glimpses that give rise to revelations of the higher realms of Mind Principle that define the Divine Laws of Existence. These glimpses allow us to realize that there is a great love that is bestowed through the presence of Light within us and around us. Without this Light of love nothing can exist—for it is genuine love that is responsible for the eternal frequency that supports existence. With this understanding, we learn to value the great perfection and diversity of life by cultivating the reverence that is due the miracle of existence. It is a sacred Light that abides within every moment and every breath, as we rediscover the beauty of the Natural Laws that sustain us.

The material world, when broken down to atomic structures, is composed mostly of space, and when physical beings break free from the construct of the body, we find that what remains is conscious awareness, or Mind—Mind that exists within space. Anyone who has ever had an out-of-body experience knows what John J. Falone speaks of in his extraordinary book, *The Genius Frequency,* where he states: "The true nature of the atom is Mind and its substance is that of Light. Thought creates Light. Light creates conscious awareness; therefore conscious awareness is Light. Thought creates form, the material worlds are form; therefore, material worlds and consciousness are Light. This is the key to understanding the Universal Center Point connecting every atom to every other atom in creation. These axioms are the foundation upon which all apparent differences are unified in God/Mind. It is a question of comprehending higher frequency dimensions while using the lower frequency, third-dimensional consciousness of the brain. The ether of space provides the medium through which the higher frequencies of Light and thought may move and have its being. The function of thought in its pure form of God/Mind remains an unfathomable mystery."

Science has also concluded that material existence cannot be explained on a purely material or mechanistic level and that the unseen forces of Mind and space must now be woven into a more balanced understanding of existence. The advanced masters have always taught that it is the duty of humanity to love and care for their Earth bodies as a home for the spirit of the God/Mind within. When the body is abused, illness and frailty overcome the body and mind, and the living Spirit within the Soul suffers in this unhappy state. The Spirit is comfortable, satisfied, joyful, and loving within its garment of the Soul when we unify the personal mind with the presence of Soul Light. To wallow in perverse carnal indulgences for the sake of merely enjoying the body and satisfying the false ego of the mind is destructive to the body, mind, and Soul.

Energizing our mental connection to our own Soul Light does not happen all by itself; we raise the frequency of our own minds through conscious resonance. Those who possess this capacity and cultivate this ability, give birth to great works upon the Earth as well as in the higher realms of influence. It is not an easy task to raise one's consciousness above the thick gloaming of untruth, chaos, and illusion that permeates the material and the mental realms of time and space. However, it is our responsibility to identify personal destructive behaviors and to understand the ramifications of certain habits in order to transmute these energies into higher reformulations. It is difficult to change the world, it is difficult to change others; but if we as individuals work on understanding the authentic power of mind, the world gains one Light Warrior at a time, and each becomes a star in the clear sky of consciousness. When we become unified in performing this task—the world is transformed.

ADOLESCENCE AND THE ART
OF COMMUNICATION

The younger generations have always relied upon the former generations for proper guidance in a world that appears to be beyond their charge. Youth is idealistic, ambitious, and inquisitive about life while being rushed toward the many distractions of the various eras. The degree to which youthful and curious minds detect the spiritual connection that is inherent within existence will vary. As time to let the mind wander, daydreaming, and leisure give way to the compulsive social networking and virtual worlds of a technologically imbalanced society, and with the culprits of violence, bullying, and emotional trauma that have always affected youth, it becomes more difficult to discern what is truth and what is illusion.

Nevertheless, there has always been a great and sacred yearning . . . and a timeless quest for verification of the formless energies of spiritual support in the surrounding worlds of matter. Eventually, everyone must ask the existential questions: What is the meaning of my life? What am I doing here? Where am I going? There is a profound and simple truth that answers all of these questions—humanity's purpose is to create a culture in which the spiritual and material exist undivided. This requires that we contact the God/Mind that exists within us, think with this Mind, and know ourselves within this reality—rather than wholly relying upon what we think ourselves to be or following what others think we should be. This is what the adage "being born again" really means. The illumination of understanding and following our higher mental faculties is the real meaning of power, or righteousness as in *right-use-ness* in life.

Cultivating higher consciousness through accessing the deeper Presence within requires recognizing that the essence of life is a spiritual force. All sacred life, visible and invisible, is set into motion by spiritual forces, the origin of which is expressed as a perfect idea. The ability to unify the higher frequencies of thought with the lower frequencies of third-dimensional existence is perfected through self-mastery of the body and the mind. When this is the main goal and practice in life, our existential inquiries are answered in a harmonious flow, step-by-step, as the flower of each unique spiritual being unfolds and becomes fruitful.

Our questions and perplexities cannot be answered all at once! Children learn to crawl, walk, and run, step-by-step. How each personal journey evolves depends upon whether we cultivate the ability to align with our own Souls and learn to trust the higher spiritual frequencies that guide and govern our lives. The meaning of one's life will be in proportion to what is earned, not in monetary terms but on the progression of the Ladder of Consciousness. Humanity's most important goal is to merge with the higher nature of the unifying principle of existence. Where a person is going in the moment depends upon his or her own volition toward and connection with the ability to access the full breath of the Soul.

It is true that today the younger generations remain as alienated as the former generations in regard to the perplexities of human evolvement. The youth of today continue to be alarmed and concerned by the fact that the diversity of life is in harm's way. The Earth's limited resources are being devastated by a draconian system that values profits and commerce over life, regardless of the destruction caused. It is a system that is ignoring and forgetting what accurately represents the true nature and processes of creation. In the current system, precious oxygen-producing forests are destroyed to make unnecessary morning papers, catalogs, and advertisements, when paper made from hemp could be a more sustainable substitute. Valuable potable water is polluted with sewage rather than implementing the composting of sewage to enrich the soil. Millions of tons of chemicals that affect the brain as insidiously as pharmaceuticals are being dumped into the environment; these chemicals contaminate food crops and waterways every year.

The youth of today—as the youth of the past—continue to be assaulted by toxic business-as-usual political corruption, while the vital resources of communities are systematically confiscated. This devastation is implemented by citizens' tax dollars funneled off to support government waste and corporate polluters degrading the vital necessities of life. There is great frustration for the majority of people in the looming specter of inheriting a future of resource wars and a desolate Earth stripped bare. Maintaining a healthy biostructure for Earth's environment and oceans is the most important human rights issue of our time. Ecologists claim that currently 90 percent of the species on Earth are in danger of becoming extinct. Although it appears that the Earth has reached a stage where it will no longer support material existence as we have known it, there is no reason to fear change when we are spiritually prepared and understand who we really are and what we are capable of achieving. It has become apparent that it is time for all of humanity to outgrow the lower nature, fear, aggression, and confusion of adolescence and cultivate a higher and more stable state of existence by dispelling the inhibiting fog looming between Natural Law and the mind of the false and dispirited human ego.

TOASTED FREQUENCY SYNDROME

The great thinker Albert Einstein possessed a powerful intuitive ability, or clairvoyant intelligence, for discerning how Natural Law works. Cultivating the intuition or the sixth sense utilized by many great thinkers is essential for all thinkers because the multidimensional universe resides in a realm of nonlinear equations that cannot be fully proven using the sciences of linear mathematics or theoretical physics. Linear mathematics does not represent the behavior of how nonlinear interactions affect the system as a whole. Outdated classical concepts of linear physics such as quantum mechanics and relativity theory have been replaced by concepts that recognize the essential underlying reality of the ethereal realm, so long spurned by the academic establishment. Subquantum kinetics is a new modality of science that is central to the new physics and espouses a cosmology of continuous matter creation rather than a single big bang event. Scientific minds have finally come to realize what the mind of the mystic has always known—that to expand and evolve beyond the limitations imposed upon the body and the mind requires the time and the space to venture into more expanded states of awareness.

For this reason, it is of great concern that many youths and adults are unusually obsessed and distracted by the all-pervasive and electromagnetically dangerous technological devices being marketed at such a rapid rate today. Rather than enhancing our telepathic and intuitive skills, the invisible electromagnetic frequencies of microwave technologies are overwhelming human cellular integrity and have the effect of hindering the awakening of our higher abilities by isolating and compartmentalizing certain areas of the brain. Technology today scrambles the natural vibratory frequencies of the body and mind and destroys the balance, resulting in weak auras, infirm bodies, and unsound minds. Much of today's technology exercises the maze of the lower frequency of the compulsive mind, and consequently we see people with their heads turned downward and their minds distracted with an array of digital technological trinkets. They do not see or feel what is happening all around them. Ironically, because of too much technology, in the space of only one generation in time we are witnessing a decline in the art of real communication. Indeed, the parents of today's children observe that the ability of young people to engage in nondigital communication has been greatly diminished.

Today we observe that memory spans are short, thinking has become more erratic, and behavior is more compulsive due to the electromagnetic incompatibility of technologies with human health on a cellular level. On a mechanical level, especially for new drivers, just reaching for a cell phone causes a sevenfold increase in the risk of crashing, and text messaging while driving increases the danger by another fourfold according to studies by the National Institutes of Health.

It is important to make note of the fact that studies by the American Academy of Environmental Medicine have shown that prolonged heat radiation from the hard drives, processors, batteries, and other internal mechanisms of digital technology can cause *toasted skin syndrome,* a painful darkening of the skin that may lead to cancer. There is a large body of scientific evidence that demonstrates the risks of radiation exposure.

The unseen downside to the supposedly great power and enrichment of our lives through technology is becoming more evident as we observe the negative health effects from EMR (electromagnetic radiation) exposure that has the effect of toasting the natural frequency balance of the body and particularly the pineal and pituitary glands in the brain that serve intuition. Of course radiation is everywhere, the sun emits radiation, and most household appliances and wiring emit EMF waves. However, today electromagnetic frequencies permeate the brain, body, and environment in an unprecedented fashion.

Perhaps the most alarming and dangerous aspect of this modern application of technology is revealed by recent research on the pineal gland. The specific gland found to link the mind with Spirit is the pineal gland. The pineal gland in the brain cannot differentiate between light waves and electromagnetic waves. This hinders its ability to produce melatonin, absorb free radicals, and initiate the healing processes that take place during sleep. When people sleep near computers, cell phones, or anywhere there is Wi-Fi, the restorative processes of sleep are dramatically diminished. Many people are waking from a night's sleep without feeling rested and refreshed. Recent studies have also confirmed the direct link between cell phone/Wi-Fi use and brain cancer. Here we see that an overabundance of technology does not replace the deeper needs of the body and the mind. Good biocompatible technology would assist humanity in the restorative processes and the further development of the valuable telepathic connections in the brain such as intuition, telepathy, and clairvoyance that are assisted through the function of the ductless pineal and pituitary glands in the brain (figure 1.1).

The art of communication occurs on many levels—the body feels and the mind thinks on the most basic of these levels. The cells of young bodies are dividing rapidly and require the natural electromagnetic frequency of the Earth and sunlight to become strong and connected. The normal

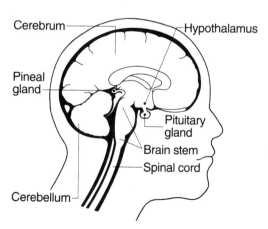

Figure 1.1. Image of the brain from the National Cancer Institute showing the location and general size of the pineal and pituitary glands.

vibratory rate of the human body has been determined to be between 62 and 68 megahertz. The brain has been determined to function optimally between 72 and 90 megahertz. As the vibratory rate lowers due to constant exposure to dissonant energies, the brain synapses slowly become more and more impaired; the flow is downward into confusion, disease, and eventually death. When the body frequency lowers to 58 megahertz the body can catch a cold, at 57 megahertz the flu, 55 megahertz candida, 52 megahertz Epstein-Barr virus and herpes, 42 megahertz cancer, and at 25 megahertz death begins.

In modern times the cacophony of new ways to lower the frequency levels of both the brain and body has reached a critical point; EMR from all digital devices and cell towers, satellites, as well as compact fluorescent bulbs (CFLs emit poisonous gases) in the home and in buildings are just the tip of the iceberg. Toxic plastic pollution; artificial sweeteners; synthesized caffeine; tainted food, skin, and beauty products; depleted uranium used in weapons; toxic vaccinations; and chemically treated mattresses, furniture, and toys are a few more that can be added to the mix.

Artificial flavorings such as MSG and maltodextrin, as well as sorbitol, sorbitan, and other sugar substitutes have been categorized as the "taste that kills" in Dr. Russell Blaylock's book *Excitotoxins*. These unregulated substances are prevalent in many manufactured products far beyond food. Excitotoxins destroy nerve endings and cross the important protection of the blood-brain barrier where the neurons in the brain are stimulated to death by the action of these chemicals. Interestingly, excitotoxin residue settles in the brain and insidiously undermines the memory aspect of the brain. Adults and especially children are demonstrating an alarming decline in memory recall and brain and bodily disease. The Rand Corporation reports that Alzheimer's disease has reached epidemic proportions. Millions of people suffer from memory loss worldwide regardless of their age. Beginning in the 1920s and continuing to the present day, the use of synthetic chemicals has released into the environment more than 100,000 new substances that have never been tested for safety. What may not be fully understood is that certain chemicals ingested through foods and other means can trigger negative emotions as well as birth new diseases. Chemical toxicity combined with radiation pollution is a recipe for disaster.

New scientific findings in human physiology conclude that we are electromagnetic beings and our memory is supported and held in place primarily by a magnetic field that exists around the brain, inside the skull, and around the head. This electromagnetic field is further connected to every cell in the brain by magnetic fields within each cell. Memory is dependent on a steady, living magnetic field. When there is little to no protection from dissonant electromagnetic fields, memory may be slowly or quickly erased as effectively as unplugging a computer in the middle of a file download. Memory loss severely limits our ability to evolve, and so we must view these dissonant electromagnetic radiations as energies that limit us from reaching higher levels of existence. Over time, microwave technologies affect the human capacity in such a way as to maintain a vibratory rate that turns people into spiritually atrophied, yet productive, automatons.

A critical factor for brain health includes maintaining the proper pH level. The brain and blood can overacidify due to a lack of alkaline-producing foods in the diet, which are mainly fruits and vegetables. Yet even the fruits and vegetables are being genetically tampered with and irradiated. Any good farmer knows that a food is only as good as the soil that it is grown in. Chemicals do nothing but destroy soil ecology and nutrients in foods. Chemicals in the environment can affect the brain as insidiously as pharmaceuticals and will pass into the placenta of a pregnant woman at a time when the developing brain of the baby is most vulnerable. Currently ten million pounds of chemical pesticides are used on U.S. farms each year that have been linked to neurodevelopmental problems. The health effects include autism, asthma, obesity, early puberty, poor reflexes, hyperactivity, high blood pressure, heart disease, diabetes, stroke, lower IQ (due to less volume in areas of the brain associated with memory and cognition), Asperger's syndrome (where children have difficulty connecting with others), and metabolic syndrome, which is a precursor to diabetes. This costs U.S. taxpayers alone roughly $51 billion annually in lost economic productivity.

Currently agricultural and manufacturing guidelines better serve corporate interests than public health and the health of the environment. When the soil nutrients are balanced and alive, healthy plants, trees, animals, and people remain impervious to pestilence and disease. Disease takes hold as a result of the Law of Cause and Effect when we misunderstand our relationship with Natural Law. We cannot escape reaping the harvest that is sown. In reshaping the crop we sow, we must choose to shape and direct our course along definite lines. All is perfection when we align our minds with Divine Intelligence, and perfection will be the result. We have the power to either free or enslave ourselves in our experience with Natural Law.

Soil remineralization has been proven to be one of the most effective remedies for balancing the energies of plant and animal life all over the world. However, it will be difficult for anything to flourish if the environment is overwhelmed and cloaked with dissonant electromagnetic radiations. Researchers have determined that animals are very magnetosensitive and are disturbed by even small changes in the magnetic field. Dogs align with the Earth's magnetic field before they defecate; birds and fish use the magnetic field to guide their migrations. When the magnetic field is altered animals have difficulty performing these tasks.

Food irradiation in the United States is a technology designed to use electron beam X-ray machines or radioactive waste products from the manufacture of weapons that uses cobalt 60. To date there is no way to determine if the foods in grocery stores have been irradiated. On the upside, food irradiation will effectively kill insect larvae; the trade-off is that food irradiation depletes the nutrients in foods up to 80 percent. Interestingly, even small family farms with high standards are finding it difficult to provide healthy living foods to their communities due to government interference.

Information regarding the dangers of microwave and digital technology radiation is easily obtainable in many European studies, well in advance of American and Canadian studies. Because cell phones work at the level where brain cells are communicating with each other across the synapse, the EMF radiation of cell phones has been referred to as a silent killer and an unseen menace in some of these studies. Microwave ovens are banned in many European countries, yet they are installed directly at head level in most American kitchens. Bioenergetic measurements indicate that all food and drink cooked in microwave ovens causes us to lose from 40 to 60 percent of our vital field following its ingestion. Even when not in use, microwave ovens emit dissonant radiations for up to six feet all around them. People rest their heads on tables directly in front of or very near to microwave ovens during break times at the workplace. People also go to sleep with cell phones and other electronic devices very near their heads. These radiations penetrate the adult brain for up to one inch and will penetrate completely through the brain of a child.

These dissonant radiations at eye level have been linked to the formation of cataracts in the eyes and other maladies such as cancerous tumors. Research reveals that the molecular structures of the elements in foods and other organic tissues are changed completely from one substance to another through microwave radiation. When food is microwaved it loses its original crystalline geometric energy structure. This results in the alteration of the crystalline energy resonance of the cell. The food that is vital for nourishing the crystalline structure of the body for life and health is destroyed. The opposite of resonance is dissonance. Dissonance is created when the polarities of the frequencies don't match. In this case the food no longer nourishes the body and mind but becomes a burden to process, store, and excrete. These disharmonic frequencies promote destructive entropy and chaos on a cellular level. Inharmonious conditions in life are evidence that we are out of harmony with the natural order of things.

ELECTROSMOG

The electrosmog emanating from such things as electromagnetic devices, cable boxes, audio players, digital picture frames, video game consoles, and electrical currents causes an excess of positively charged ions that disturb the balance between the positive and the negative particles in matter. Further, these also create an excess of positively charged chemically unbound particles in the air. Even more concerning—it takes just thirty seconds on a cell phone to weaken the blood-brain barrier tissue that protects the brain from toxins, and this effect lingers for eight hours. This means that a thirty-second cell phone call in the morning renders the brain especially vulnerable when foods or products containing toxins are eaten or used throughout the day.

Studies also reveal that when animals are subject to long-term exposure to the emanations of Wi-Fi, they become violent and begin to fight. Interestingly, a Swedish study concluded that uterine cancer developed in 90 percent of women who used a copper IUD for birth control while simultaneously using cell phones, the cause being that the IUD functioned as a transmitter and receiver of the unnatural, dissonant frequencies of digital technology. This suggests that any metal in or on the body may be conductive to receiving these unregulated and unpredictable radiations. Canadian school teachers are observing that the children are exhibiting alarming symptoms after the schools installed Wi-Fi. The eyes, skin, brains, and visual fields of sensitive youngsters are being adversely affected, prompting further inquiry into EMF research. The French and Italian governments have gone a step further and ordered all Wi-Fi in schools to be replaced with hardwired Internet connections. It is not uncommon to have on average between 150 and 6000 microwatts of radio frequency per square foot in the urban home. Radio frequency health effects include dizziness, headaches, irritability, memory problems, inability to concentrate, violent behavior, lethargy, and poor appetite. Electric-field health effects include night sweats, disturbed sleep, insomnia, heart palpitations, muscle and nerve pain, waking tired, aggravated allergies, depression, anxiety, moodiness, lack of social development, and bed-wetting in children. The experts agree that Wi-Fi routers, baby monitors, electric blankets, electric alarm clocks, cordless phones, and cell phones are all dangerous. Professor Leif Salford, head of research at Lund University in Sweden, has stated, "The voluntary exposure of the brain to microwaves from handheld mobile phones is the largest human biological experiment ever." We must recognize that technology is a tool with benefits and also carries inherent risks, especially for children.

In 2002 a young man of 19 years old came for an iridology reading.

The science of iridology is used as an uninvasive way to read the iris in the eye, which functions like a map of the inner body. This young man was unable to work due to debilitating dizziness and lack of energy. In the area of his iris that reflects the brain I observed an alarming black degenerative lacuna that correlated with the side of the head that he used his cell phone on. I recommended he adjust his diet and use his cell phone on speaker mode, and only for emergencies. The young man was not happy with my advice, but he followed it anyway. Six months later we did another reading. He had returned to work and was functioning well. Best of all—it was thrilling to see healing signs in the brain tissue. This was when I realized that the brain can, and does, heal itself if given a chance. I wondered what the biological damage to the brain tissue looked like. Thanks to the latest brain scan devices we can now observe what damage to the brain actually looks like (see figure 1.2).

In 2014 I discovered that, although I do not subscribe to Wi-Fi, my apartment in San Francisco had become saturated with it. A strong signal over my bed and signals from multiple neighbors, as well as a new citywide signal turned on at the turn of the new year had made my

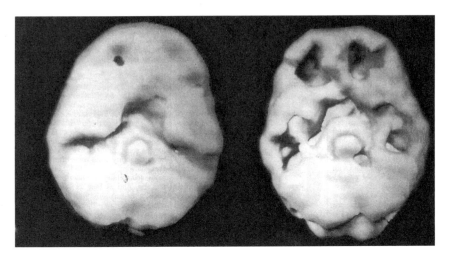

Figure 1.2. The image on the left is the brain of a nonviolent person and the image on the right is the brain of a violent person. The damage you can see in this brain would also be reflected in the eyes of the person and would be visible to an iridologist. From The Biology of Transcendence *by Joseph Chilton Pearce.*

home of thirty years unfit to live in. During that time I made a dream journal entry that read:

Jan. 2014: Feeling exhausted and unable to sleep soundly since the city turned on the new Wi-Fi signal. This is aura shattering stuff, and it is more difficult to remember my dreams. I'm having shooting, sharp pains in my brain, dull headaches with a dull undertone of nausea, and insomnia, and I seem to sleep, but I wake still feeling tired, an uneasy feeling, and a lack of euphoria. The rents in San Francisco have tripled and many people have been evicted. The young well-paid tech workers flooding into the neighborhood have cut down a huge, old shade tree and ripped out a well-established hedge of jasmine that has perfumed the air for more than fifty years only to be replaced with a funky party deck. The tender vegetation that depended upon the shade tree has withered and died in the heat of the summer sun, and yards are looking bleak. I have noticed that the birds and birdsong have been greatly diminished in the neighborhood resulting in a deathly silence. This is a disrespectful violation of people's rights to live and thrive as they choose. This unnatural technological paradigm is being forced into this world and everyone is expected to adopt the robotic lifestyle that goes with it, without question. The titans of tech are quick to espouse how much people love the new technology, but the voices that question its safety are ignored.

Immersed in a microwave soup of frequencies that are incompatible with the human energy system, the body and mind are unable to adequately recharge, repair, and refresh during sleep. Deep sleep is no longer possible, and we awake feeling fatigued, off balance, and unstable. The body, mind, and immune system are weakened and depressed. This is beyond ignorance; it is the path to extinction. It occurred to me that the only alternative was to move away—but there is really no place to hide anymore in this world. There is a great deal of healing work to do with plastic-polluted oceans and marine life, chemical trails, and pesticides undermining the natural cycles of life. People created these problems, and there are good people working hard to heal our planet, but healing the Earth must now be the responsibility of every man, woman, and child. It is imperative that we alter the path that we are on before the damage to life in all forms becomes irreversible.

In the midst of this dilemma I received a book from my publisher, Inner Traditions, that offered hope, *Shungite* by the French geobiologist Regina Martino. Shungite is a silver/black stone found only in one place on Earth: the Russian part of Karelia. Due to its stable tensional integrity shungite is the only mineral known to balance EMF radiation without taking on negative charges. Unlike crystals or metals that will eventually take on the resonance of EMF radiation after about three months, shungite creates a lasting, active, and protective microvortex of energy. I now use shungite to help balance the bioenergetic equilibrium of living in what has become a hostile environment for the well-being of life. Martino explains that EMF radiation is a principal source of left torsion fields. Torsion fields are transmitted by electromagnetic waves, and left torsion fields are very harmful to health. They are especially detrimental to our overall energetic balance, which includes all the following levels: physical, energetic, emotional, psychic, and Spiritual. Shungite transforms a left torsion influence to a right torsion influence helping us to reconnect with homeostasis and the natural energy of life. I find that shungite also alleviates pain, perhaps because it has the additional property of activating energetic circulation. There are many other uses for shungite; for instance, shungite also supports humidity retention, resulting in a decrease in water consumption and enhanced productivity in farming. Martino's book is fascinating and offers charts to illustrate how EMF frequencies cause imbalance in the vital energy fields of the body and the science to back it up.

Because we are children of nature—not technology—it is essential that the human vital energy field be rebalanced when the integrity of the body and brain is being violated by technopollution—especially when the major portion of one's time is spent within close range of technological devices. When we no longer resonate with nature, we experience dissonance, an unbalanced state of being. Electronics are designed to create dissonant static that jams the harmonic human frequency, which in turn causes the inability to get beyond a certain frequency rate. So it is very important to balance technoactivities with an equal amount of time outdoors, take the shoes off and connect with the Earth, and take actions to avoid and neutralize the health dangers of radiation exposure. We are electromagnetic creatures, and if we wish to evolve we must recognize that modern technology must be altered to harmonize with the well-being of all sentient life in general.

Fortunately, the wisdom of timeless intuition is still observable in some people who limit and avoid being overly and unreasonably influenced by the use of addictive techie pastimes. Many of the more creative youth dislike the impersonal aspects of technocommunication and wisely steer clear of it. Conversely, some misinformed parents are shipping their children off for summer vacation to technology camps. This means that many young bodies and minds are not only bombarded with dangerous electromagnetic frequencies during the school year; they are cuddling up to these dangerous devices for summer vacation, rather than enjoying the natural outdoor activities that define the carefree and restorative season of summertime. If the child is to become healthy and well balanced, it is essential for the child to be introduced to creation through the inspiring beauty of natural surroundings in nature's outdoors. Nature is a refuge with the sublime power to transmute lower-frequency thoughts and emotions. Connecting with nature bolsters the body's defenses against physical and mental illnesses. Natural settings give children an awareness of their interaction with life and an appreciation of their own existence. Will the children of the future become more like the technologies that represent such an imbalance in their lives? We observe that mental and developmental disabilities such as autism, Alzheimer's disease, clinical depression, and bone and muscle ailments are on the rise in both children and adults. A recent study by the Obama administration indicates that 40 percent of school age children are lacking in empathy, a factor that contributes to violence in young people. According to a recent study by the Pew Research Center in Washington, D.C., 92 percent of teens go online daily. The nonprofit Common Sense Media based in San Francisco found that teens average about 9 hours of media use per day.

To remain viable stewards of our lives and this world, it must also be recognized that the more technology that is used, the greater the resources that will be required to maintain them. Consider that the unused laptop computer left plugged into the electrical outlet eats up enough power each day to run a small refrigerator. The so-called cloud requires massive rooms of servers from floor to ceiling whirling with unprecedented amounts of energy in huge buildings to store information relayed via satellite. The word *cloud* simply adds a wow factor to describe information storage. It is misleading and romanticizes the perceived mystique of machinery—machinery that requires more energy than ever . . . to support a larger population than ever . . . in a world that is already on information and energy overload. This is insanity.

We must wake up and ask: Where is the balance here? Where is the overwhelming impetus for digital technology coming from? Where is this unnatural dance with the stray energies of science and technology leading us? We know these energies can alter human DNA as proven in experiments conducted in the field of transhumanism. *Transhumanism* is the term used to define research in the area of the genetically modified human being. It is a combination of science and technology that is attempting to create hybrid supersoldiers, superanimals, and superintelligence using the living matrix of the human genome. Interestingly, even the most prominent tech titans recognize the dangers inherent in the mad pace of technological advancement. Elon Musk of Tesla, SolarCity, and SpaceX fame has commented on the potentially scary outcomes regarding artificial intelligence. In a 2014 interview with the *Epoch Times,* Musk referenced the *Terminator* movies, in which machines can think and act independently, turning against their human producers and commanding the future. Musk stated that we are looking at roughly fifteen years before this nightmarish scenario could become a reality.

If we care about our humanity we must realize that it is the pathway that the human family chooses that will make the difference in limiting the influence of technological machinery. We must come to the understanding that machinery is incapable of superseding the vastness of biological spirituality. To neglect the development of the higher Self through dependence upon anything outside of self, such as overreliance on technology, is to weaken one's own nature. As Earth's population pulses beyond seven billion people, truth seeking requires that we find ourselves facing a formidable foe—our own free will. We can choose to be blindly guided without a compass, or we can choose to follow our destiny: self-mastery.

Generation after generation strives to seek out the real meaning of their lives and find that it can be both challenging and disappointing to struggle with how best to proceed in a world that is uncertain as to what to value. As the meandering paths of life unfold before us amid diverse lives, personalities, preferences, belief systems, cultures, and traditions we must learn to alter and reinterpret what we think we know if we are to truly evolve with the passing of time.

Eventually the deeper journey of life reveals itself, and we discover that no one is immune from error and that life itself is the Master Teacher. Unless there is recognition that we are immersed in the unlimited creativity that infuses existence, the age-old questions will continue to remain enigmas. There is a great need for openness regarding the unimaginable—not the vulnerable openness of ignorance and naïveté, but rather, openness to exploring the realities of both the material and the ethereal forces that uphold and sustain life, as well as other forces to be reckoned with that we may not be aware of or fully understand.

BIOGEOMETRY AND BIOSIGNATURES

Let us now consider more creative solutions to some of these serious technological dilemmas. According to Dr. Ibrahim Karim, founder of the modern science of BioGeometry, the electromagnetic fields produced by the stray energies of digital electronics and satellites are a thousand times more powerful than the frequencies of human cells. This distorts and confuses our energy fields (auras) and weakens the immune system. The ever-increasing exposure to electromagnetic energy hinders our ability to cope or adapt beyond our biological threshold, threatening an imminent collapse that he claims could lead to global extinction. This is a real threat that we are hardly aware of because the dangers of EMR frequencies are not being relentlessly promoted; yet these microwaves are continually passing through the auric fields of our bodies, causing headaches, dizziness, memory loss, hyperactivity, sleep disorders, tingling, numbness, and pain in arms, fingers, and legs, as well as contributing to ailments such as chronic fatigue, vision problems, disorientation, instability, stress, nausea, depression, listlessness, allergies, and inability to heal.

A promising solution for balancing the dissonant radiations of digital technology and modern electrical devices has been brought forth by Dr. Karim. In 1973 Dr. Karim was appropriately the fortunate recipient of all the scientific works in the field of French radiesthesia (energy wave measurement) that were buried for decades in the cellar of the Maison de la Radiesthésie in Rue St. Roch in Paris. The owner, Madame Lambert, gave Dr. Karim all of the old books and instruments of the great scientists of radiesthesia that included her husband, Alfred Lambert, as well as scientists Chaumery, de Belizal, and Turrenne.

This windfall began a long journey for Dr. Karim that eventually sprouted a new energy design language that interacts with the forces of nature through the use of forms called biosignatures. Biosignatures use shapes, color, motion, and sound to produce energy balance in all living and inert systems in the environment. For example, the simple L-shaped biosignature is made of light clear plastic with an adhesive backing that may be applied to the battery area of a cell phone or computer and even the corners of a mirror to balance the resonance of dissonant frequencies. The difference in energy balance can be felt and also measured with a pendulum.

Dr. Karim states that the energy produced through the use of BioGeometry and biosignatures offers the same vibratory energies as sacred power sites. The design methods of this science offer a holistic way to enhance and balance the energy fields of people using technology, resulting in the balance of the biological functions of the human body and mind, as well as plants and animals. Dr. Karim explains that time and space equal balanced motion that manifests on many levels. All matter can only exist in time and space because we need the polarity of opposites to perceive the various vibratory realms of existence. The actual essence of energy (which he claims is an unanswerable question) beyond time and space produces the *primary motion* that transforms the energy into the different forms that create the duality of opposites. This motion is balanced in a way that could be called geometrical— a balance that creates complementarities out of opposition. It is this harmonic opposition, or polarity, that seeds the field for all levels of creation.

The application of BioGeometry and the various biosignatures also offer excellent energy support for many types of medical treatment devices because they cancel out the harmful electromagnetic fields that diagnostic and treatment devices emit. Some biosignatures are so simple they can be drawn on a Band-Aid or be permanently applied like a tattoo. Tattoos are an ancient Egyptian tradition that have been greatly misunderstood and misapplied in modern society. Geometric symbols transfer information through resonance and have been drawn on the body to stimulate self-healing for thousands of years. The most ancient example was discovered in 1991, when the 5,000-year-old iceman, Ötzi, was found to have tattoos over his arthritic joints. The use of tattoos for healing was the original purpose for painting the body. When properly applied, energy balancing biosignatures are beneficial for any form of life.

Energy balancing BioGeometrical designs can be incorporated into many products that have obvious or suspected dangerous potential. Some products that create long-term stress effects that would be good candidates for this application are cell phones, computers, microwave ovens, airplanes, cars, cigarettes, cosmetics, pharmaceuticals, furniture, and machinery. BioGeometry has also been tested with positive effects in jewelry design, tableware, bottles, and to enhance the growth of plants. To learn more about Dr. Karim's work, please refer to the resources section at the back of the book.

TESLA TECHNOLOGY

Technology is not necessarily the culprit; it is how technology is currently being used that is objectionable. From the time that Nikola Tesla introduced his free energy and antigravity technology to the world, people have been experimenting with it—fascinated with the beauty and purity of working with natural forces. The atom bomb is one example of the misuse of Tesla technology in destructive hands. There are constructive working prototypes of Tesla technology that must be brought forth and no longer suppressed for the balance to return to technology. Nikola Tesla exemplifies a man who lit the world by following the inner genius that shapes the Soul's purposeful path in life. Global warming would not be a problem if Tesla's technology were properly implemented on a global scale for generating power.

ENLIGHTENMENT

Our unique life experiences are a reflection of our ability to read the signs and follow the nuances that lead us toward or distance us from the Soul's purposeful path in life. The quality of this great journey is dependent upon alignment with the Spiritual Laws of Existence to create balance. It may be said that true balance is a form of enlightenment. Enlightenment is a way of freeing oneself from ignorance in order to act, operate, and contribute as a Light in the world. It is through the balanced integration of body, mind, and spirit that a deeper and more profound Intelligence is expressed. Those with inflexible minds will be hindered in seeking this deeper journey because evolvement is rooted in dedication and flexibility. Cultivating the unifying connection to the higher realms of consciousness is the most important and valuable endeavor one can possibly pursue in life.

It is also imperative to acknowledge that the physical relationship that we have with the Earth is intimately connected to the relationship that we have with our own bodies, minds, and spirits. Both the body and the mind are fallible. The body and the mind must come into proper relationship with the higher inner Light of the Spirit for the individual to become unified and more balanced in both the inner and the outer machinations of life. This forms the natural foundation that embodies a real and balanced working relationship between the physical body, the ego intellect, and the higher frequencies of Spiritual

Intelligence. This is the original foundation that humankind strives toward in religion.

True spirituality embodies a very personal relationship that depends upon the ability of the individual to receive guidance inwardly through authentic experience. This is a form of communication that does not require idols, a guru, priests, great pageantry and ceremony, righteousness, war, or technology. However, it does require that the individual cultivate respect and reverence for discerning the inherent gifts to be found within the self, and the presence of mind to follow through and trust the Inner Teacher, or Spirit. It requires a knowing awareness that is freshly alive in the moment.

Spirit is the primary power of vibratory life seated right within your Self. Acknowledging its existence does not take long years of suffering and study. Spirit is already flowing through you; feel it—and become that pureness of Intelligence in thought, word, and deed. We are allied with the Intelligence of the Universal Mind that supports us in perfect harmony. Without constant book learning we can draw upon this perpetual well of knowledge when we accept that we are part of the Universal Mind. Aligning with the inner Light of Cosmic Intelligence can be effortless, or it can require courage, dedication, and fortitude because the human struggle with the personal psyche, the false ego, and the book-learned intellect are strong and prone to self-deception, self-obsession, self-service, self-avoidance, distraction, laziness, weakness, arrogance, and illusion. The lessons in books of truth are only necessary to bring us to the understanding of unity with higher forces of intelligence.

For humanity to evolve and make a contribution of value toward real progress, it must become unified in the cultivation of its most valuable assets. Regardless of one's personal religious belief, or lack thereof, we are all inherently endowed with the same gifts of Spiritual Light to draw upon. It is the responsibility of the individual to learn to recognize the difference between personal and culturally driven patterns of thought and authentic spiritual guidance, or inner knowing. There is no one who would not benefit from cultivating a deeper understanding of how the sacred is revealed in everyday existence as a higher order of life that serves to guide and to protect the Soul of life.

The journey of each human being is unique and it is incumbent upon the individual to recognize the power and the wisdom in the higher guiding forces. This is a most fascinating, uplifting, and challenging journey. It requires an honest evaluation of the pitfalls permeating how one thinks, which can be fraught with confusion. There is a corollary between confusion, suffering, and fear, which can be a catalyst for much misunderstanding and unnecessary destruction in the world of human affairs.

It is no secret that the human family has arrived at a critical threshold in regard to great challenges unlike any other. The world stage has been set for irreversible loss due to arrogance, ignorance, unreasonable corruption and greed, cultural clashes, and warlike behavior. This is a tipping point in time where the differences between gender, race, and religion must no longer be accepted as barriers to progressive change. It is reasonable to say that the solution to the unfolding crisis of the planet is—at its core—a spiritual one.

Many illusions abound in discovering where and how to find spiritual guidance. The world has always been full of illogical misconceptions that separate people and that lead them away from the reality of Natural Law. Real religion does not separate people; it forms a common thread for all. Fundamentally life itself is multidimensional. The atoms in all living things operate as multidimensional units of awareness, alternating between the material realms and the ethereal realms. The multidimensional consciousness of the atom produces many effects: waves, patterns, shapes, sound, cold, heat, electricity, chemical action, magnetism, color, and light.

There exists a complex interplay between conscious vibration, color, and light. The higher the vibration, the higher the consciousness that in turn increases one's ability to attune to the Cosmic Mind. The multidimensional intelligence in human beings reveals itself on a personal level through fascinating experiences that encompass a wide range of intensities delivering powerful effects. Many people have had extraordinary experiences that they cannot explain and therefore may be reluctant to share with others. A person's most profound insights and experiences must no longer be regarded as socially unacceptable or discounted as delusional.

Proof abounds in the profound experiences of millions of people that are gifted with prophetic dreams, visions, miraculous healings, out-of-body adventures, and the ability to channel knowledge from higher dimensions of existence. Skills and talents are automatically acquired in proportion to the frequency of the consciousness one abides in.

Due to a lack of strengthening our connection to the ethereal realms, we may experience a void in this crucial area altogether. One may be inclined to ignore or be intimidated by inexplicable experiences. We may undervalue or misinterpret these gifts, especially when thinking is limited and vibratory acceleration is blocked by third-dimensional linear logic. It takes time and quiet contemplation to appreciate the true significance of multidimensional experiences that communicate in both subtle and powerful ways, as well as with unlimited variety.

Some spiritual insights are crystal clear, while others are sublimely subtle and thus more challenging to interpret and implement. The subtler feelings whisper—and they are easily dissipated as the linear thinking of the intellectual mind intervenes or fear arises. The false ego is challenged as the opportunity to correct mistakes is presented; it may be difficult sometimes to accept a sobering truth. The opportunity to transcend the frequencies of one's own mind cannot be forced . . . the individual must be a willing participant in the transmutation of both individual and collective evolvement.

Learning to pay more attention to the finer impressions that we receive will help us to honor what we experience, even if we don't always understand it. Everyone's mind and energy operates uniquely, and so our own perceptive abilities will vary. We may perceive impressions that are abstractly fragmented or quite precise and complete. Ideas and thoughts may be accompanied by imagery, physical sensations, emotions, symbols, or déjà vu. Auditory sounds such as ringing, buzzing, or words may be heard in the inner ear. One may also experience certain tastes or fragrances that speak to us in familiar ways or that have a message. All of these assist us in recognizing the larger patterns in life that may be accessed through multiple levels of consciousness. It is useful to explore the areas of the brain and the superconscious mind that help us to shift from normal consciousness to that which is more transcendent.

Our ability to perceive on multiple levels can be awakened, activated, and stimulated by establishing a more direct link with the sources of our subtle, intuitive perceptions.

Throughout history the true spiritual sages, spiritual messengers, and powerful spiritual shamans have taught that all people must contemplate the true significance of the guidance that not only surrounds us but abides within us, and we must be responsible for the field of action, or inaction, this may require on a personal level. A deeper understanding of this inherent ability is essential for achieving the inner joy that is so elusive in the ever competitive and fleeting world of material existence. Yet even in times of plenty it would be difficult, frustrating, and perilous to live without honoring the eternally loyal spiritual assets that serve as our most valuable tools for traversing life with wisdom and enduring success. The human condition will spiral upward and humanity will advance if it will pause, look within, and learn to strengthen the pure essence of a sacred reality that is inherent in the inner Light of each human life. It is our dedication to the inherent Light of the Soul and our quest in understanding the higher frequency of the Universal Mind Principle that inhabits the Soul that requires much more exploration.

INCOGNITO

The ego is a marvelous fiction . . .
A false mirror . . .
A novel written by ourselves, about ourselves,
And the very first step on the Quest is to disentangle oneself
from its seductions.

YATRI (UNKNOWN MAN)

Incognito *(adjective or adverb): With one's identity kept secret; pretended identity.*

Oftentimes, the knowledge we think we have regarding what is right for us or wrong for us is rooted in the false mirror of the dispirited ego and is part of the ignorance that must be addressed through self-evaluation. It requires focus to see beyond what we think is reality. Usually, we are so paralyzed by our own ideas, emotional habits, the opinions of others, fears, expectations, and the noise of our own thoughts that we forget to consult the higher Light within. The false ego of the personality is so distracted and busy—building its reputation, wielding its power, and accumulating wealth—that it becomes so much a part of our nature that we are not aware of it.

The world at large remains overwhelmed by the influences of

material and commercial bondage and world opinion, and this has been mainly what is believed, practiced, and developed rather than the Spiritual Law of one's own being. When hyperconsumerism dominates the world, it cannot do otherwise than consume those that worship materialism. So long as one's higher inner Presence is ignored and the current imbalances endure, no really effective mode of the evolvement of life can be carried to a successful conclusion. History has borne out the fact that, as Lincoln said, "a house divided against itself cannot stand." Life processes cannot unfold any faster than the physical metamorphosis of a planet will allow. We have no control over our geologic evolution. All physical life is time conditioned and delayed by time and space. There is no escaping to another planet of origin to evolve.

People can elect to use the life force in a degenerate way, in which it is not allowed to manifest toward its greatest degree of potency. They can elect to waste the riches of nature and alter the work of Creation or try to overthrow it. This is not the fault of the higher Mind Principle; it is the fault of those small minds that allow degeneration. Degeneration is rooted in the personal desire for self-gratification. It was Plato who said, "The first and best victory is to conquer self. To be conquered by self is, of all things, the most shameful and vile."

Because people are distracted from, or not interested in, conquering the small self that Plato referred to—many people are living under a kind of hypnotic spell that perpetuates the idea that humanity is sinful and must be controlled through manipulation, extortion, and usury while surviving in a merely material world. A world experienced under this spell is one that is escaped only upon death and from which—if one is righteous and believes in certain saviors—one may be redeemed and delivered to what has been termed *heaven*. For centuries people have struggled in a system designed by those who despise spiritual independence and affirm a person's animal nature rather than one's humanity. The egocentric, selfish ideas and ingrained beliefs of this paltry system of limited existence do not represent the original plan and purpose of the Universal Mind Principle.

INTUITION

When you have a talent, it's a gift from God. When you
use your talent, it's a gift to God.

RED SKELTON

Intuition is one inherent aspect of higher consciousness that communicates via mental telepathy. Intuitive insights offer an expanded vision of reality that instills a greater degree of certainty and truth in our lives. When we experience this level of wholeness, we are penetrating multilevels of consciousness. The inner expression of life as the true spiritual nature allows one to intuitively feel it and to follow it, is the basic foundation of the Universal Mind Principle, and offers access to a true mode of living. There are those who claim that intuition is unreliable, and therefore impotent. It is naive to expect that intuition would be handed to us. To access the power of intuition, it must be given the proper environment in which to operate, it must be cultivated, utilized, strengthened, and exercised like a muscle until the intuitive ability of living through consulting one's "inner voice" becomes second nature. It is a sacred mode of living—a lifestyle and a frame of mind. Accessing information that is beyond the surface mind requires bypassing the intellect and the false ego to read the vibratory energies of emotions, feelings, and knowledge that permeate our multidimensional energy bodies. The great artist's hands and the wisdom of intuition work together, creating in harmony without the mediation of the surface mind. In times past, illiteracy was not an obstacle to accessing intuition, talent, and wisdom; the toughest and wisest people are the gentlest, and the superstrength of intuition and wisdom has always been applied to live in peace, rather than to foment war—evil deeds that destroy Creation.

The locked boundary of the ego/intellect strives to categorize everything and everyone—but Spirit must simply be experienced. The intellectual belief system of the surface mind wants to take over; it is a portion of the self that is human. Intuitive wisdom teaches what we *know* on a Soul level. This appears to be a duality, or polarity, of mind; but ideally, and in the purest sense, it is a unity of mind. Our beliefs tether us to a certain frequency of mind. Breaking free of these tethers allows us to become more in tune with the lighter, and therefore subtle, qualities of intuition: the Inner Teacher. This achievement constitutes an authentic level of strength toward self-mastery and spiritual advancement. The intuitive part of the Self is built through first acknowledging and honoring the Universal Mind Principle, allowing a clear avenue of access and building trust as insights are translated into action. This true mode of living is an unlimited adventure and a source of quiet joy in every moment, even in difficult times. Consciousness in its purest form is a state of bliss, or perfect happiness. When people align with the freedom and the liberation of this deeper presence of being, they will not be bored, lonely, or lacking or be induced to relinquish this pure creative power very easily. A quote by J. D. Walters helps to further describe the deeper meaning of joy: "True joy is not an emotional state. It is not that which one feels when some desire is satisfied . . . it is inward; it is of the Soul."

Ignorance and arrogance are distressing states of mind for humanity. Ignorance and arrogance that cause a sense of separation, entitlement, and aloneness are erased from one's consciousness when the true nature of one's unity with the Spiritual Mind Principle is restored. It is not easy for everyone to suddenly shift their self-centered, self-deceiving, self-pitying, and self-destructive thoughts, actions, and beliefs into something that is very far and very different from where they are and have been for a long time. Personal mental processes become habitual, ingrained and embedded in the mind, which greatly inhibits the fluid nature of learning new things. Elbert Hubbard's insightful adage is ever so true in describing human nature: "It has always been a mystery to me why people spend so much time deliberately fooling themselves by creating alibis to cover their weaknesses. If used differently, this same time would be sufficient to cure the weakness, then no alibis would be needed."

Because the human psyche is so deeply entrenched in its own machinations, vibratory shifts of frequency are usually a gradual process. People become discouraged when they are unable to achieve instant gratification in gradual processes. This causes people to conclude that they really have no control over their own thoughts, behavior, and actions. However, control of the mind through willpower may be achieved instantly or through persistence and practice, depending on the genuine desire and proclivities of the individual. There is no other way to work toward self-mastery than through voluntary self-effort and through observing personal experiences. If one does not conquer the false ego, one will be at the mercy of negative personality traits, such as those that give rise to the many disharmonies in life. And yet disharmonies are inescapable and a natural part of the learning process. Mistakes occur as life progresses. Progress toward correcting mistakes provides new and varied challenges that must be lived into wisdom. One level of self-mastery always opens to yet another level of existence to master.

There are some who claim to be masters or modern-day prophets . . . yet true mastery is living the instruction of the higher Self—the higher consciousness—rather than seeking the adoration of others in order to establish one's worth. A great deal of human insecurity is brought about through subjection to the beliefs of others—beliefs that in reality have no power.

One cannot successfully bring forth political, economic, or religious rules and regulations that govern the human family while under the spell of the false ego/mind. In this state of confusion people become arrogantly greedy and power hungry, others overtly selfish; some become demanding, intimidating, or abusive. Conversely, others become weak and focused only on material welfare, forgetting the guidance found in spiritual wisdom. How can such divergent thoughts be organized into a synchronized and harmonious whole?

What appears to be dual mindedness and separation is merely a dual set of ideas and beliefs proliferated and projected by the mortal mind. It is the mortal mind that sets the stage for duality, and this causes deviation, misuse, and abuse of our inherent spiritual gifts. Some people become so obsessed with satisfying temporal desires that the true Spiritual Light is not allowed to surface and manifest. The human psyche struggles with the false ego—the "I want" nature that is self-important, presumptuous, envious, gluttonous, possessive, intolerant, shortsighted, and rapacious.

The ego also controls aspects such as willpower, instinctual compulsion, self-preservation, self-satisfaction, egocentricity, intellect, ideology, and outbursts of anger and antisocial behavior. When the ego is altered from its pure state of being, the mind becomes the soil where greed and selfishness are cultivated. It is through balancing the pure ego/mind of the Soul with the intellectual/mind of the brain that we obtain the invaluable tool of whole mind thinking essential for a joyous evolving human adventure. We must ask ourselves where our own minds are taking us! The tortured mind gives way to the tortured life, and the balanced mind gives way to the balanced life. It is the mind that is either tortured or soundly balanced that determines how the living Light of the Soul energy will manifest.

Reading the energy of a person's mental psyche is the ability to sense the energy surrounding the individual. If one is sensitive to energy, this happens instantly and is helpful in making intelligent decisions or offering healing empathy. However, the habit of constantly judging others can be detrimental to spiritual prescience. Sometimes we think we know things when they are merely the ideas, beliefs, and opinions of the false ego. Some people cannot imagine what it is like to be inwardly guided. Sometimes people listen to the inner voice of the Soul, and sometimes they do not listen. The reality of achieving unity with this higher Wisdom and Intelligence is that there is not one personal inner consciousness or outer Universal Consciousness: it is all one perfectly sound and whole Mind Principle. To harmonize with this Reality, one must allow one's personal thoughts to be unselfish and pure through transmutation of the lower forms of ego/mind.

There is a rather humorous adage in Hindu lore that states, "If God wished to hide, God would choose man to hide in. That is the last place man would look for God." The sad truth is that people seek and search everywhere outside of the self for God, when the whole time every human being—bar none—is imbued with this God/Mind quality that resides within each person as the fulfillment of Natural Law. It has been said that humanity's greatest folly is in the attempt to overpower Natural Law, rather than simply aligning with its natural flow through a pure feeling awareness. It is not the pure ego of the natural individual that we wish to change, but the false ego that the individual has assumed.

The advanced masters teach that it is the belief in separation from Spirit that has caused our biological bodies to age and die. There is a Natural Law that transcends death; there are realms beyond third-dimensional existence on which the Soul depends, and human evolution is slowly moving toward understanding how to honor it and use it. It is a higher expression of consciousness and, in turn, a geometrical spiritualization of the cellular biology of the flesh.

Although there are forces attempting to block the attainment of higher consciousness, the resistance one has to cultivating higher consciousness is really the only thing standing in the way of building a better life, a better world, and a future that will strengthen our ability to advance in worlds beyond the physical. The only way forward is through working with one's own personal level of conscious awareness to produce the frequencies required to transcend the limitations of the mortal mind.

The advanced masters teach that heaven is in the always-present harmony within the individual, wherever one may be. Herein lies the art—the ability, even in the throes of chaos, to calmly celebrate being. In a state of panic, it is a matter of asking the Higher Self for guidance and taking the time to feel and to listen for the appropriate action. It is a skill that is cultivated through reprogramming the consciousness to be keenly aware and active in present time.

People often separate themselves from being present in the moment by living in the past, or in the future. The past cannot be changed, but how one holds the past can be transmuted and then released through forgiveness. The success of the future must be implemented through understanding the eternal in this moment. Human endeavors are often out of sync with the reality of Natural Law, and this results in difficulty and imbalance.

Although the human condition has demonstrated growth and expansion in the course of its slow evolution, it is now urgently essential to strive to obtain a substantial equilibrium that functions at the level of stability and balance, rather than perpetual population growth, materialism, technology, competition, and war—all resulting in environmental stress, destruction, and Spiritual imbalance. This represents a very challenging endeavor given the climate of the current state of existence on Earth.

Progress and evolvement come about through our own efforts to align with Natural Laws and not by the efforts of others who will claim to be our saviors. The capacity of the brain becomes limited and restricted when one succumbs to the desire to be rescued by a source outside of the Higher Self. This is a form of victim consciousness that hinders the internal process of self-mastery. Life requires action on the part of the individual, as well as self-expression in bringing forth one's natural gifts and talents. It is as necessary to develop the talents of the Soul self as it is to inhale and exhale in the process of breathing. To receive from Creation without giving to Creation exhausts life, dries it out, and consequently one loses the ability to create. Some beings have perfected the habit of becoming needy predators in the world; they are more like parasites than human beings. This parasitic state of mind demonstrates the ways in which human existence can sink lower than the animal. There is nothing in the attitude of the higher Mind Principle that relegates humanity to this kind of limitation. The individual must simply work toward eliminating that which obstructs life's higher purpose.

Through intuition one knows when the Laws of one's true nature are being violated just as easily as one knows when the harmonic notes of music are discordant. We can feel the moment when discord arises in and around our whole being. This initiates a feeling of discomfort and unease that causes the nervous system to register apprehension, anxiety, and concern. Before the harmony in one's life can be reestablished, the cause of the obstruction must be uncovered, demystified, and corrected. No one else can truly initiate this for the individual. In this respect, the individual is in competition with only the false ego of the self—and no one else.

Beyond learning reading, writing, and arithmetic, many family structures, educational systems, and religious institutions inadequately prepare most people to evolve into Spiritually mature and well-balanced adults. Shaped by centuries of patriarchal elitist culture, children are rarely taught about the deeper things that they really *need* to know—this is not an accident, it is merely a strategy for control. Learning is not only derived from books and the intellect: we must also ask the Inner Teacher (Universal Mind Principle) to guide the intellect so that we may begin to interact with Natural Law. This subdues the intellect's appetite for competition, arrogance, and greed. All people who have created something of real value that serves humankind have done so as catalysts that are aligned with existing Creative Spiritual Forces. It is through the higher forces that we learn such things as self-realization, self-worth, self-love, empathy, love of others, intuition, inner knowing, how to express feelings, and how these things are connected to who we really are on a Spiritual level. This additional level of learning must become part of all educational systems if the human race is to advance and evolve in its current evolutionary position. This manner of learning may be disconcerting to purely scientific minds, but it is clear as day to those who incorporate the underlying facet of mysticism and multidimensional realities into the equation of life.

There are many distractions and intrusions that hinder the expanding and upward spiral of evolvement; and we must explore why the human family remains stuck in the continuing circle of ignorance, abuse, and spiritual strangulation—so that the flowering point of spiritual maturity may develop fruit.

The progression of higher consciousness is constantly thwarted by the misdirected ambition, arrogance, manipulation, willfulness, and stubbornness of those who employ the false mirror of the ego/mind. Shattering this false mirror is very liberating. Many people strive to make sense of the outer world that does not resonate with a truer sense of what is inwardly felt. People seek the ways and means to reclaim this inborn power of trusting what comes naturally. And yet—the false ego will look elsewhere for what it thinks it needs, pursuing religious ideals, romantic relationships, marriage, sexual trysts, children, money, material goods, addictions, superficial distractions, and the like. When people begin to operate with the Light of higher consciousness, it becomes increasingly difficult for false influences to intervene and take over. When enough people shatter the false mirror of the ego, those who attempt to manipulate, control, and frighten the masses will be seen for what they truly are—spiritually bankrupt and unevolved beings.

It is evident that society is conspicuously encouraged to strive for more than is materially needed, and this creates unceasing competition to get ahead. This appeals to the false ego hard at work creating a great illusion. Paradoxically, there is immense suffering and poverty in life in the midst of very small groups of obscenely wealthy people who indulge themselves to excess in their own pleasures and eccentricities. This paradigm starkly contrasts with the more Earth-based cultural societies that teach that no one wins the game unless everyone's needs are met.

In spiritually balanced societies, those who claim more than their fair share are seen as selfish and unwise. Today, all people must temper their striving for material clutter and learn to contribute to the greater good. This will allow time for a greater focus on the art of cultivating the Inner Teacher to guide one's actions. This in turn will assist in the ability to become the intellectual candle guided by the inner voice of the Soul, rather than just the intellect. Live life as the artist working toward understanding Creation, rather than following the crowd. This is a way of integrating the sacred into daily existence so that life becomes rich in quality. It is a spiritual ethic for governing society that facilitates everyone's evolution.

FREE WILL LOSING ITSELF

We are obligated to experience the outworkings of our choices. One's progression can be thwarted through the misuse of the human will. The darkness associated with evil—the devil and sin—is merely free will losing itself in relationship to the Light. When the intellectual powers of the mind and the spiritual powers of Universal Knowledge are combined, both good and evil become clear as moral choices. The trend of the linear intellect will occasionally embrace and explore evil, departing from the way of the Inner Teacher. In living a wholly self-determined life— seeking only one's whims and desires—one becomes less and less aware of the guiding Presence within. This unconscious separation leads to a wilderness of misguided ambition, misfortune, uncertainty, and fallibility.

For these reasons, real progress is slow and suffering is great. Evil and sin may best be defined as that which impedes evolutionary development.

The inner Light of the Soul is a different kind of wilderness of open truth that is simply trusted, practiced, and followed by those with an enlarged awareness and awakened outlook on life. Light brings forth knowledge, learning, and guidance. Darkness withholds information, which engenders ignorance. Discern which frequencies you are harboring and encountering. Seek to awaken the higher Self and begin to trust the reality that the plane of Light is a living Law of a Spiritual nature that offers continuous support in casting aside the veils of illusion and replacing delusion with Cosmic Consciousness.

The support and influence of higher forces manifests from an unknown stimulus that may not necessarily be received from any definite place or personage. Some people receive inner guidance consciously, some unconsciously—and some know, acknowledge, and cultivate a partnership with Spiritual guidance daily, with reverent gratitude. Spirit may best be described as the central control of the Universe and the space within the atom and is often referred to as Principle, or God/Mind. This Principle governs with sublime creativity and serene Intelligence. For this reason it may be considered to be a Mind Principle that permeates all sentient beings and organic life. Humanity's real dominion is to align with and not overrule the focal point of the Mind Principle that activates all conditions of life.

The ephemeral essence of Mind Principle and the manifestation of matter work in unity with each other. As physical beings we live within the Laws of nature and are subject to the consequences of violating the Laws of nature. If we cultivate a connection to whom we really are, we see that reality lives at a level that is above the mortal mind; there is a greater guiding force that we must trust and align with in our lives, for we are truly and gently held in this embrace. When we fail to see this, the Universal Law of Cause and Effect serves as an inspiring teacher for greater self-awakening.

Self-awakening requires the ability to transcend one's judgments, preferences, compulsions, ideas, beliefs, and customs at the level of cultural conditioning. Accepting what must be learned, transformed, and transmuted depends on one's ability to align with the higher Spiritual gift of Mind that is allowed expression through the self. This is the true and proper use for the Universal Law of Allowance. Not only does free will allow the reception of higher expression of Mind, it chooses to act on behalf of this higher Spiritual authority.

THE HUMAN BODY

If the body and the mind are not in alignment with Spirit, how can the body and the mind express Spiritual values? It is the inexplicable force of Spirit that makes life possible. In turn, the body and mind reciprocate by allowing Spirit its expression. Otherwise we become entrenched in the idea that we are separate from this reality and we are alone, expressing ourselves autonomously. It is only when we believe that we are separate and alone that fear, panic, and dysfunction create the impression that things are out of sync and therefore out of control.

Because the physical body resides in the third dimension, at the surface, the body appears to be a dense and limited vibratory force existing only in space and time. The body and the mind must also be honored and understood for their intrinsic value as vehicles for the multidimensional Spiritual forces. It is the Spiritual forces that allow the human body and mind to become capable of much more than is currently accepted. Spirit always remains Spirit and so the body that contains Spirit is already Spiritualized, radiant, and limitless. Denial of this fact perpetuates a limiting influence of materiality; and some do deny the reality of the Spiritual Light of Mind Principle. When we are told that we are sinful limited beings for long enough, we begin to believe it. We become lost and estranged to the breath of Soul in our lives. This leaves us defenseless, hollow, and without our inner compass to guide us past the forces that attempt to set us on a course of destruction and slavery.

When the Presence of Spiritual Light manifests into one's being, the individual automatically resonates with the frequency of Love, and one's cells become lighter and less dense. Light is really a current of Love that galvanizes and balances every cell in the body. How can true Love be expressed unless it flows through one that is aligned with, and expressing, the harmony of Spiritual Light—the Soul of Life? Pure Consciousness at its highest resonant level creates intoxicating new dimensions of Intelligence; a true marriage of Love and unity that protects and gently guides us through every twist and turn in life. Real Love may not always be kind and reassuring. Real fear, rather than imaginary fear, is nature's way of alerting us to danger. Anxiety and discomfort are often signs that something needs to be attended to and acted upon in life. To ignore and deny these red flags is to deny the reality, Wisdom, benefits, and full range of experience in life.

It takes time and effort to alter the negative images, attitudes of sickness, deterioration, and traumatic events that become so ingrained that they dominate our lives. The stabilizing Principle of Universal Mind must be self-generated from one's Spiritual center of power through consistency and integrated into the lifestyle as a self-imposed discipline, rather than total freedom marred by compulsive behavior. When the influence behind disease is altered and transmuted to a true state of unification, the flesh radiates with a higher frequency of harmony. The false ego can greatly affect the health of the body, and some diseases truly arise from the belief that one is separate physically, mentally, and spiritually. Therefore, the false ego can be the greatest violation of the Natural Law of one's well-being and can produce devastating results.

When we allow Spirit to express through us in the ideal way, the flowering of the human family will manifest as a blaze of real beauty and authentic Love—is this not what we are all really looking for? The inner Light of the Soul harbors the perfect potential, just as the potential of the flower and the fruit is wrought from the seed in its perfect image. The flower develops step-by-step, day by day; it expands, unfolds, and brings forth fruit. The Mind Principle from which this expression emanates is reflected in the same deep, inner drive that compels all advancing life forms.

For humanity, it is a matter of cultivating what is inherent. It is a higher expression of consciousness that in turn Spiritualizes the flesh. The highest expression of the flesh is found in the example of the advanced masters who have cultivated the very real ability to create a Superlight body. When the body is infused with the Light of higher frequencies it levitates, or Spiritualizes, the flesh rendering it lighter than air.

In her book *Aboriginal Men of High Degree,* Australian anthropologist A. P. Elkin documented the sacred practices of the *karadji*—Aboriginal shamans who heal disease, make rain, intuit future events, and demonstrate the amazing ability to appear and disappear at will. These isolated tribal shamans exhibited the same skills as advanced masters. The advanced masters insist that all people are capable of achieving these skills through mastering frequency. Mastering frequency requires properly managing the energies of the so-called light and dark side. This is achieved through learning to navigate multidimensional energies and continuously working to transmute the darkness that, in truth, inspires and awakens the inner Light.

The ability to willfully appear and disappear is actually a fundamental teaching in learning self-mastery. The phenomenon of free-will thought aligned with Spirit, or God/Mind, and united with the atomic hive we call a body determines the lightness of one's being in life. The advanced masters demonstrate that the power of higher thoughts and deeds loosens the hydrogen bonds from their natural state to a point where a seemingly solid body can transfigure itself by creating a higher body of Light.

The advanced masters are able to rest their atomic or purely physical bodies where they lay. The higher body, a Spiritual replica that floats along in a manner lighter than air, is derived from Original Substance, or One Mind Principle, of existence. The Light body allows the masters to travel in the invisible and arrive at the intended destination, then lower the vibratory frequency to appear as visible in order to proceed with the task at hand. Later, the master realigns the ethereal life energy to the waiting, inanimate physical body. This same ability of transmutation was applied when food, shelter, heat, clothing, money, or any material need was required for the higher good. It is with this ability that one's difficulties in the world of material existence disappear!

In self-mastery, the body is indeed a tool to be merged with the biomagnetic energy of Light and mastered so that it does not die. The biomagnetic force field of the body is not to be destroyed, but lifted to a higher vibratory dimension of existence. Otherwise, the body will eventually die and the Soul incarnates into another body to begin again.

The body of a master may also be renewed and refreshed upon death—and reawakened. This is the mastery that we are all meant to aspire toward.

However, most people simply do not believe that self-mastery is possible. This implies that people do not know whom they really are and what they are capable of. This is the crucial teaching that has been suppressed in religious doctrine to keep people under control and in a state of servitude as slaves, rather than masters. It is a state of living without death that has nothing to do with being "saved" by a Savior. It is purely the responsibility of the individual to do the work of transmutation from the lower to the higher states of frequency in order to project conditions of perfection into life, the Earth, and the Universe. Exalt life, and you will be a master. Thinking that you cannot achieve or are not capable of the work of self-mastery builds a self-imposed prison of limitation.

When we speak of the advanced masters, we speak of the striking resemblance between the works that have been attributed to all known and unknown enlightened ones—those who are the oldest known Spiritual Teachers of humankind. The masters, seers, prophets, sages, and visionaries of history all demonstrate, to a greater or lesser degree, the higher condition of life that higher consciousness brings forth. Universally, higher consciousness is referred to as *Christ Consciousness*. This is not attributed to the worship of any one being; rather, Christ Consciousness is achieved through realization of the living God within. The lives and experiences of those who have mastered the body and the mind through aligning with the God within are genuine demonstrations of this original teaching. This is the ultimate adventure, as the advanced masters have always insisted that there is no mystery to their works.

Reference to the advanced masters does not constitute any one religion or institution. The body and mind must simply express through its Spiritual foundation in order to learn to express the power of the Spirit. This is achieved in the manner by which all things are brought forth—through cultivating this desire, focusing one's attention on this work, and experiencing the fruits of Spirit. Through this focus the flesh is harmonized, the Soul is seeded with radiant joy, the thoughts are keenly enlightened, the words are true, acts are constructive, and all things assume a harmonious position in this life and beyond.

BODY BASICS

Purification of the body and the mind is an essential step that assists the individual to receive and maintain higher vibratory frequencies. The body and the mind must be cleansed to support higher frequencies. There is a great wealth of information in the world regarding the basics of purification and self-nurturing that I have written about at length in my first book, *The Seasonal Detox Diet* (originally titled *The Ancient Cookfire*). For those who wish to discover the finer points of purification and prevention, these books cover in detail how to support the health of the body. Toxins greatly retard the efforts of the spiritual realm to exult the material mind. A comment that I often hear from those who simplify their diets by abstaining from low-quality food and drink and allowing the body to detoxify is the profound alteration they experience on a vibratory level, resulting in improved functioning on all levels. When we choose discordant processed diets, rather than food and drink in a more natural state, we worship discord rather than harmony, which depletes energy and lowers the vibratory potential of the body and mind.

The body cannot maintain a stable state of health without an environment of sufficient energy to support and sustain a healthy condition. The irises in the eyes of each individual are unique, and so too does each body deal differently with the same nutrients. Good health is closely related to the enzymatic assimilative ability of the individual. A body that supports bacteria and disease-causing entities can be changed to one that does not support deterioration.

When the environment is altered by the ever-increasing effects of toxic chemicals and electromagnetic pollution, we see that the resulting depletion of the body's bioenergetic balance contributes to new disease conditions. The good news is that each degree of effort on the part of the individual is met with a correspondingly higher degree of assistance;

when we choose to consciously resonate with the frequency of Light, results are forthcoming. For people who are experiencing overwhelming stress in regard to managing their health, I have listed some new products made with integrity and quality to support healthy frequencies in the Resources section at the back of the book; these are simple additions to the recipes that are offered in *The Seasonal Detox Diet*.

WHAT IS FREQUENCY?

Frequency is a wave form of resonance that creates a pulsated electrical energy construct. Various frequencies generate different shapes, sound waves, colors and patterns, viruses, fungi, and bacteria that appear within the space of mind, body, and ether. Life begins with encoded molecules having a frequency designed to survive within their own energy support system. The human body has its own electromagnetic frequency that harmonizes with the electromagnetic frequency of the Earth: a frequency that pulses at about the same rate as the hands of people who are healers, about 8 hertz. Electromagnetic energy is defined as the various waves of electricity and magnetism emanating from many objects and forms of life.

ROYAL R. RIFE

A great deal of bodywork entails working toward balancing electromagnetic frequencies. The genius inventor Royal R. Rife knew this and invented a safe way to neutralize cancer and many other maladies using a frequency wave machine with separate settings for various frequencies of disease. By increasing the intensity of the frequency at which a particular microbe resonates, Rife discovered that the natural oscillation of the microbe also increases, causing it to die. Rife named this intensified frequency the mortal oscillatory rate—MOR—and isolated the frequencies of fifty-two harmful organisms, including typhoid, tuberculosis, pneumonia, syphilis, candida, and cancer. Although Royal Rife's work was undeniable proof that the use of biofrequency healing is a nontoxic way to kill disease, the wave machine was disallowed for use in hospitals by AMA and FDA regulations. However, personal experimentation with the current-frequency instrument is permitted and lists settings for over eight hundred diseases, disorders, and pain relief. (See the Resources section for more on Rife's work.)

Although emergency medical services are certainly essential for saving lives, the first time that I consulted a medical doctor for a simple stomach ailment, I discerned that it would be up to me to take responsibility for my own health. From the beginning, practicing the art of detoxifying and balancing the body with the proper food and drink, as well as simplifying the diet, is very uplifting. Once we begin to master the art of self-nurturing, we naturally come to ask: where do we go from here? It is difficult to remain balanced in an unbalanced world. This inquiry led me toward the next step—the exploration of the mind and a deeper, more thorough investigation of the many astonishing Spiritual experiences that I have had throughout my life.

THE HUMAN MIND

Mind is always above matter for the simple reason that mind exists one level above the third dimension, in the fourth dimension. There is a great body of evidence that indicates consciousness exists at frequencies above the biological body. According to the work of Albert Einstein and Herman Minkowski, time is the fourth dimension of space. In time-space, conscious thought does not depend solely on the brain; the near-death experience demonstrates that Universal Intelligence and the human mind are inseparable. The near-death experience is only one way that teaches us that mind remains functional beyond the death of the physical body. People have had experiences of life beyond the death of the body that predate organized religion. The fourth dimension serves as a transitional arena for the evolution of consciousness. It is a holographic storehouse for the living blueprints of the elemental kingdoms of nature. These blueprints govern and maintain the integrity and intricate workings of the physical systems of Earth. The fourth dimension functions as the mind of the Earth.

Just as what one eats and drinks seeds the environment for the body, so too do thoughts and emotions seed the environment for the energetic mental bodies. Because the biological human brain does not possess an innate sense of moral ethics, higher conscience is the Soul's responsibility.

People are very determined to exercise the free will aspect of the body and mind, and life reflects both the failures and the successes of these efforts. The mind is a creature of habit and feeds on the dominating influences and thoughts with which it is nourished. Strong feelings of emotion are not always the equivalent of the leadings of higher Spiritual guidance. To be strongly and overwhelmingly compelled to do a certain thing or to go to a certain place does not necessarily mean that such impulses are the inspiration of the indwelling Spirit. All people experience uncertainty in discerning issues between matter and Spirit. Nevertheless, one cannot escape the responsibility for maintaining balance between the multilevels of living. Our thoughts, feelings, and emotions all radiate out in electromagnetic waves that imprint our intent. Ultimately, the living bridge that we are building must be one that raises our frequency.

The pinnacle of human experience is when we begin to vibrate with sovereignty and self-knowledge. It is a matter of getting beyond the mortal self, above the influences of psychic intrusion and the false ego that are apt to mislead. The biological mind by itself is a poor master and cannot create a stable, meaningful foundation until it is energized with the frequencies of Spiritual inspiration. The brain is the intermediary between the physical and the Spiritual realities. When we accept higher consciousness as a reality, then all things are interpreted from the perspective of the Spiritual ideal underlying them. It is not an exercise of material power for the exaltation of the false ego—a smaller self that cannot do Spiritual work in the absence of Spiritual power.

THE NEW BRAIN SCIENCE

Thought carries a potent radiation due to its effect over the vibratory field. Thought moving concurrently with Mind generates electrons that produce movement in the plane of manifest substances. The energizing principle of material creation exists as a polarized electronic field of positive and negative energy points. The electron that is the foundation of this principle functions as a multidimensional particle/wave unit of communication and awareness in all life forms. Individual consciousness is created through the electron, and all matter has awareness through the function of the electron, including water, air, fire, and even rocks and minerals. The electron is the frequency from which thought is created, and through the condensation of thought, the various degrees of consciousness are formed.

Consciousness is ongoing and eternal; thought does not die with the death of the biological body. When the individual consciousness attains a high enough electronic frequency, it ascends through the spiral of frequencies to the next higher dimension. Here the entropic cycles of birth and decay, night and day, and other polarities of third-dimensional existence are transcended and transmuted. The individual Soul has earned the right to co-create through aligning with Consciousness in such a way that the created and the creator merge as one to continue creation in higher dimensions of thought.

This is the realization of the God/Self within. Every human entity co-creates within the frequency of his or her own creations. However, when one has realized the genius within Self and moves within the infinite levels of self-mastery, one becomes a true co-creator merging as one with Principle. Teaching, healing, and learning on this level requires cultivating peace and balance within the self before one can broadcast healing energy on a global and universal scale.

The biological mechanism of the brain is an important circuitry of compartments and glands that are portals serving both the physical worlds of form and the Spiritual worlds of the formless. Interestingly, the new brain science has indeed confirmed that the function of thought and the Spiritual footprint cannot be fully attributed to brain physiology. It has been determined that the brain is basically a biophysical substrate for the mental and Spiritual energetic processes. Science has also confirmed that the actual vibratory energies of thought exist one layer above the body in the fourth astral dimension, creating what has been termed the *psychic,* or the mental environment. And so the brain is more like a mediator between one's Spiritual reality and one's physical reality. This upholds the claim that the vibratory Spiritual forces do not replace the mind, but instead will employ or influence the mind. The more separated we are from higher Spiritual influences, the more differentiated and departmentalized and unsound does the mortal mind become.

Mentally unsound minds are easily herded into organizations and institutions, and this ultimately becomes a form of bondage. Mental soundness is wholeness—knowing that we move with and are included in the operations of the whole. No one is sound until he or she operates as a complete unit, in and with the higher Mind Principle. The advanced masters state that "whenever one group, race, or nation segregate themselves as a chosen people favored by God, they are not sound people, and their doctrines are never sound. All people are chosen of God. All people are God's Soul Seeds in manifestation just as all forms of plant and animal life are manifestations of Nature."

Vibratory energies that are formless, yet capable of communication, exist everywhere. The ancient and mysterious force that animates life is known as subtle energy by metaphysicians, *prana* (breath) by Eastern healers, and chi (life force) by the Chinese. It is a free flow of information carried by the biochemicals of emotion. Emotions exist in the body as informational chemicals: the neuropeptides and thin receptors that assist the circulation of emotional and spiritual information that connects the physical and the nonphysical realms of existence. A person's perceptual capacity determines how revelations of these forces are brought to light. These revelations assist the individual with insightful solutions when challenge arises and guide us toward adjustments in relationships and changes that must be made in life. To facilitate this process, the average person is capable of feeling, hearing, seeing, and experiencing energies that run the gamut of emotions. We are also surrounded by colors that many people cannot see and sounds that many people cannot hear. Nevertheless, these vibratory energies exist as a reality and communicate in many forms.

In working toward balance it is of chief importance to cultivate the ability to emit one's own frequency of love, rather than searching outside of the self for love and thereby absorbing the oftentimes dissonant, self-serving frequencies of fickle, unfaithful partners who seek love through the manufactured, hypnotized illusion of what people think is love. True Love is unconditional and emanates from the Soul.

It is reasonable to suggest that the manner in which a person cares for the physical body and utilizes the mental forces will determine the aptitude for expansive awareness, or conversely the potential for limitation and narrowness. And it is essential to focus on balancing the physical and the Spiritual in our daily lives to counteract the destructive influences that weaken human consciousness. When the few that influence the many are unbalanced, then the greater population is thrust toward imbalance. Currently, people are struggling to live a balanced life in an imbalanced world.

THE FEW THAT INFLUENCE THE MANY

One ring to rule them all,
One ring to find them,
One ring to bring them all,
And in the darkness bind them.

J. R. R. TOLKIEN,
THE FELLOWSHIP OF THE RING

There are many good people in the world that are unaware of some of the causes behind the effect of many shocking world events. It is with a heavy heart that I include the following paragraphs. However, this information is necessary to bring people to a fuller understanding of the invisible few that influence the many. This information illustrates the false ego at work in the world in its saddest and most dangerous state. It personifies the phrase, "The scum rises to the top." When the underlying sources that promote darkness and destruction in the historical evolution of the world are brought into the light, we can begin to direct our efforts toward unification and healing rather than hurting each other.

Because more and more information is being leaked in the news and revealed in various books, in documentaries, and through people's experiences, a greater understanding and uncovering of the cause behind the effect of corrupt institutions will better assist us in creating balance. Throughout history many true Spiritual teachers have appeared among the various races to challenge the priests of any age who oppose real education and attempt to thwart Spiritual evolution. It has always been imperative to overcome tyranny by resisting the deceptive teachings that foster imbalance.

One of America's most eminent constitutional attorneys, Edwin Vieira is helping to explain part of the imbalance in his two-volume book *Pieces of Eight: The Monetary Powers and Disabilities of the United States Constitution*. Mr. Vieira reveals why the work forces of the world, the taxpayers, and those who save money are unable to get ahead due to income inequality. Vieira explains that the Federal Reserve System (a private corporation, often termed the *Fed*) functions as a de facto world bank and is run by a very small number of people—potentially just one: the chair of the board of governors.

It is supposedly a secret exactly who, or what, actually owns this parasitical system that lords over policy and economics in Washington, D.C., and the world. It is fundamentally a system of foreign private member banks that are below the regional Fed banks using the pyramidal structure. These banks create currency out of nothing (credit creation by banks), then lend it out and charge interest on it. This gives the illusion that there is money flowing into the economy. Consequently the cost of living increases faster than people's wages, and the standard of living decreases. Here the majority of people are held in a downward spiral of usury and extortion. Ironically Washington, D.C., can print money without the involvement of the Federal Reserve, rather than borrowing money and paying interest. When this system fails, the banks are bailed out by the government using taxpayers' money (the public purse).

The interest on the debt exists to give the Federal Reserve and the bankers a partnership interest—a piece of the public purse. Technically, the debt on this interest is an illusion, created from nothing. However, it is not an illusion to those who must work and labor their lives away to bail out the banks. When the interest on debt balloons out of control due to overspending, the debt is simply unpayable. The only way out of enormous debt is for the Federal Reserve to ultimately forgive the interest on the debt.

Interestingly, the Federal Reserve has no responsibility to Congress—rather the Fed is committed to maintaining their own entrenched economic advantage and makes policy that quickly turns into direct operations in the local and foreign financial worlds. Although unelected by the people, the chair of the Fed wields great influence over the important economic variables of the world. The Federal Reserve does not pay taxes and will never be audited. World governments pay the Federal Reserve a fee for running this system—a system that is designed to control and impoverish people. Before the financial crisis began in the 1990s, the Fed owned more than nine hundred billion dollars in assets. By the end of 2013, it owned more than four trillion dollars in assets. Oxfam International reports that by 2016 the richest 1 percent of the population will control more than half of the world's wealth. This is an unjust and dangerous predicament that is unprecedented in both American and world history.

Essentially, a worldwide imperialist corporation has been carefully and methodically created over many centuries whereby the corruption of the administration robs the wages of the people to line the pockets of those in positions of power. Imperialist control embodies a warlike system that secretly aims at dominion over the Earth's resources through political means. It is not recorded in the history books, but all democracies are designed with two separate organizations that play the political game: the visible government and the invisible leaders that control the workings of both government and finance behind the scenes. The visible government is at the mercy of the invisible leaders who enjoy immunity from the irresponsible consequences of the government policies that they control.

Currently, America is an unwitting partner in the unsustainable and sad game of war and corruption. A large percentage of taxpayer money is used to establish control over the taxpayers and to engineer the needless wars that destroy so many lives and lands. The governments of resource-rich countries are methodically taken over and used. When we hear Hillary Clinton say, "The emperor has no clothes," or

President Obama say, "Make no mistake . . . evil exists in the world," they are inviting people to read between the lines. In Native American culture, it is believed that true sorcerers know how to steal power. The sorcerer understands that to kill is to lose one's power, and so to maintain power the sorcerer knows how to make people kill each other and themselves. They conceal the fact that the true might and power of the individual is rooted in the wisdom of self-mastery, not in war.

If we follow the money and connect the dots it becomes evident that there is only one place in the world that is allowed to operate in this imperialist manner: Vatican City in Rome, Italy. No significant political or world event can be fully evaluated without considering the dominant role the Vatican plays in it. Recall the old adage, "All roads lead to Rome." The Vatican is actually a private corporation and military order, operating under the guise of religion—various historical records have long warned of this proverbial wolf in sheep's clothing. With all the bloodshed, destruction, and war wrought in the name of God, it would not be unreasonable to conclude that the perpetrators of these heinous acts would be akin to a military order acting under the cloak of religion. This is precisely what we must consider if we are to recognize the truth. How else over the course of thousands of years could these sorcerers achieve control over the finances of the world's governments, industry, religion, education, people, and the media?

The Vatican is one of the world's largest corporations, and we must look at the corporate influence on everything that takes place regarding the world's resources and the human family. The current pontiff, Pope Francis, appears to be genuinely attempting concrete action to heal and eradicate the terrible scourge of modern slavery in all of its forms. Pope Francis is the first Latin American pope in history, and he is wise and brave enough to rise above the Roman political hotbed of corruption. We would do well to pray for Pope Francis as he requested, to give him strength and protection against those who do not wish to see him succeed.

The advanced masters teach that no one should presume to stand as interpreters, intermediaries, or intercessors between humanity and the indwelling God/Mind within the individual. However, we observe that the current protocols often condemn freedom of consciousness, freedom of the press, and national sovereignty. It appears as if the ultimate goal is a one-world government of economically socialist police states. This is a plan that has utterly exhausted the human family with hatred, disease, struggle, dissension, war, and torture.

The Federal Reserve Bank is but one aspect of this system of control. Popes, monarchs, and government leaders that resist the protocols are often punished. Withholding information is standard practice, as secrecy has always been essential to the successful practice of fraudulent activities. Important books are suppressed, the truth is suppressed through lies, and campaigns are launched to pervert and vilify. This system also seeks to control the fortunes of those who resist them.

This is how much those in control fear the creative power that is inherent within the individual. When people are deceived into believing that others wield authority over every aspect of their lives, generation after generation, the world becomes shaped in the image of those with a soulless and coldly manipulative upper hand. Culturally, we have inherited a collective memory that influences our behavior and beliefs. This collective memory has been largely fashioned by the overbearing, self-appointed imperialists that build the fortunes of the so-called elite. The mechanics of physical survival have been carefully systematized so that the people inadvertently preserve these power structures and follow the archaic and outmoded rules that inhibit conscious evolution.

Without conscious evolution, dehumanization sets in; futility and the *why try* attitude overshadow the enthusiasm and joy that is a natural gift of a life well lived. When one group denies basic freedoms to a part of the whole there is always inequality. It is becoming overtly obvious that a certain group is attempting to arrogate power and advantage to itself, while attempting to penalize, or virtually enslave, others— especially if they do not support the dominant element. All of this has been omitted from history books; we have been taught little of how Rome terrorized Western Europe for over a thousand years and why our ancestors sought freedom by fleeing from Europe to America.

It appears that the propagators of untruths and the irresponsible policy makers have quite a foothold on the world; however, this system could not be carried out for ages without the cooperation of the human family. It takes many so-called little people, or worker bees, to carry out the rules and regulations of this stuffy, officious regime. Remember the old adage of the 1960s, "What if they gave a war and nobody came?" When we *wake up*—we will use our consciousness properly and will no longer allow ourselves to be willing pawns in a game of endless suffering!

The tyranny of fear and anxiety that is currently rampant in the world will be transmuted through the conscience intention of each individual to enhance their skills in mind power, contemplation, and meditation and to resonate with the frequency of Spiritual Intelligence—which is synchronous with Love. The subtle power of love is our real strength. The energy of all highly developed spiritual individuals is focused in the heart! At the threshold of no return, the sorcerers of war and greed must resort to morality and sanity—or the natural order and cycles of life will be destroyed. We are all made or unmade by our choices. Every Soul in its purity houses a miniature God to be merged with right now, right here on Earth—not waiting and hoping for the death of the body and another life cycle of suffering. If we cannot master consciousness in this realm, how then do we expect to master consciousness in higher realms?

It takes courage to resist becoming lost in a world that encourages one to lavish so much time, attention, and importance on material acquisitions, egocentric insecurities, the latest trends in technology, and warlike behavior. And many people do become lost while chasing after little that is of true and lasting value.

Placing great value on that which can be easily destroyed or taken away does not constitute real security. Real security requires a refocusing of consciousness on reclaiming our deeper wisdom and authentic power. Real security is Spiritual security. Spiritual security is the ability to respond to problems and concerns with the power of the deeper resources of one's higher inner authority rather than responding with hopelessness and helplessness—a "tell me what to do" victim mentality. The whole process of Becoming is difficult and lost when the greater majority of people are incognito.

MINDLESSNESS

There exists real potential for self-destruction when thought becomes fixated in a world of perpetual persuasion, seductive distractions, and divisive deceptions—a world that is banking on the premise that people will mindlessly think and believe what others influence them to think and believe. Mindlessness may very well be the most dangerous disturbance that life on Earth can endure. The great eighteenth-century German poet, philosopher, and natural scientist J. W. von Goethe described mindlessness succinctly when he made the statement, "There is nothing more terrifying than ignorance in action."

Mindless thinking is often the culprit in causing one to judge or reject the natural creative outgrowth of the higher Self. This information often requires a change in direction that the person would be wise to follow—yet, this may be perceived by some to be a threat to free will. If we are unwilling to receive real Spiritual assistance, we render a self-imposed impotency of limitation and pain upon ourselves that also reverberates on others.

A life well lived requires a modicum of humility. So it is reasonable to accept that without humility the mortal mind is prone to sham identities fashioned by the misdirected desires and dreams of illusion that are engraved upon the false ego of the human psyche. The false ego demands attention, will seek out attention, and will compete for attention in a myriad of ways. The false ego in its unbalanced state will foster victim consciousness, as well as become addicted to power, manipulation, and control—all of which inhibit one's ability to perceive logically. The implementation of rigid control constitutes a deviation from the Universal Law of Allowance—that, in turn, causes chaos, destruction, and imbalance. Natural Laws always work regardless of whether we understand them or not.

Humanity has been perennially called to awaken from the self-imposed nightmare of the egocentric mortal mind. This nightmare represents the popular ideas and the illusory conventional thinking that people rely on . . . and mistakenly call truth.

The solution to imbalance lies in the deliberate intention to resolve imbalance by cultivating balance. It is a great endeavor to follow the challenge of what we must do—rather than taking the easy path of what we want to do. To follow the truth of one's higher Mind is both humbling and thrilling as we awaken to something more accomplished than the mundane. The higher Mind is a subtle force that comforts with steadiness and reassurance. If we accept the existence of our higher Mind—seek it out and learn to use it—we then become the recipients of a power that is beyond the temporal world. Here, life is no longer mindlessly governed by damaging decisions, empty drives, misdirected ambitions, self-doubt, raging fears, betrayal, and deception.

For the human race to align itself with the flow of life and create an effective alliance to protect life and live with wisdom on a finite planet, the seed of Spiritual maturity must be nurtured. The seed of Spiritual maturity is a great ally, which is hidden beneath the darkened soil of the formidable foe of the false ego. Rather than sacrifice our Earthly Eden, it is time to sacrifice the limiting thought patterns, destructive actions, and the futile dramas that drain the energy out of life and living.

With the potency of free will to choose which energies we will be most devoted to, we see that civilization has been "incognito" for far too long in service to illusory gods, parasitic structures of power, dangerous technologies, epidemic addictions, sexual deviance, and other self-destructive distractions that cloud our ability to navigate through life with clarity and balance. These are challenging and misguided distractions that compel us to waste a great deal of time creating a discordant life, rather than aligning with the destiny of our true work in the world.

Recognition that we have roots in the realm of the Spiritual is relegated to repetitive and robotic prayer and traditional rituals that are only verisimilitudes of true religion. That we must remain balanced and connected within the realm of Earth through the fluid movement of Spirit is a lost art. The institutions of organized religion have perpetuated a monopoly on universal Spiritual meaning cloaked in assiduous book learning and ritual. The cost has been a dangerous lack of nurturing a more personal experiential discovery, resulting in a suppression and estrangement from the deeper inward avenues of Spiritual prescience. To be "managed" in regard to our private Spiritual lives stifles the experiential essence of inner religion. The Inner Teacher is different for each of us, and it can only be discovered on a personal level and as the unique experience that it is.

Through a deeper inquiry and contemplation of one's own spiritual gifts, it is possible to rebalance, restructure, and resolve what must be learned and what must fall away. The cultural obsession with scientific fact and overreliance on linear logic and mental reasoning is due to a failure to view life at its deeply layered, multidimensional level. Connecting with our multidimensionality requires tapping into the essential skills that our ancestors relied on. It is a dynamic relationship with the fullness of one's total environment.

In order to survive, the fading cultures of our ancestors developed the faculties that could mesh with and perceive the Soul of their environment. They trained themselves to discern with their inner eyes and relied upon oracular dreams to know how to find what was needed—a place to find water underground, where to find their prey on the other side of the mountain, and even how to find their way home to their tribe across hundreds of miles. Animals too are inherently endowed with the qualities of the inner eye. The valuable ability to find one's way home across many miles without a compass or a map has been achieved by magnetically homing in on, or *feeling,* the beacon of their nomadic group Soul. In times past, telepathic skills were developed and relied on as a matter of survival, and the human family will greatly benefit now from resurrecting this talent.

Everyone in a conscious physical state contemplates the mysteries of life. Eventually the most profound questions can be answered if we are honest with ourselves; it becomes clear that we bear a great portion of the responsibility for whom we ultimately become and why we find ourselves in a particular predicament in time. The realization of truth requires courage if we are to change, and change personifies the monumental journey of life. The development and the advancement of each life ebbs and flows with the ability to discern that which is constructive and what is needed, in contrast to that which is destructive and does not serve life.

People are perennially struggling for balance in a world that is unbalanced. Currently, it is a world where strong influences encourage living life on a base and superficial level. It is a world where people are led to believe that they are "creating their own reality"—a reality driven by the desires of the false ego, where the greater focus of thought shifts to material acquisition, social status, self-gratification, and the personal fantasies and compulsions that drive human misery. This constitutes a misguided use of both the mental and the spiritual energies and results in a vain movement toward false satisfaction.

No one entirely escapes these alluring influences. The ramifications of creating your own reality using the false ego are evident all around us. There is also a tendency to blame others for the unhappiness and the hardships that living a shallow life presents. However, we may be assured that life is truly the Master Teacher, so it would be wise to accept responsibility, learn from life's lessons, and rise to the challenges. It is the Spiritual Mind Principle that creates the reality of life. It is the mortal mind that fosters illusion.

The finite material brain cannot possibly fathom the volume of information inherent in the hierarchy of the creative process and the various planes of being. It is difficult enough to decipher an imprecise past shaded by myth, as well as the mental and spiritual contamination that has been wreaked upon the world. To achieve a solid standing in life, both the material and the spiritual must be cultivated in equal measure. When one predominates over the other there can be a significant lack of balance, confusion, and deterioration, which is largely what we currently struggle with in the world.

BEYOND RELIGION

People are advised that there is always a fine line to walk when it comes to discussing religion. The constant warning not to question its validity and purpose is replete throughout society. Yet the edicts of the institution of religion suffer from the same misinterpretations and poor translations of the surface consciousness and false ego as all things do over time. This matters not when one follows the Inner Teacher of the higher Self. Religion when properly implemented offers hope, charity, and Spiritual advancement. But true goodness is unconscious and emanates from the wisdom of the heart/mind. Wisdom and goodness then are really beyond religion. They are inherent endowments. People don't require religion to simply act from a loving heart. When theological laws are misused in the name of authority and tradition, then religion becomes an unwilling accomplice for those who would use it to misguide and manipulate others.

When the world is governed and influenced by a very small percentage of people that impact human development and determine its activities, we must be vigilant and question all areas of human endeavor. An important law of living is that stronger minds influence and dominate weaker minds. And the strength of stronger minds stems from a function of both concentration and motivation. We know that working toward, thinking about, and concentrating on one thing for a long period of time produces a result that could not otherwise be achieved. Anyone who has crafted, composed, or invented anything worthwhile knows that concentration, matched with skill, planning, and perseverance, will produce results.

Despite this, people are not generally taught the essential skills of concentration, contemplation, patience, and single-mindedness when it comes to both secular and religious education; here the main focus is memorizing information in order to meet certain educational requirements. Consequently, rather than learning to concentrate the mental energies of the mind to create self-confidence and self-mastery through aligning with Spirit, we experience all manner of deception, confusion, dysfunction, estrangement, war, and alienation on both an individual and a collective level.

Opening a dialogue regarding religion is essential for exploring how the deeper connections between matter and Spirit are formed. The right of each individual to choose or not choose a religion is a personal matter of free will. And there is no intention of denigrating anyone's belief system in this exploration. Attacking the various belief systems and exhibiting disappointment, frustration, hostility, impatience, and anger does not help people. Genuine truth has universal application and transcends fixed ideas, customs, and beliefs. Universal Spirituality directs us to the great fabric of life into which we are interwoven and interdependent. It is not bound by devotion to one deity, person, or idea; rather it is a fundamental wisdom that all intelligent, sentient life forms share on a universal Spiritual level.

Scientific evidence and historical artifacts related to inherited religion were actually left unchallenged until the seventeenth century. It is well documented that real physical evidence of biblical texts is hard to come by. The closest examples that science is aware of are the Dead Sea Scrolls, the Silver Scrolls, and the Bhagavad Gita. The Bhagavad Gita is perhaps the oldest surviving religion of the Nag Hammadi codex banished to obscurity. It has been established that the first five books of the Bible are attributed to Moses. However, the advanced masters claim that Moses received the biblical teachings from Babylonian records; then these records were badly distorted by translators—some holy, some not so holy. There are many mistakes in the translations from the original texts in the context of the Bible, as well as many false prophecies.

There is also strong evidence that the general outline of the Babylonian and biblical texts emerged from the oldest original records kept in the Temple of the Great Tau Cross by the Siddha masters of the Himalayas. It is claimed that some of these records date back to the period of the advent of humanity upon this Earth. These records are those of the Naacals, or Holy Brothers, as they were called, and they came direct from the Motherland of the human family. It is also claimed that these Holy Brothers came direct to Burma and taught the Nagas. These records also prove that the forefathers of these people were the authors of the Surya Siddhanta and the earlier Vedas. The Surya Siddhanta is the oldest known work on astronomy. These records date back 25,000 years and the earlier Vedas date back 45,000 years. It is not claimed that these were all original records. Rather, these were copied from the same records that the Babylonian records were taken from. It is also claimed that the originals from which these were copied are the original Osirian and Atlantean records, and some of these tablets date back hundreds of thousands of years.

These records preserved by the Siddha masters of the Himalayas are the oldest known Spiritual guidelines that antedate all religious history. It is said that the system of rulers inadvertently sprang from this original teaching. People soon wandered away from the original teaching and realization that life is God expressing through people, animals, and plants—that through the step-down process, God serves creation and creation serves God. If God served only God, the material worlds would be nonexistent. Erroneously falling prey to the wants and desires of the false ego, people lost sight of the Spiritual aspect of life and created an overriding hypnotic influence of materiality and psychic prowess. This gave rise to a greater separation in beliefs and an ever-widening diversity of thought regarding religion. The focus of the original Siddha text is on Natural Law and the great Father/Mother Principle of sentient life. The idea of a racial or national God of a specific gender has been inserted by people and promoted by governing sources, resulting in further separation between men and women, as well as religious wars.

We give our power away when we forfeit what we know to be right and true. Irresponsible leadership, maladministration, tyranny, religious fanaticism, oppression in all its forms—of women and children, of people of color, of people with various sexual orientations, and all dissonant states of being—is an example of people attempting to exert their power, without knowing how to carry power. With no belief in the separatism of power there can be no separation in race, nation, or creed . . . and thus no strife or war. True Spirituality would invalidate war and necessitate that war be outlawed. The difference between the religion of the false ego and the religion of God/Mind is that while the former is upheld by political and ecclesiastical authority, the latter is based on human experience and the ability to unite the presence of the Spiritual Light of Knowledge with the intellect and the body of one's own Being.

The original religious books of antiquity were intended to serve the evolution of intelligent sentient life on a universal level based on Universal Law. Over many centuries we observe that the various alterations and mistranslations of the Bible have resulted in inconsistencies and lack of detail. For example, there are several different versions of the great flood and many obvious discrepancies created by people attempting to exert their influence regarding gender, morality, and ethics through rewriting these records over the course of history. The Christian position regarding reincarnation and psychic phenomena has been contradictory. Because one's power ends where one's fear begins, fear has long been used as a tool to control people. In the sixth century, Emperor Justinius forced the church fathers to remove the Law of Reincarnation from the Bible because he worried that reincarnation removed the fear of death. Only a few overlooked vestiges of the great magnet of evolution called reincarnation remain. Reincarnation is the Law of Rebirth—a process that allows the invisible God to experience its polar opposite through material existence.

People reincarnate at the same rate of vibration as where they left off. Reincarnation is a tool for perfecting one's physical, mental, and emotional nature through experience, which leads to self-mastery. Through cultivating self-mastery we work toward discipline, self-regulation, self-control, and the betterment of humanity until we recognize that heaven is a state of being: The Kingdom of Heaven manifests within us when we recognize that we are held in the embrace of the nature of God. The legacy of the institution of religion is not exempt from human deception and frailty and may encompass discord, strife, and special interest groups overriding the needs, concerns, education, and rights of the general population. This results in instability, is antagonistic to Spirituality, and has a retrogressive influence on civilization.

It is interesting to note that the Easter Bunny originated, according to English historian Venerable Bede (672–735 CE), with the Anglo-Saxons, who worshipped the pagan goddess Eastre, symbolized by the hare. The original symbol for Christ Consciousness was the dolphin, considered to be the most intelligent animal being on Earth. This significant symbolism was carelessly changed from the dolphin to the fish during the time of the Greek Orthodoxy.

There are many pagan (Earth) symbols and myths that dovetail with the historical stories of religion. For example, the beliefs and rites of Christianity are very similar to those of the ancient Roman Sun God Mithra, who was born of a virgin mortal on December 25, the birth witnessed by shepherds and magi. Mithra went forth to perform a bevy of miracles, including raising the dead and healing the blind. There was also a last supper held with the twelve disciples of Mithraism who represented the twelve signs of the zodiac. It was the Roman Catholic Church that declared December 25 to be Christ's mass in the last half of the first millennium—uniting the old intercalary days of Brumalia, Saturnalia, and Opalia into the "twelve days of Christmas" and the birth of Jesus coordinating with the time of the winter solstice. The underlying point is that when scrutinized, many of these myths and misrepresentations serve to placate tradition-minded people, alter the truth, and separate people, leading them away from the simplicity of Natural Law.

The three predominant monotheistic religions of history, Judaism, Christianity, and Islam, have been used to offer hope, but also misused as a source of great misunderstanding, competition, war, and strife by igniting hatred to pit people against one another. If we are to evolve rather than devolve, and create balance in a world that now requires a more mature human stewardship, it is essential to question just where these various forms of long established religion are taking us.

It is not unreasonable to conclude that the more fanatical orders of Judaism, Christianity, Islam, Hinduism, Buddhism, Taoism, and the like are often used as political tools that have the effect of creating division and destruction in the world. This has hindered the evolution of the human family, destroys precious resources, and prevents proper relationships among people of all beliefs. Religious fanaticism exemplifies how religion becomes a mortal ego/mind creation that works against human evolvement by morphing into competitive political parties within a religious institution that ultimately creates separation. To argue and war over which God has the last word regarding the character of Creation does not serve the deeper journey of the Soul.

All around us is a great sea of energy—cosmic, solar, lunar, and planetary energies that are highly beneficial. This world of subtle cosmic energies that are beyond the electromagnetic spectrum are lucidly described in the Hindu Vedas, yet they are largely ignored by the science of orthodox religion. The keepers of the original texts claim that all could profit from wading through the folklore and misinterpretations of the Bible by reading the Bhagavad Gita, the Mahabharata, and the Vedas. It is suggested that the Vedanta philosophy is the best exposition of the teachings of the advanced masters. These works predate the Bible and are the original source for the authentic parts of the six thousand versions of the Bible.

Another very interesting and unique publication called the *Urantia Book* may be likened to a cosmic bible with the word *Urantia* used as the term for the original universal name for Earth. This extraordinary resource informs the human race of the process and organization of both local and uncharted galaxies and universes.

From the *Urantia Book* we learn that humanity's nature is the cosmic consequence of the blending of creature and Creator. Therefore, humanity's ability to transcend the lower self is the one thing that distinguishes humanity from the animal kingdom. This distinction allows for a profound partnership between Creator Spirit and material creature. The creative central Force (Spirit) is the highest known manifestation of life fused with the lowest form of intelligent life (human being) capable of comprehending and attaining cosmic advancement. The *Urantia Book* speaks of super-Self attainment, which is one's ability to recognize the truth of God's indwelling presence within the human being. It is the essence of the living God within each—not separate from the individual. It is the inner guidance system. This eternal bestowal of Cosmic Divinity upon the human family explains the multidimensional experiences that people have when they align themselves with the limitless possibilities inherent in the supernal partnership with the Sacred. It is through the superconscious or Spiritual spheres of human experience that civilization advances. Aligning with the higher levels of the superconscious mind is nothing more or less than the willingness of the individual to share one's inner life with the Creator that makes life possible. Because humanity is so endowed, the celestial supervisors of Earth have complete confidence in the ultimate evolutionary triumph of the Human Race. Due to the innate striving for perfection, Mind and Spirit, when fully united, achieve a level of personality realization of the highest attainable order.

The scholars of Christian theology claim that there is little evidence of the life of Jesus in his youth. However, one of the most intimate, moving, and detailed accounts of the life of Joshua Ben Joseph

(Jesus) and his apostles is lovingly recorded in the *Urantia Book*. This fascinating story begins in the Spiritual realm, well before Jesus is born on Earth in the flesh, and documents details beyond human invention and imagination. It is claimed that Jesus, the Spiritual Master, was very careful not to leave any written material of his own teachings behind. Jesus proclaimed that God had already gifted humanity with inner knowledge that would be written on the hearts of those that choose to align with this gift. Jesus observed that his apostles were not fully assimilating and understanding his teachings, and therefore they could not be relied on to properly translate the truth of the new Spiritual teachings brought forth. This may explain why the Gospels of John and Thomas are in conflict with each other as written.

The twelve apostles steadfastly persisted in attaching the new Spiritual teachings of Jesus directly onto their old and entrenched literal concepts of the Hebrew prophets and Greek moralists. Jesus did not attack what the Hebrew prophets and Greek moralists stood for; he came to teach something additional—the voluntary conformity of humanity's will to God's will, allowing each Soul to develop in its own way, not simply to produce a religious puppet molded and enslaved in the bondage of a preset pattern of beliefs and traditions.

Jesus taught that the greatest of all Spiritual errors is to worship the idol rather than aligning directly as one with the principal Source and cultivating wisdom and knowledge through the experience of bringing forth the God within. When we directly align with the God within us, we become our own saviors. Jesus's life on Earth was devoted to pointing out the great danger of replacing religious experience with mere religious formalities, ceremony, and repetitive prayer. Jesus wisely taught that the only worship required is living a self-aware life and cultivating the Christ Consciousness that is aligned with the harmonious laws that support the expansive expression of Creation. All advanced masters teach that Christ Consciousness is God flowing through the individual. Awareness of this law allows us to give conscious expression to it.

Entraining our thoughts and attitudes toward the science of expressing Christ Consciousness empowers us to free ourselves from negative conditions that are self-generated. In expressing the Christ-like attributes rather than destructive thoughts, we are transformed, uplifted, and saved from ourselves, and others are saved from us!

Through this conscious direction, our bodies are transmuted from a lower to a higher vibratory frequency of Light. Transmutation is creation in a higher sense. This understanding has become inactive in mainstream religion, and many people are unaware that drinking deeply of the waters of this great power is how the true flow of universal abundance works. Jesus explained that the Kingdom of Heaven is an evolutionary experience, beginning here on Earth and progressing up through successive life stations. Jesus taught his associates to recognize and administer to all who suffer the afflictions of disease, mental and physical difficulties, and insanity. Our final destiny on Earth is to achieve perfect mastery over any condition and circumstance through Spiritual illumination. Humanity's only contact with a master will be through the mastery of the Self. Life is meant to be boundless bliss, ceaseless happiness, and unending joy. Jesus perceived heaven as being right here on Earth—a place of learning among people and nature, rather than a place of dread, desolation, and ruin.

Many modern leaders of Christian thought continue to divert the followers of Jesus and his teaching to the experiences of the apostles after his time, rather than teaching that the Law upon which those teachings were based was an exact science that could be understood and experienced as Spirit flowing through the life of the individual. The institutionalized version of Christianity also results in the idol, or personage of Jesus, being worshipped rather than people doing the work of cultivating Christ Consciousness, or God/Mind, within the self. This is how many religions end up losing their primary Spiritual focus. They lose the true Spiritual essence and become vehicles for worshiping the idol, the institution, or the race itself as being superior over other nations and people.

The sad fact is that some teachers of the various religions know the truth but choose to support a perpetual form of false religion, as well as intellectual dishonesty. When people refuse to follow false religions they are branded as heathens, heretics, and witches. And there are many saints and mystics who were excommunicated from the church and condemned to death because their spiritual revelations did not fully conform to the orthodox teachings of a certain religion. Attempting to control people through the improper use of religion results in wicked inquisitions, horrifying holocausts, and crusades of terrible suffering. All this and more has been done in the name of God. Let us be reminded that the Law of Spirit is the Law of Love. If you are truly in Love, then you are in God and God is in you.

It is interesting that the *Urantia Book* has no author listed as its source and is described as being presented by a legion of celestial beings as a revelation to instruct humankind in regard to its genesis, destiny, and relationship to God. This epic work is the integration of science, philosophy, and religion, although it is not a religion. The detail in the more than two thousand pages of the *Urantia Book* is extraordinary, and the life experience of Jesus on Earth is only one small part of it. According to these writings, the birth of Jesus was claimed to have taken place in Bethlehem at noon on August 21, in 7 BCE. The birth took place with the help and kind ministrations of fellow women travelers. According to the Jewish practice, Jesus was circumcised and formally named Joshua (Jesus). There was no star of Bethlehem to guide the wise men. There were, however, a series of extraordinary but natural conjunctions of Jupiter and Saturn in the constellation of Pisces. However, Jesus later taught that although astronomy is well suited to science, astrology has no value in discerning Spiritual truths.

Like all people born and living in this hypnotized world of the human psyche, Jesus was in grave danger from the moment of his birth due to the fact that Moses had taught the Jewish people that every firstborn son belonged to the Lord and that in lieu of his sacrifice, which was the custom, such a son might live provided his parents would redeem him by the payment of five shekels to any authorized priest. There was also a Mosaic ordinance that the mother of the child must make a proper sacrifice at the temple to insure her (in this case Mary's) ceremonial purification from the alleged uncleanness of childbirth. And the Soul of Jesus did indeed come into the world in the same manner that all children do. Part of the mission of Jesus was to be born and live as all people do and to submit his Self to the natural course of human events just as any mortal creature must.

According to the *Urantia Book,* even Jesus, while in the flesh, struggled with his own mortal mind; he laughed and cried and experienced disgust and disappointment with his family, as well as disbelief about the way that people were conducting themselves. He understood the Law of Reincarnation and knew that the price of the flesh and the mortal coil of uncertainty would be passing. Jesus steadfastly drew upon and relied on the fruits of Spirit—Beauty, Love, Hope, Knowledge, Wisdom, and Faith—as eternal aspects of Light in his life.

At the tender age of fourteen the life of Jesus became very challenging after the death of his father, but Jesus cheerfully accepted his responsibilities as head of the family. Jesus suffered financial difficulties, made his home in parks during his travels, and was one of the homeless of the Earth during his wanderings. Jesus avoided the larger cities, preferring to commune with God amidst the trees, animals, and starry realms. Jesus did not marry or father children. There was, however, one woman from a wealthy family named Rebecca, the daughter of Ezra, who showed Jesus an indefinable devotion.

Counter to the cultural conditioning of the day, Jesus exhibited the most astonishing and revolutionary attitude toward women. In a time when men were not supposed to salute even their own wives in a public place, Jesus dared to talk to women in any circumstance and bravely included them as teachers in his second tour in Galilee. Through his example, the teachings of Jesus accorded women equality with men. Jesus taught that one is not "saved" by living a righteous life; rather one lives a righteous life *because* one has already recognized the gift of Spiritual Light within. He taught that the Spirit-Born life is incompatible with sin. Jesus taught that male and female are created to complement each other, not oppose each other; working against each other in any manner does not accelerate human evolution.

People use religion to complicate gender and transgender issues; however, I have lived in San Francisco long enough to come to the understanding that people do not choose to be homosexual, transgender, and bisexual. Medical research on Olympic athletes has verified that sex chromosome variations occur as frequently as 1 in 400 births. People that have XX chromosomes are considered to be male. People with XY chromosomes appear to be female; but they may be insensitive to the hormone testosterone and may be genetically male. We are all a combination of both male and female in differing proportions, and people have been medically classified as being intersex with characteristics of both sexes. Religious beliefs are not always based on an understanding of what a person really is. As Martin Luther King, Jr. explained, the integrity of a person's character is far more important than race, gender, or religion. All people are faced with the challenge of integrating balance into their lives regardless of the diversity and variation in people's lives. We must use the unique gifts that are given to us with reverence, rather than looking elsewhere for acceptance.

In modern times it is important that the male of the species work to evolve from overfocusing energy in the base chakra, or sexual mind center, in order to heal the distorted sexual view of the masculine and the feminine. When men are encouraged to shut down the feeling and emotional mind centers, in order to give away one's power by accepting orders to kill and war over others, this prevents them from integrating and balancing the male and female aspects that create wholeness in the character. Women suffer greatly when they abdicate power over their lives to unbalanced men. Being a willing pawn in the hands of an ignoble man will not protect a woman or assist her in developing real personal power.

During my many years of research, imagine my disdain when I came across a book called *The Home Hand-Book of Domestic Hygiene and Rational Medicine* by J. H. Kellogg from 1896. In the section on childbirth he wrote, "The pains of childbirth are part of the curse pronounced upon Eve, and the use of anesthetics for the purpose of mitigating the pain prevents the execution of the penalty." This statement is from a man writing a book titled *Rational Medicine*, made irrational by following an unbalanced patriarchal belief system. Both religion and society have erred in their treatment of women. Rather than denigrating women, the modern world would greatly benefit from learning that women possess a unique ability to shift between the rational (left brain) and the intuitive (right brain) with fluidity. The ability to shift from intellect to intuition, and from linear to nonlinear thought, enhances psychic abilities. The prevalence of this ability in women is due to having a thicker bundle of nerves called the corpus callosum, connecting the left and right lobes of the brain. The root of the word *psychic* means "of the Soul, Soul abilities, or Wisdom from within." This is the reason women have been marginalized and feared by ecclesiastical bureaucrats. It is as though there has been a conspiracy all along to conceal how much power women potentially yield. With fewer nerves connecting the left and right hemispheres of the brain, men tend to operate mainly in one hemisphere or the other. All people are born with psychic abilities, but we are bombarded by belief systems that associate psychic abilities with mental disease, witchcraft, or worse. When people lose faith in the authentic power of the Higher Self, they tend to give away their power in a myriad of ways. They become warlike, desperate, needy, confused, and blameful and consequently run the risk of living mundane and unremarkable lives. People hold on tightly to the identity that they create or that is created for them; the traditional male role includes the concept of superiority and the right of entitlement to control others. Psychic abilities challenge those who attempt to control others. Even though males and females have survived by sharing each other's bioadvantages, there is still an ancient formula being implemented in modern society: divide and rule.

SOUL BREATHING

Authentic power for a man, woman, or child arises from cultivating the deepest relationship possible in life—the ability to draw the breath of life and power from the God/Mind within one's own Soul. Both male and female are here to learn to master the ego/mind in a very difficult world system that is not forthcoming with information regarding the true essence of self-mastery—self-mastery is Soul Breathing. Soul Breathing is entraining the mind to remember that every drawn breath of life's sacred feast is supported by the legacy of Light of the Force that propels life, and then exhaling forth this divine expression of Light as a sacred gift to both the Self and the world, forsaking the many prophesies of doom and gloom. Soul Breathing arises from the ability to discern whether created frequencies emanate from the false ego or from the true ego. Soul Breathing is the ability to create a balanced life on Earth through a conscious connection to Spirit. It is a state of grace achieved through action and experience.

In the *Urantia Book,* it is recorded that the only prophecy that Jesus conveyed to humanity is that no one is immune to the accidents of time or to the ordinary catastrophes of nature. However, cultivating the Light of Spiritual maturity insures that you shall be unafraid when trouble does arrive or so-called death may claim you.

From his birth to his death, each year of the life of Jesus is lovingly described in rich detail in the *Urantia Book,* and after this intimate journey one can barely endure the brutal ending to the Spiritually beautiful Earth life of the One whom the advanced masters recognize as the greatest Teacher of humankind. "The Human heart cannot possibly conceive of the shudder of indignation that swept over a vast Universe as the Celestial Intelligences witnessed the sight of their beloved Sovereign submitting Himself to the will of His ignorant and misguided creatures on the sin-darkened sphere of Urantia."

It is said that many people living in the time of Jesus were not at all bothered in conscience by his murder; however, they were nonetheless scrupulous regarding their ceremonies and traditions. What Jesus was teaching was in conflict with the Roman Empire, and in essence, Jesus was a heretic, which is punishable by death. What Jesus was doing was politically dangerous. Let us not forget that Jesus was to die under the watch of the controlling Roman, Pontius Pilate, governor of Judea. In truth, Jesus did not die as a sacrifice for human sin; Jesus was crucified by the false egos of men who wished to remain in power.

The real and pure intention of Jesus was to exemplify *how to live* a Spiritually beautiful life and to leave only the memory of a human life dedicated to the highest Spiritual ideals. Jesus came to proclaim the "good news" that the Spirit of God lives within each human being, and this Light of life allows all to access the attributes of a Spiritual life well lived. The essence of this message is that we are in bondage to no one in regard to the liberties of the Soul, and everyone who commits sin merely chooses to worship sin. When we worship sin, darkness, destruction, and ignorance, we can hardly walk in the Light of truth . . . and yet we must not judge others, for the Spiritual Laws of Creation will judge for us.

The death of Jesus on Earth ended a day of tragedy and sorrow for the myriad of Cosmic Intelligences witnessing the shocking spectacle and exhibition of mortal callousness and human perversity. The savagery of His death implies that nothing can appeal to the unfeeling hearts of those who are victims of intense emotional hatred and slaves to religious prejudice.

There are new Spiritual works that have come to Earth since the *Urantia Book* was translated into the world. Automatic writing is one way that some of the most ancient records were rendered into being. And the Earthbound people who received the information experienced altered states of genius while transmitting profound information from the hierarchy of Spiritual realms.

The Spiritual Light that emanates within our being is a Light of unity and wholeness. This Light has been referred to in the original ancient doctrines as Christ Light. The advanced masters teach that the much-heralded Second Coming of Christ is not in the "arrival" of one particular personage; rather the Christ is a state of higher consciousness or power that is felt moving within one's own higher nature as knowledge, wisdom, and love . . . the God within. This is the authentic inner and secret doctrine for all time. When we accept this, we stand on the Mount of Transmutation.

According to the advanced masters, the Ark of the Covenant is really the silent acceptance of the secret relationship that exists between the Creator and the created. This is why the material Ark of the Covenant will never be found. The definition of the word *ark* is a boat, or vessel, that also includes the body as a vessel. A simple change in spelling offers the definition of the word *arc* as a luminous electric current crossing a gap between terminals. This implies that the arc is of an energetic quality such as between matter and Spirit. The meaning for the word *covenant* is simply a formal agreement. If the material rendering of the Ark of the Covenant is ever to be found as being the Ten Commandments given to Moses by God, it would still only be a symbolic map for the human journey; good words have little value unless they are lived into being.

The habit of attributing certain powers to others and denying them for oneself is the practice that forever keeps the human family from self-mastery and in perpetual victim consciousness. When truth is formulated into a creed or doctrine dictated by the false ego, it becomes spiritually stagnant. It is in casting one's lot blindly with religious authority that individuality is compromised and the most thrilling and inspiring aspects of human experience are surrendered. The personal quest for truth and the exhilaration of facing the perils of intellectual discovery are rooted in the determination to explore the realities of personal religious experience.

When we hear the acclamation, "Behold the Avatar," or the Savior, this means that the individual is aligned with and lives closely to God/Mind. All those who work for peace and freedom on Earth are Avatars and Saviors. The inner Light of God/Mind is the savior of every man, woman, and child's total being. When this is accepted and lived into Being, we can view all people as the potential embodiment of the same Light. When we live this Light, we are imbued with grace, wisdom, intelligence, knowledge, and authentic power: Love. This is the Spiritual doctrine in which true peace and goodwill shall be established on the Earth. This is the same original Spiritual doctrine that has been taught by every spiritually advanced master.

Both Eastern and Western cultures for many centuries understood that the personality passes through many stages of moral reason. From amoral, immature, and violent to patient, forgiving, honest, and loving. The important thing is to recognize our errors, avoid victim consciousness, and have the courage and the self-sufficiency to make constant adjustments in our lives. People often define themselves by their beliefs. The need to define confines. Resisting self-defining beliefs allows us to become more like open vessels through which the fruits of Spirit can flow and be obtained. Beliefs that hold us back are not to be held in paralyzing perpetuity. Sometimes we are only able to unlearn things when we experience the truth of a false outcome.

All of the creation stories are wrought from the deep yearning of civilization to understand itself; however diverse, these stories all ultimately lead to the Source of Creation, which reveals itself both externally and internally—visible and invisible. Perhaps the most modern Spiritual religions on Earth were set into motion by the Aboriginal cultures, such as those found in Australia, Tibet, Peru, Mexico, Africa, and others throughout the world, including Native American Spirituality. These, as well as some of the newest Spiritual renderings continue to be greatly inspirational despite the effort to destroy and suppress them. The foundations of these intuitive practices tend to be all encompassing in regard to honoring all of life. Those suffering from lack of intuition and higher knowledge may wish to consider opening the floodgates of higher consciousness.

Human civilization has resorted to false hopes of what has been prophesied as "the end times," when the various saviors will relieve humanity from burden. It is unwise to align with the destructive prophecies of the human psyche or dangerous claims of unworldly alien beings foretelling that, when we are ready, the Masters will arrive in a spaceship! Prophecies of doom are projections of limited thought, and time has proven this. Why would we hope to end the flowering of a higher consciousness for the human family when it is only just beginning? Necessity is truly the mother of invention. Innovative and creative inventions arise from aligning with insights from the higher mind faculties. Spirit moves harmoniously to promote the well-being and advancement of all intelligent sentient life. When the human family looks to the Light of Spirit, the dark shadows will vanish, and we will know how to do the right thing at the right time. This is the real meaning of righteousness, or right-use-ness. This is the real substance of proper social functioning in the future.

REALIGNMENT

The purpose of education is to break down barriers, to overcome obstacles, to open doors, minds, and possibilities, to be an empowering tool to change the world as we find it.
WILLIAM AYERS

Realignment *(verb): 1. place or bring into line. 2. join as an ally.*

Consciousness is more than simply thinking thoughts. Consciousness is a nonlocalized body of Spiritual knowledge, or Universal Mind, that is omnipresent within existence. When we entrain our minds to receive the natural presence of Universal Consciousness, our electrons shift to a higher resonant frequency that in turn triggers a carrier wave of informational Light. Certain thoughts and emotions can strangle and impede the breath of Universal Consciousness. When the mortal mind desires to be in control, the cosmic flow of information is inhibited as we continuously insert our own will, thoughts, and ideas. When the mind is closed, compressed, stressed, and tense there is a lack of fluidity in thinking that blocks the free-flow function of Universal Consciousness.

When we claim that we are creating our own reality, we must be careful that we are not saying that we are attempting to control the primal force that sustains us and instead do things our own way. Here we are worshiping the desires of the dispirited false ego, rather than opening the mind to align with the natural Presence of Spiritual Intelligence. When we desire that our lives unfold in only one way and no other, the potential for superconsciousness is thwarted and the illusory ego/mind remains in charge. The belief that Spiritual guidance can be coaxed into servitude for fulfilling selfish wants and desires does not align with Spiritual principles. Each person is guided only toward the information that is needed to fulfill the Life Contract during the Earth visit. Faith is not so much about religion as working to fulfill one's Life Contract. An Angel, Elder, or Spirit Guide may only communicate once or twice in a person's whole life during times of crises to ensure that we are able to fulfill our highest potential and may not appear again. So it is up to us to maintain our faith and connection to Spirit on a daily basis. True Spiritual guidance arises when least expected. These experiences are profoundly personal and creative and confirm the existence of the miraculous. Real solutions to problems and new ideas to act on are earned through synchronization and willful alignment with the original template of God/Mind that is in sync with the true ego—the pure ego that helps us to fulfill our Spiritual contracts in life.

Our bodies exist within an encapsulated field of Intelligence that knows everything before the senses of the surface mind can pick it up. When we align with the higher Mind, we open to real intuition and authentic precognitive and psychic experiences. Intuition is the power of knowing without book learning or mental reasoning. Direct, nonverbal telepathic intuition is the language of the Universe and is our innate connection to real knowledge through a step-down process. For example, we experience nonverbal telepathic communication when we dream at night. In dreams we experience ourselves as mental bodies—in a holographic setting rather than physical settings.

Universal Mind is the formless force manifesting through matter spoken of in the I Ching; the God/Mind referred to in John J. Falone's book, *Genius Frequency;* and the mysterious principle, or Cause that Charles Darwin acknowledged in his work. It is the call to knowledge peppered throughout the work of Marshall Vian Summers, and it is the "Power of Now" referred to in Eckhart Tolle's book of the same name.

Paving the way for a new civilization are the Light energies that effect a transformation in conscious attitude. The human family must now look upon each new year as a period of ongoing Spiritual attainment, achievement, and enlightenment. There are definite lessons for those who do not grasp the meaning of the goal of a life well lived. We must make self-mastery a priority and important branch of study so as to become stronger from each succeeding experience.

Creation encompasses a vast array of Spiritual expressions. From the beginning, the work of Souls has always been to align with Spirit in order to fulfill a great mission and destiny—the unlimited and eternal plan of Creation. Alignment with the Universal Laws of Knowledge and Wisdom is essential for self-empowerment. Real empowerment emanates from within one's own self-awareness; this is a great shift in self-perception for those who look elsewhere.

THE GEOMETRY OF THOUGHT

Life's adventures encompass the age-old struggle between light and dark energies. Dark thoughts create geometries of lower frequency and separation from the geometrical regions of Light. The battles that rage over people's minds and Souls exist in both the physical and nonphysical realms. The destruction of the life force is the serious issue surrounding conscious choice and free will.

The ability to take charge of one's own conscious frequency is the ultimate resource and is essential for cultivating self-mastery. The lower third and fourth dimensions harbor many Souls existing at various frequency levels ranging from the dark and ignorant to enlightened, progressive personalities. Spiritual growth may manifest in slow steps, and no one has control over another's consciousness evolution, or lack of it. The individual is responsible for aligning with higher consciousness simply by training one's thought processes and holding Light within as one's ultimate intention. Practicing the conscious act of aligning with the Light of Universal Mind while going about daily life transmutes the denser energies into vistas of higher influence. Knowing thy Self is an intense journey that requires a reevaluation of the power of words, actions, and commitments.

When the mind and body resonate with the vistas of Light, they rise to a higher level of Spiritual understanding and knowledge. This state is enhanced by a peaceful lifestyle free of stressful energies. The natural and restful places such as the silence of the deserts, calm bodies of water, serene mountain forests, and the softening and balancing energies of nature in general enhance our ability to resonate with the pure energies of Creation. Earth magnetism draws out impurities and negative energies in our systems. In a more balanced state, we become more sensitive to the discordant energies and the disharmony of others: arguments, roaring engines, wailing sirens, discordant music, noisy crowds, barking dogs, gunfire, and the like. The base misuse of sound can alter one's frequency by jarring focused conscious thought. Yet the mind can override disturbing sounds regardless of the noise emanating from disruptive sources. Through toning, singing, and humming, the mind can invoke peace by creating an instrument for sound and a still mind.

The human body has the ability to be lifted into ecstatic states through proper breathing, a harmonious environment, and quiet meditation. When the molecules of breath are energized through deep breathing they emit spikes of infrared radiations that release toxins from the body. For example, when the mantra *A-U-M* is breathed repeatedly, it clears the body of carbon monoxide. This in turn alters the body chemistry, along with one's state of consciousness. The molecules from good quality essential oils also absorb infrared radiations from the breath. This was discovered by the nineteenth-century Irish scientific genius, John Tyndall, who actually discovered the beneficial effects of penicillin eighty years before Alexander Fleming.

Interestingly, sick plants signal their impending death by means of exhaling infrared radiation. The sicker the plant, the more powerful the scent, which attracts waiting bugs. The various kinds of radiations at the upper end of the electromagnetic spectrum can be quite dangerous: ultraviolet light, X-rays, beta and gamma radiations. The lower frequencies create a narrow band of light visible to the human eye, such as infrared colors and ELF (extremely low frequency), a frequency emitted from the brain. Extra-high-frequency emissions to be avoided are radar beams and microwave beams from satellites used for long-distance communication.

BETA-ALPHA-THETA-DELTA

It is through modulating and protecting our own frequency that we explore the various electromagnetic spectrums of darkness and light. Thought travels on electromagnetic wavelengths measured by science as cycles per second, or CPS. The slower the brainwave activity is, the higher the brain function. The beta state (14 CPS and higher) color is yellow and is the most common state of mind for people and is referred to as the surface mind. People spend most of their waking hours in the beta state, which carries the lowest frequency for awareness, learning, and performing physical skills. Here the mind rambles with repetitive internal dialogue, seeks distraction, projects illusions, becomes delusional, and performs mundane tasks that may lead to muscular tension and a reduced capacity for healing. The alpha state (7–14 CPS) color is green and resonates at a wavelength that allows a higher potential for learning, including intuition and artistic and creative abilities. In the alpha state we begin to perform skills such as inventing, composing, painting, and planning that is well thought out. Here the Intelligence and the Wisdom of the Soul begins to shine through the mind, and the two begin to work together in unity. In the theta state (4–7 CPS), blue in color, the mind begins to resonate with the frequency of genius, and we come to know things without being formally taught. The mind receives higher knowledge through symbols, images, dreams; waking visions, meditations, and Spiritual teachers. Here our self-healing abilities also increase. In the delta state (4 CPS and lower), purple in color, the frequency of one's consciousness unites as one with Universal Mind Substance as a harmonic of pure joy, peace, and limitless love. Here there are no words or thoughts, but a pure, organic, somatic Knowledge.

In the delta state we have reached the pinnacle of fluid learning and conscious co-creation with the authentic power of Creation. The delta state may also be attained while asleep or in a state of deep relaxation in a natural setting. The delta state may manifest for several seconds to minutes or hours depending on one's capacity to hold the delta frequency. Delta states are rare, and for this reason scientists do not have much data to help them understand more about this natural euphoric state of pure genius. However, we learn more about the delta state through personal experience and by taking into account the abilities of the advanced masters. It is here that we observe that the delta state is a frequency of limitless transcendence. Humanity is innately endowed with these abilities, but few make an effort to cultivate these gifts.

Although there are those who attempt to diminish the magnificence of life, we see that the value we place on Mind seeds our existence. This is key to understanding that the long-awaited Second Coming of a Christ-Being is truly one of cultivating higher consciousness, rather than awaiting the arrival of a savior. A savior cannot save people from what is cultivated in their own minds through free will. Universal Law commands that all striving must originate from the inner seed of original awareness, or Mind in relationship with free will. When Light is not received from within the expansiveness of mind, it tends to become darkness and ignorance. It is up to us to cultivate and discover the innate brilliance of Universal Mind.

LIGHT AND ENERGY

Intuition is a prime expression of the source of our guiding Light in life. Intuition is meant to lead people to the threshold where going deeper becomes very important and not only worthy of focusing more time and effort on understanding the source of this inspiration but also for taking responsibility for one's own Spiritual advancement. It is rare that people come to this change in perception. It is challenging to balance the activities and obsessions of a visible material realm with an invisible Spiritual realm that seems so subtle, evasive, and ephemeral.

Yet it is true that the most powerful energy is subtle. This energy does not originate from the false ego of the surface mind. We must quiet the mental noise in the mind to allow superconsciousness to surface. Here, we are allowing the physical body and mind to serve as mediums for the expansive Spiritual energies. For this reason, it is a great honor and privilege for humankind to express this Spiritual language of Light through the physical body and mind. We feel good and happy when we are aligned with the Light. Limiting thought forms lower our capacity for joy, and this is due to densification of the Light frequency within the body and mind.

Evolvement of consciousness in a physical body is prone to retro-gressive violations that are not aligned with the subconscious Soul force. People are much more preoccupied with self-perpetuation, self-maintenance, and self-gratification than self-realization. The work of self-mastery is worthy of much more time and attention in our lives. Human consciousness was originally created to resonate with the Soul Self. The Spiritual Soul can overcome time and space, communicates telepathically, and awaits the awakening of the superficial conscious-ness. The Soul is seeking to emerge and to be acknowledged. It com-municates in many inspiring ways to reveal the essence of its existence through experience. The Soul's genius and creativity operates above rational, logical thinking. The advanced masters teach that suffering begins when we lose our connection to the Divine.

MASTER EQUATIONS

Sacred geometry is an evolved intelligence considered to be the root of all language in the Universe. A profound legacy of Light and creation may be accessed through certain geometric codes. A geometric form such as a pyramid gathers energies from the Earth, as well as receiving cosmic energies; the sphere symbolizes unity, completeness, or the God form; the five-sided figure of the Merkabah represents the human being in its most unlimited and free state. Geometric expansiveness in the form of a spiral circular motion is a repetitive form that is observable in many cre-ations on Earth, including the structure of DNA. In 1953, two scientists, Francis Crick and James Watson, discovered the double helix of DNA at Oxford University in London. The double helix is two strands coiling around each other. The newborn receives one strand from each parent. The emotional state of the mother before birth is very important because trauma can alter the genetic makeup of DNA. Every brain is unique in regard to the organization of neurons, and every human being is endowed with a unique sequence of DNA that belongs to no one else. This is why it is referred to as a DNA fingerprint. The acronym *DNA* stands for deoxyribonucleic acid, the genetic part of a cell—a code divided up into units called genes that dictate physical characteristics.

DNA is a living genetic blueprint of identity condensed into light-encoded filaments of information. The modulation of frequencies in DNA can expand and evolve. The energy of the spiral also forms the shape of the galaxies and is considered to be the basis of how creation expands and contracts. When viewed from space, our galaxy resembles a giant rotating spiral pinwheel. The spiral is accomplished by interlacing the polarities with the circular motion to widen the circle and to either lift or lower the continuity of vibratory frequencies. The shift of energy that is necessary to accomplish the transition between polarities is similar to an electrical charge. These energy fields are in motion and move through our bodies and galaxies in cycles that coordinate with all other cycles with mathematical precision.

The common language of creation is based on the sacred geometry of mathematical formulation. These mathematical equations determine the many cycles of the solar systems, synchronizing them with the master equations of the galaxies. Both the Mayan calendar and the I Ching, or Book of Changes, are excellent studies of the mathematical precision of the cycles of life. The I Ching is precisely synchronized with our genetic codes, and the Mayan Tzolk'in is synchronized with our galactic codes.

The genetic codes govern information concerning the operation of all levels of the life cycle, inclusive of all plant and animal forms. The galactic codes govern all information affecting the operations of the cycles of Light that inform the self-generative functions of all phenomena, organic or inorganic. In his fascinating book *The Mayan Factor,* José Argüelles explains how the codes are interpenetrating and complementary. These cycles of evolvement are also a natural constituent of experience. Without these brilliant and firm guidelines for expression, creation and experience would express only as incomprehensible chaos.

SUN CYCLES

All levels and dimensions of creation are cyclical. The pulsations of the cycles are alive and may be likened to intervals of cosmic breath. The sun cycles are readily observable in the seasons of renewal and decay—spring and summer, autumn and winter. The entropic cycles of renewal and decay in third-dimensional reality are natural processes of the twin primary light rays of creation. The cycles of renewal and decay are not good or bad; they work together in unison to fulfill the Natural Laws of Creation.

Physics has demonstrated that the electron can simultaneously exist as a particle as well as a wave, which bears witness to the scientific revelation that life is multidimensional. The particle/wave revelation is the key to understanding the universality of Light as free awareness, a nonpolarized universal language. The electron operates in a spherical domain creating the space-time continuum. This is a Law from which no form of material creation is exempt. Free awareness is the critical mass of electron function that forms consciousness in varying degrees and becomes operative on a self-perpetuating basis—the thinking of thoughts, functioning in body and mind. In other words, life will unfold without trying too hard to move it along. We align with life through Spirit; therefore we allow the mind to be led by the Spirit.

The calculations of the Mayan calendar are based on galactic sun cycles of about 26,000 years each. December 21, 2012, signified the close of the cycle termed the Fourth Sun, setting the stage for Earth's passage through the portal of the Fifth Sun beginning with the year 2013. Interestingly, the number *13* is significant as a cosmic key to a new doorway of momentous energy and power as the Earth passes into a region of highly charged particles called the Photon Belt; this is estimated to last for about two thousand years and will usher in unprecedented challenges on a global scale. The most important and worthwhile task for each member of the human family in this new 26,000-year cycle is to transmute the lower, denser energies of the body and mind through choosing to cultivate the higher frequencies of Light through consciousness, understanding that locked into every atom is the potential for accessing higher dimensions. This understanding seeds the Soul connection to the Spiritual vistas of inner knowledge and power through integration of the intellect with Spirit.

The time of the Fifth Sun promotes the understanding that Souls are priceless conscious beings vibrating with an energetic range of frequencies that are produced regardless of whether a Soul resides within a live biological body or lives in the nonphysical realms. The art of life is to master the frequency that you broadcast regardless of the theater being presented and to know that the indestructible Spirit within you serves as your inner guiding Light.

Linear time is constructed around a cyclical calendar that is set into motion and remains consistent enough to create realities of matter from thought forms. Matter is created as ideas are transmitted on various frequencies of Light. Cultivating a solid foundation for living while navigating the frequencies of third-dimensional existence is a very challenging test.

Discovering one's journey from the density of the surface consciousness to the Light of interdimensional communication is an unpredictable adventure. Yet the nature of all realities is to discover what is truth and what is illusion. When the thought patterns of creative living become more linear and logical, people tend to embrace materialism, and they begin to lose the knowledge and the significance of the cyclical spiritual seasons.

Purely linear and logical intellectualism can hinder the frequency of the vitality of love. As the lower aspects of the surface mind prevail, a shift occurs from whole-brain thinking (intellect and intuition) to the intellectual compartmentalization of thinking that results in partial equations of consciousness. This is where people begin to give away their authentic power by accepting that their Spiritual connection can only be maintained through organizations, middlemen, and intermediaries.

WHAT IS SOUL?

As far as we can ascertain from experience, we know the Soul to be a living Spiritual thought form that works in conjunction with the Spiritual hierarchy and the biological brain. The pure ego of the Soul can evolve regardless of mental culture, but not in the absence of mental capacity and desire. Unlike Spirit, the higher Self of the Soul may be limited and delayed, as there is an association between free will, time, and space. The Soul is the unifying principle between Spirit and matter that provides consciousness as a microcosmic seed of the infinite

Intelligence that may be termed God. Consciousness is given within the Soul as a power of expression. The Soul is a living Intelligence that gives personality and quality of character to all Godly Creations. Each Soul is composed of a Superlight that remains dormant until the proper steps are taken to resonate with one's true origins. The foundation of this original Intelligence, or pure ego, is Love, Light, Peace, Wisdom, and Truth. The Soul advances through the embodiment of the flesh. Being human means that we will make mistakes and may deviate from the subconscious guidance of the Soul. In our youthfulness we are not expected to be perfect.

The ancient word for the Soul, *Anima,* is drawn from the Latin language to describe the invisible force that animates the body, yet is absent in the corpse. From experiential memory, people describe the most outstanding characteristic of the "Soul world" as a powerful spiritual force directing everything in perfect harmony. All biological sentient beings are gifted with Soul fragments in varying degrees.

Although the essence of the Soul is Light that endures beyond the biological body, the substance of the Soul is enlivened by the manner in which it expresses in any sphere of existence. The Soul is a fragment of intelligent energy arranged by precedence in life. For example, some animals may have very simple fragments of mind energy vibrating in the lower frequency color of red, and yet the animal may be very intelligent. A more advanced Soul may have a far-reaching Spiritual consciousness vibrating in the higher mind frequencies of blue and violet. From simple to complex, the journey of the Soul is an eternal process.

The Soul also performs as a kind of vibratory reducing valve that regulates a step-down process of higher Spiritual powers that align us with the prescience of inner knowing. True power is within the Light of energy formed by the intentions of the Soul. From the depths of our own being we begin to understand that the word *Christ* is synonymous with the divinity within the Soul, the Light of the higher Self.

In the extraordinary book *Journey of Souls,* by Michael Newton, reincarnation for the Soul is explained by describing how the Souls of young children who die soon after birth may choose to stay within family bloodlines and return to the same parents as the next baby born into the family. A dying man or woman may also choose to return as the next baby in the family to restore a broken life connection.

The Soul knows if a baby will be carried to full term or not; if not, the Soul will not enter the body, and there will be many other options for the Soul. Considering that the Soul field will not enter a biological body when it is known that the baby will not be gestated for the full term, the issue of choice must always be open for people in regard to choosing or not choosing childbirth. Unwanted or forced pregnancies are not a welcoming beginning for the Souls of children. Unwanted pregnancies are a normal circumstance of life, and there is no spiritual judgment involved. The Soul is imbued with the multidimensional ability to move in and out of a biological body at will and will leave at such time that it is known that the body will perish. The multidimensionality of Souls is and has been experienced in a variety of ways, by many individuals, throughout time immemorial.

The Soul enjoys a relationship of interdependence through a symbiosis that unifies the biological brain with the Cosmic Mind. The modern scholar and philosopher Immanuel Kant wrote that the human brain is only a function of consciousness, not the source of real knowledge. When we become obsessed with our physical bodies and are carried away on an unstable mental and emotional roller coaster, the wisdom of the Soul can be submerged by the false ego of the surface mind. Because every brain has a unique pattern like a fingerprint, through brainwaves, the Soul is alerted to crisis and disturbing vibrations and will quiet the individual through the vibration of peace, love, and healing.

Those who claim to seek peace and love through the use of mind-altering drugs discover that destructive habits act as a thief to one's own higher consciousness. A long held belief that habitual pot smoking impairs memory, learning capability, and the ability to make rational decisions has been confirmed by Australian scientists. Long-term cannabis use is hazardous to white matter in the brain, especially when the brain is still developing. Drugs diminish drive, dull psychic abilities, destroy patience, and lessen willpower—inhibiting the creative aspects required for a productive life. Patience, resiliency, and flexibility are the true attributes that keep us from breaking under the strains of life. The responsibility for the evolution of our own Soul is ours.

The frequency level of the Soul ranges from beginner to advanced. A beginner Soul is highly intelligent, yet has a limited attitude and a closed, inflexible mind in regard to adjusting to new situations. Advanced Souls exhibit a broad capacity of abilities directed toward helping human progress and seeking personal truths beyond the false ego. When we humbly pray for guidance in aligning with the authentic path of our Souls, we open a channel of communication with our Spiritual teachers, guides, and masters that help us to both earn and be empowered by wisdom. Releasing the false ego in exchange for a partnership with Spiritual guidance challenges us to explore the full breadth of our authentic power and responsibility.

The Soul may be considered to be one of the most important guidelines for expression. Just as the body is sheltered in a home or nest, the enigmatic Soul is home for the Spiritual energies. The Soul is a Spiritual jewel box where the eternal ancestor of Spirit lives. The jewel of Spirit that indwells the Soul is the impetus for the higher and advancing Self— the authentic human being. The evolving Soul is what determines the potential of the spiritual capacity for receptivity. Because the Soul exists beyond time and space, it serves as the ladder on which the liberated Spirit may ascend to perfection. The multidimensional Self must become the most important subject of study for humanity if we are to learn about our true heritage and relationship to Creation through Spirit and Soul.

When we are in alignment with the authentic power of our Soul's path, our thoughts, words, actions, and lifestyle will both serve the Self and contribute to the flowering of every Soul. Serving the greater purpose of the Soul imbues life with a higher purpose that will blossom with the fullness of an ebullient satisfaction. This feeling of ebullience is reflective in a buoyant personality that exudes compassion, peace, love, and a quiet, childlike inner joy. This is not to say that life will not be challenging, and sometimes rough. Sometimes even the most negatively perceived experience becomes a catalyst for beneficial lessons that serve to teach us of higher laws. Each experience, regardless of one's perception of failure or success, can be of great value in bringing one into alignment with the Universal Laws of Existence.

The Light of Christ Consciousness is inherent within the Soul. This Spiritual energy waits for unity with the will of the individual. To be at one with Christ Consciousness is to know thyself. It was Edgar Cayce who said, "God's desire for companionship and expression is the reason for Creation." With the human Soul as the replica of the Spiritual Mind, and a gift from Spirit, we begin a matchless adventure of ever-widening opportunities, sublime uncertainties, and boundless attainments through experience.

The Soul serves as both the pyramidal receiver and the projector through which the human intellect can be transmuted into Divine Intelligence. Thus, it has always been very important that children be guided to trust the inner authority of wisdom emanating from the Soul, due to the preponderance of deception in life. The Soul contains the potential for the human being's perfection. When the energies of human intelligence are grounded through the Soul, the energy of Divine Knowledge is channeled; this transforms the quality of the human experience and greatly accelerates individual growth.

The frequency of the Soul is exquisitely delicate, sensitive, and tender. The Soul reacts to every thought by shifting its color and wave pattern as the opportunities presented to the individual are used properly, or abused. Souls with the same awareness level recognize each other because the Soul emanates with the mind frequency and physical condition in which it exists. A person's state of mind is the main governing factor for the Soul; however, food, environment, and other conditions also affect the Soul's experience in the body. Each Soul must experience fulfilling the purpose, or Life Contract, for which it has entered—irrespective of the temporal and carnal desires of illusion that permeate existence. Allowing one's higher Self, or Christ Consciousness, to be guided by Spirit is the ultimate goal in fulfillment of the Soul. The Soul is the "I am" presence of pure ego, the part of the Self that knows it exists. After the death of the body and during sleep, the Soul operates as an ethereal body that experiences, learns, and endures in the various dimensions beyond Earthly and physical existence.

Just as each person projects their own color aura—as found in

Kirlian photography and proven in studies in parapsychology at UCLA—Souls project their own color in the spiritual realms as well. The darker the Soul energy becomes, the denser the mind frequency. The highest frequency of Soul Light is said to be in the ultraviolet range. Deeper hues ranging from black to gray and brown characterize the frequencies of impure Souls. In Native American teachings, black is the home of the void or what is not yet in form. Black is void of color and therefore is void of Light. Black does not always denote evil; however, the darker hues in the aura and Soul represent illness, toxicity, or ignorance. The advanced masters teach that there is only one plane of existence: the plane of Light. Our challenge is to enliven any darkness of the Soul with Light through conscious choice and free will.

THE SOUL AURA

The Soul aura is linked to the chakra system and is the outward expression of the individual's energetic body. The color of the enlivened Soul begins with crystal white Light. The intensity of the Soul's frequency determines the brilliance and intensity of white, a color that radiates all colors. From the color white, the spectrum range of colors is harmonically arranged by frequency from lowest to highest: reddish, to orange white, to golden yellow white, green, and from light blue to indigo blue and the range of violets. Souls that have attained varying degrees of self-mastery radiate with the colors of Spiritual teachers: the gold of authentic royalty and the range of blues to violets. The golden halos depicted around the heads of saints in many spiritual paintings are renderings that show how Spiritually aligned Souls radiate with the strength of the aura Light.

Transient and ever-changing emotions, such as joy and sorrow, are a combination of energies affecting the aura light and are accumulated cellular reactions to the past and present experience, the psychic climate of the individual, as well as the external environment affecting the Soul. The Soul communicates through feeling and intuition, not necessarily emotions. Emotions can block the present-tense "feeling" of intuition. Feeling is also a present-tense awareness of the immediate internal and external environment.

The Soul is personal, and you are acting on behalf of your own Soul; you have a role to play. The question is . . . who is the director? People become such victims of their own self-defeating thoughts that they do not entertain the idea of helping themselves, which is the one thing that is required to effect the change and recovery of the Soul. We are self-deceived and stuck in victim consciousness when we are unwilling to be Spiritually directed. The Soul will not carry all imperfect conditions of the human psyche over to new vistas of existence, as many imperfections live as an integral part of the temporal and the carnal mind.

The Soul is a ray of uncorrupted original crystal Light that preserves the best of the wisdom of experience. The ultimate objective of the Soul is to unify its actions with superconsciousness, which is a supreme source of creative energy. This source does not dwell in one central space in the spirit world. The Source *is* the Spiritual hierarchy of Light. The body lives in a space with time limitations. Soul lives in nonspace that is timeless. There are, however, thresholds between realities that are interconnected spiritual doorways that Souls can pass through into various physical planes of time and space. Time expresses itself as change, and universes are created to live and to die in order to express Creation. Human laughter, good humor, and playfulness are hallmarks of Soul life in the temporal worlds, as well as in the realm of Spirit. Every Soul enjoys genuine and hearty laughter as a form of good medicine.

In his interesting study of the Soul, Robert Siblerud explains in his book *The Science of the Soul* that the Bible and the Koran offer very little understanding regarding the Soul. Of Earth's two most ancient religions, Hinduism and Buddhism, only Hinduism has elaborated on the nature of the Soul. The 5,000-year-old doctrine of the Bhagavad Gita encourages every individual to use Earthly experience to evolve his or her Soul to its greatest potential. All Souls have equal potential to achieve self-mastery and the realization of what is termed the supreme reality—an ineffable Truth that transcends all boundaries.

Brahmanic scripture also touches upon the Soul quality and speaks of two fires: the spiritual energy that descends from the higher planes and the Earthly ether of energy that ascends from matter. It is here in this perceived duality or separation that the difficulty, confusion, and challenge arises. We can either resist the interchange of the two fires of energy (matter and spirit), or else we can accept the flow and be lifted into the immense harmonic balance of the secret inner world of the higher Self that guides and protects the lower self. The Spirit is willing, but the false ego and the flesh are weak. The spiritual energies of the Soul are subject to free will, which in turn is subject to the personality of the individual. All of these determine the survival value of the Soul. There are some personalities that are virtually disqualified for eternal survival through unfit frequencies. In this case the Soul is then assigned to a new life or higher type of race in another realm, as all Souls must be lived into being through experience.

A Soul is the individualized nucleus of a nonphysical higher conscious awareness that is aligned with the original cause or substance from which it sprang. What is the difference between Soul and Spirit? Spirit is original Source; Soul is the individual spark or seed of Spirit that is uniquely yours as it is given personality. Soul and Spirit may be thought of as child and parent. The Soul interacts with physical matter, and the Soul also develops with help from Spiritual Knowledge. The Soul fragment cannot carry all of Creation's luminous energy fully, and so it must grow and expand in capacity. The Soul is a free-will eternal entity that provides a deeper inner direction for a physical being's mind and body through maintaining contact with the higher spiritual planes beyond time and space.

The Soul is resonant with the higher good and lives for the universal expansion of creation. The greater majority of Souls enter the physical world to work toward perfection while aligning the activities with a higher meaning and purpose. Once the Soul develops a modicum of mental perfection, it liberates itself from the bonds of materialism, freely moving within the realms of matter and Spirit through embodying the unity of the Whole.

The intensity of the Soul's contact with Spirit is in direct proportion to the mind's receptive capacity. The Soul is strengthened by constant Spiritual renewing of the mind, and personal prayer is a spontaneous and heartfelt expression of the attitude of the mind toward Spirit. Prayer is not to win favor with God, but to enlarge the Soul's capacity for Spirit receptivity. Advanced Souls are very rare. The mark of an advanced Soul is one who has patience with society and shows extraordinary coping skills and insight. The advanced Soul radiates peace, composure, compassion, kindness, and understanding toward others. Not being motivated by self-interest, advanced Souls may disregard their own physical needs and live in reduced circumstances. However, the advanced Soul is not above administering tough love in dire circumstances.

Light and color identify the quality of a Soul's spiritual attainment. The master equation or essence of a Soul can be identified as a geometric figure, as a number, and as a harmony of color and vibratory rate. This speaks to the power of time to perfect the existence of all Souls. This also speaks to the fact that the Earth is not so much a place for humanity to develop—more correctly Earth is a school for the development of humanity. This drives home the importance of our ability to live in a sustainable manner on the Earth. In the vitality and the variety of physical life on Earth, we see the concrete manifestations of numerical powers and the transformation that evolution allows. People must not fail to increase in love and grow in spiritual grace through the Soul energy. When we work with the natural energies with clarity in life, we become a co-creative partner with the Divine Mind, or Spirit through the power of the Soul.

WHAT IS SPIRIT?

The word *Spirit* is interchangeable with the word *God*. Spirit is the Universal Principle, the central Light of the Law of One. The ruling Intelligence of Light and life is a vibratory "Master Radiation" that pervades everything. This Master Vibration is also that which may be termed God. Spirit, or God; is the name given to describe Creation that is all knowing (omniscient), all powerful (omnipotent), and always present (omnipresent). Spirit is the creative force of Intelligence and the Soul's core identity, as well as the deepest part of the Self. Spirit may be likened to a vibratory presence of Love that connects all Souls to everything. Spirit is the existential Cause of the entire cosmos, for all forms of biological life. The Mind Principle behind the cause of all things that we see about us may be attributed to Spirit. Without the undying support of Spirit the Universes and all they hold would vaporize into nonexistence.

Ancient Medicine also describes the conscious presence, or breath, living within the body, but void in the corpse, as *Spiritus.* This Latin essence of Spirit is understood as being exhaled in the last breath. This is the pure energy of a high and Divine Plan. In Spirit there are no polarities to be mediated. The fusion of Spirit with the mortal Soul is an unprecedented and unimaginable partnership. The task of this partnership is to spiritualize and eternalize the personality of the individual. One's real path to heaven is the path of Spiritual advancement within this partnership, and this, as always, is subject to the human will.

The Native American meaning for Spirit is the nonphysical energy of the creative Source. A person with sufficient purity of thought to communicate with the dimensions of the forces of Light is referred to as shaman, seer, or visionary. The spiritual voice takes form as thoughts, images, and feelings that occur as an integration of the timeless Self with the personal self. When the mind and emotions become entrained to perceiving the higher dimensions of genius, the energies are drawn upon as needed. This requires intention and commitment. When the mind discerns spiritual insights, the result is *prajna,* as the Buddhists call it, or Wisdom.

There are varying degrees of spiritual luminosities, angelic helpers, and divine entities that sustain a nurturing connection with humankind. A spiritual entity can be invisible to the human eye and yet also has the holonomic ability to appear solid in order to be viewed. Spiritual experiences may be dismissed and misunderstood by those who refuse to accept realities beyond the physical realm—until they are confronted with the absolute proof of their own experiences. A few charming examples are lovingly depicted in the heartwarming character of Ebenezer Scrooge, in the Charles Dickens novel *A Christmas Carol,* and the wonderful holiday story by Dr. Seuss, *The Grinch Who Stole Christmas.*

One's spiritual perception, or the lack thereof, quantifies the varying degrees of ability to comprehend Truth and respond to spiritual teachings. The harmonic frequency of spiritual energy is very high and is felt as being superlatively fine and subtle—rather like an ethereal veil. To discern spiritual prescience it is important to step aside from the rush of life and escape the harassments and appendages of the temporal world to refresh and inspire the mind's receptivity to Spirit. Whether one is conscious or unconscious of this creative process, Spirit is the supreme essence underlying the human being.

To describe Spirit, Plato used the term *daemon,* a Greek word for Spirit that means hierarchical law. This term was used to speak of higher beings that guide the Soul's ability to integrate corporeal existence into a divine pattern. The daemon, or Spirit, oversees the individual life of the Soul.

Although the word *Spirit* truly defies definition, the late clairvoyant Edgar Cayce characterized Spirit as "focused awareness." The extraordinary modern-day spiritual messenger Marshall Vian Summers describes Spirit as being the equivalent of a knowledge that is beyond the intellect. This knowledge, he says, transcends theology and devotional ritual. It represents each Soul's intrinsic relationship with all life. The late clairvoyant Jeane Dixon was the only one who portrayed Spirit as being what she called the "Aura Flame." "The Aura Flame always burns in even the darkest hour, bringing Light and hope to the Soul in the blackest night of negativity and despair."

THE SPIRITUAL CARRIER WAVE

In 1932, the Russian researcher Scariatin, who wrote under the pen name Enel, discovered that the energy around the tombs of the ancient Coptic Christian saints in Egypt emanated with great concentrations of what he termed the "Spiritual Carrier Wave." His research in radiesthesia led him to create a scale by which to measure spiritual energies. His measurements revealed that through deep spiritual work and prayer, the saints had created great concentrations of the spiritual high harmonic in their bodies and the energy fields surrounding their bodies. This he deemed to be the incorruptible and optimal energy quality of spirituality that permeates all matter and carries energy and information, as well as consciousness, from one location to another.

Enel's scale of measure for the Spiritual Carrier Wave revealed that in the average person, the electromagnetic spiritual wavelength measured between 7 and 25 in saturation.* Spiritual healers tended to measure in the range of 70 to 100 in saturation. The level of Spiritual Carrier Wave saturation required for angelic connection was determined to be 195 wavelengths. The most potent reading reached up to 350 wavelengths, which is the level of the most advanced spiritual masters and prophets.

The golden ray is linked with this divine wave energy and is depicted in religious iconography around the heads of saints or in the energy fields of high masters. This quality of energy is known as the "higher harmonic of gold." This higher harmonic has the capacity to transmute toxic energies to beneficial energies and transform lower elements to higher elements. The higher harmonic of gold is also created when a person prays in a personal heartfelt manner or engages in harmonic meditation or other kinds of spiritual work, such as communing with nature on a devic level. This energy quality has a strong vitalizing effect on the human immune system.

A person's level of spiritual saturation will be high during times of spiritual practice, then fade in intensity unless the spiritual connectivity is held at all times. The Spiritual Carrier Wave is a transcendental energy that occupies empty space. It has the shortest wavelength in respect to all other invisible energy wavelengths. The ancient Egyptians were fully aware of this energy and designed the pyramids for optimal spiritual saturation of the initiate. The ability to connect with and hold a high level of spiritual saturation is the goal in self-mastery. The Spiritual master manifests the divine energy quality of perfect balance by holding this energy effortlessly at all times. This quality of energy may be felt while visiting certain historical spiritual sites such as the Great Pyramid in Egypt and Stonehenge in England.

In 1934, French researchers Leon Chaumery and Andre de Belizal stated that the Spiritual Carrier Wave, otherwise known as Negative Green (−G), is the most powerful wave vibration with the shortest wavelength in the Universe. Interestingly, Negative Green is generally beneficial in its horizontal wave form and detrimental in its vertical

---

*Enel had his own scale of measurement, but this is likely similar to the electromagnetic current or wavelength of the delta state.

wave form. One is the archetype of the green energy of life, and the other represents the dehydrating energy of death. Here again, we find a profound correlation between the upward and downward polarities of the spiral energies that constitute and are inherent within existence, demonstrating that energy can be both created and destroyed.

The many items made of gold unearthed from the pyramids in Egypt are reflective of the fact that gold as a metal is higher in energy quality than all other metals. The higher harmonic of gold is the energy of tremendously deep wisdom and ultimate balance. It has a soothing and calming effect that reduces stress in the body. The higher harmonic of gold is also the divine harmonic of Christ Consciousness.

The work of Enel dovetails with the work of scientist and researcher Royal R. Rife who made a truly amazing discovery in the area of frequency when he proved in the 1920s that specific frequencies could kill deadly microscopic organisms. Rife discovered how to make normally invisible microbes visible by illuminating each one with the light frequency that matched their own unique resonance frequency, causing them to glow in their own natural color. Rife killed viruses, cancer, bacteria, and fungi with the same natural principle that made them visible—resonance. Resonance also permeates our thoughts, words, and deeds.

THE SEED AND THE WORD

The Spirit acts as the intermediary between cosmic power and those sentient beings that are able to receive the potent Truth. Spirit strives to create synergistic relationships between body, mind, and Soul. Through the word, Spirit creates a language of Light that creates harmony out of discord; our words are potent only in as much as Spirit is the operative Cause backing the words. One's conscious awareness is the focal point in the power of the word. Space is no barrier to words and thoughts; they can travel anywhere. As heat remains in a room after a fire has died out, so do thought forms remain long after the one who has created them has left. Idle words are impotent and do not create much, though they may add to the hypnotic energies of the false ego. The antiquated false-ego idea of the devil is a direct transgression of the fact that there is only the reality of Spirit, Cause, or God. The purpose of the spiritual word is to dissolve ignorance, just as Light dissolves darkness. The more we employ higher consciousness in our thoughts, words, and deeds, the greater the power involved in the process of cultivating higher wavelengths of consciousness.

It is the activity of the spiritual forces of nature that compels the seed to grow, for no seed has volition within itself without Spirit. The seed is the container, or vessel, for that force . . . and so it is with words. Our words are determined by our consciousness, and our consciousness is determined by one's state of awakening. One may be awakened to the truth, or one may develop a sense of a so-called reality that is entirely false. The highest attributes of consciousness are demonstrated when we acquire the ability to perceive the truth through all conditions and circumstances. The advanced masters teach that cultivating higher consciousness completely removes the vibratory veil between the mortal mind and the Spiritual Mind. There is no longer a conscious, subconscious, or superconsciousness, just One radiant living conscious Light of reality. This is a state of complete freedom from mortality and therefore from hypnosis. The silent words of conscious thought are more potent and travel more rapidly on a vibratory scale than spoken words, as silent thoughts are not subject to time and space; a spoken word must traverse space and time to reach its destination.

THE WILD CARD

Humanity's relationship to Natural Law is reciprocal, and evolvement within Creation is a constantly exchanging cooperative process of the wisdom inherent in these forces and of personal experience in relationship with this wisdom. The wild card in this evolving game of exchange is the gift of free will. The free-will aspect of thought is considered to be both the thorn and the blossom of the flowering process of experience. The constructive and destructive use of free will holds both emanations of creative energy. Free will has at its essence both positive and negative polarities and is not bound by the cyclical Galactic Laws that are in motion. Essentially, free will is designed with great pitfalls that ignite the challenges that each person must learn about and overcome through experience. This process is not easy, painless, or without confusion or despair. In simple terms, as in Buddhist spirituality, free will teaches us that we reap what we sow, and that which we choose creates a pattern that must be experienced both individually and collectively.

It is in properly utilizing the Law of Free Will that we develop a method of working with the system of the invisible life forces that maintain life, and we learn to accept the unity the invisible spiritual blueprint shares with the physical blueprint. It is a method of mediating between the world of everyday experiences in cooperation with Eternal Law, rather than against it.

THE AGE OF CRYSTAL

The word *crystal* is partly derived from the Greek term *kristos* or *christos,* meaning "the one with Spiritual Light," or having raised one's consciousness through initiation with the Light. These words are much older than Christianity and are the original definition for the purpose of life, which is to raise one's consciousness to the level of Divine Knowledge—or *krist-all,* which may also be defined as *christ-all,* or crystal. The spiritual beings that understand the metaphysical laws of the cosmos patiently await the time that has been termed "The Age of Crystal," when all people understand the real purpose of life and implement it.

Recent discoveries in genetics, quantum physics, and electrochemistry reveal that the physical body is actually a crystallization of vibrations. One's entire biology is shaped by the intelligence of each of our fifty trillion cells, and the single most important way to influence them is through the energy of our thoughts and beliefs. Because Creation is fundamentally intelligence in pursuit of understanding itself, it is necessary to discern that certain beliefs reach a tipping point of limiting our opportunity to evolve. It is then a perpetual process of transcending and leaving behind each learned understanding and transmuting it into wisdom of higher accomplishment. The exception to this process is the immutable Universal Law that supports the integral processes of life as a whole. At the foundation of changing thoughts and beliefs, there is always a greater understanding of utilizing the Natural Laws through wisdom gained by living the experience.

The negative polarity, or downward spiral of experience, is brought about by failure to use Natural Law. Nature exists in harmony with these laws and contains the same element of programmed push to exist and evolve that is universal in all creation. All real solutions to problems dovetail within the flow of the expansive energies of the Natural Laws that maintain the reality of existence and allow it to continue within these laws.

Through free will, the purity or impurity of one's thoughts find the most effective path, like any stream in nature. Free will is limited; it can be overthrown and influenced by greater forces within certain boundaries. One's thoughts can create a perceived experience, and thought can change its perception into another experience entirely. Combined focus of thought is all-powerful when it operates within the Spiritual Laws and is supported by personal and collective commitment. The interactive complexity of these laws will multiply as they are understood. Underlying all this is how much advantage the individual takes in seeding the fertility of the Soul's ability to resonate with Spirit and the absolute potentiality that is inherent in the Soul of each human being.

The third-dimensional wave form of the human body is the densest frequency for human existence, and it is the most difficult to transcend because of its slow vibratory resonance. And like many areas of thought in third-dimensional illusion, the real meanings of the four basic Universal Laws have been altered to mislead people by influencing selfish gain that further contributes to the hypnotic effect of a disingenuous human experience.

Real personal growth is dependent upon the ability to align with the higher knowledge that is available and live it into and through the flow of experience. The flow of this spiritual path is ideally an upward spiral. Rarely is it a smooth upward spiral! A spiral downward leads into the lower vibratory activities of greater technological control, violence, and denigration of the body and mental faculties. Self-awareness is a magnetic frequency, and the desire for a higher experience must be self-directed. The desire for and the resolve to move through various forms of manipulation, violence, abuse, and the like must be conceptualized to bring forth a new stepping-stone leading out of a downward spiral.

Human beings are designed to move into a much higher frequency of existence. However, this is not going to be handed to people. It must be earned through cultivating self-mastery and understanding that the transmutation of energy is a personal conscious act. Thinking good thoughts for the sake of thinking good thoughts will not propel the individual toward clairvoyance or crystal-clear thinking. Rather, cultivating the art of perception through discernment and asking for assistance from your higher inner Source is a more all-encompassing process of unfolding and awakening.

The journey as pioneers of this expanding consciousness may require the exploration of some dark, foreboding places. Do not fear darkness; Light overcomes darkness. We would do well to thank the inner Light for loving and guiding us as nothing else can. When we align with a deeper natural rhythm that can be felt as an inner resonance of truth and inward depth of Knowing, we automatically understand how to advance forward. When we view life from this broader scope and acknowledge that which is larger than ourselves, we are opening to the guidance of a fresher perspective and great prospects for success.

The human growth process begins with the self-awareness of pure ego; this is the magnetic aspect of the Mind that knows that it exists. The awareness of the self progresses through the various stages of self-realization, self-acknowledgment, self-transformation, and awakening. This process is facilitated and accelerated through listening to the deeper sense out of which our thoughts and actions arise. Yet we are so often encouraged to distance ourselves from our feelings, rather than experience what we feel. We must learn to recognize and value the subtle feelings, thoughts, and emotions as doorways leading to the entry points of transformation beyond what is programmed into our lives. Recognition of this deeper inner process allows time to listen to what Spirit thinks. We are then free to follow the mental process originating from this deeper core. This is a very abundant way of living!

Many people wonder why God does not give them what they want. This is because God, or Spirit, is fulfilling its own universal purpose, and it is the responsibility of humankind to come into harmony with this purpose. Adverse thought patterns limit people; when this inefficiency is removed, we will begin to receive more perfect results. With practice, cultivation, and in healing separation, we will learn to finely focus the mind like a laser beam to manifest things into holographic form from the higher to the lower material dimensions and to manifest what is needed for the higher good. A true holograph is projected by thought, not by a mechanism, a camera, or the manipulation of virtual reality. The true hologram is the vehicle in which thought forms from higher dimensions are seeded and planted into lower dimensions, and vice versa. For example, when food is needed, one thinks the idea of a loaf of bread into a thought form. The thought attains the constituency of Light in its respective dimension, and the loaf of bread begins to build up by attracting molecular particles of ether that gives substance to materialization. This is a way of tapping into the secret of the Universal Mind Principle and building from cause to effect by mastering thought projection! However, Earth's environmental frequency is currently so distorted and unpure that the process of lifting the frequency must occur on a planetary scale to accomplish the expansive expression of this transcendent process. The good news is that one spiritually mature person has the power to dispel the negative frequencies of one hundred destructive people, or more.

Thought projection gives us the confidence to overcome difficulties and limitations. It is self-confidence rather than egotism that gives power to thought projection. Having confidence that dwells within Self is the essential element in all creative action. However, the desire to rid ourselves of selfish motives and narrow attitudes to transcend our limitations is also fundamental. The following affirmation exemplifies the attitude required in bringing forth power from Universal Substance.

God, I am expressing in my affairs that which will satisfy every good desire. As a seed, my desire is planted in my Soul and is quickened by the life of Spirit. In the fullness of time I ask to express Love and realize harmony, happiness, and abundant prosperity; this is not for myself, but that I may have the understanding direct from Spirit of the

*method of bringing forth from Universal Substance that I may be of
service to all of your children.*

THE ART OF THE HEART

Abundance is not the same thing to each person—as each journey is
unique to the individual. Fundamentally, abundance means living
within the law of allowing the mind to follow the Spirit within the
Soul, for this allows all people to live in abundance. It is not allowed
within the laws to take another's abundance to add to one's own.
Beyond the basic needs, such as water, food, clothing, and shelter, long-
term happiness is not found in abundant material possessions. It does
not take much time at all to discover that too many material possessions can become quite burdensome. Nor does living within the Law
of Abundance require that everyone become a monk or a missionary
in pursuit of performing thoughtful acts of compassion, kindness, and
love. Sometimes the simplest act can have a most powerful effect. The
following story shared by my friend Lois S. is one perfect example.

> *It was a bitterly cold night in rural Minnesota. The location was our
> motel, which I was managing on my own that night. The shrill sound of
> the doorbell in the middle of the night always meant that someone needed
> help. I opened the door to find a young couple with an older woman,
> shivering in the cold night, and I noticed they were certainly not dressed
> for walking almost the half mile they said that it took them to reach the
> motel.*
>
> *The couple checked into their chilly room while I placed a chair by the
> heater and covered the older woman with a blanket. Then I proceeded to
> make her a cup of hot tea, and as I handed her the tea, she said, in a very
> gentle voice, "I love you." Thirty years later I can close my eyes and picture
> this quiet, gentle woman who turned a very cold night into one of the most
> memorable and meaningful moments of my life.*

Lois's story demonstrates how the simplest acts of kindness can
ignite heartfelt and abundant satisfaction. Achieving satisfaction and

aligning with one's true Self within the growth process encompasses the art of the Heart. To incorporate the art of the Heart into our lifestyle so that it is not neglected or ignored is a great achievement. When the heart/mind directs the devotions and commitments in our lives, we are following the Light of a higher intelligence within us.

There is a misconception that what we seek is entirely beyond ourselves—in the material things, faraway places, games, and theme parks of the world. When we allow ourselves to be carried in a more spiritual way, it softens the strain and the yearning that we have for a purely materialistic pursuit of abundance and satisfaction. After all . . . it is a long journey on an evolutionary scale; we would be unwise to cut ourselves off from the real meaning of Love and lose the ability to draw from the larger context of Creation.

Without spiritual support, the mental processes are less empowered, which leads us to the false conclusion that we must be saved from our own mental processes! If this were true, we would be absolved from free will and from taking responsibility for our choices, for our beliefs, and for our actions. This flows against the current of Natural Law. If we are attentive only to our misguided desires and drives, we can miss the signs that are truly meant to guide us out of harm's way. People who are devoted to working toward the noble causes in the world will be thwarted unless they accept that help is available, and though at times we may believe that we are alone, we must listen very carefully to the voice of Spirit—the ka energy, the vague, ephemeral presence the Egyptians so valued. Knowing that we are blessed with the eloquence of the ephemeral Light of Love to achieve our goals, we must consciously align with our deeper senses and ask the higher mind to guide us when we ask, "What am I here to accomplish?"

All physical life must contend with the work of survival, competition for resources, the deprivation of resources, and hardship. Innovation and certain technologies solve some of these problems, but when unchecked, these also create imbalance. Technology is not to be entrusted with the spiritual evolvement and the redemption of human life.

To come into alignment with a deeper understanding of the greater order of life that is available requires discerning friend from foe. To develop the art of distinguishing personal thoughts from true Spiritual Guidance is the only path worth pursuing with eternal dedication. This deeper awareness is the practice of listening to your inner knowing in order to discern whether the truth is rising within you or if it is your own mental projection, the mental projection of another being, or a fabrication of the imagination. In times past, the instinct of heightened awareness was essential for survival. Exercising the faculty of deeper awareness is like exercising a muscle; it is not wise to be pacified into the belief that one does not need instinct to discern the truth. The truth is a deeply felt experience of feeling that resonates through the entire body and mind.

EXPERIENCE

Experience is the epitome of learning in life. It is through experience that the mysteries are revealed. It is through experience that our inner knowing is validated or invalidated. It is through experience that we learn maturity, and it is through experience that the personal Soul earns advancement.

Irrespective of scientific data, political edicts, philosophical postulations, or the world's eclectic religious attunements, experience is our greatest teacher. It is through experience that we allow our successes and our errors to teach us the way toward evolvement. The Universal Law of Knowledge is the Sacred Intelligence that is woven throughout the fabric of existence. If it were not, there would be little hope of advancement and achieving balance for sentient life. From this Source emanates a creative universal grammar of Light and spiritual forces that uphold the unchanging laws that infuse life with the gift of existence. This is where the essence of truth and the foundation for a pure and uncorrupted reality lives.

Human history has recorded the experiences of exceptional Souls that have served as sages, shamans, seers, prophets, visionaries, and spiritual messengers for the advancement of the human race. These exceptional men and women exemplify and teach the reality of how Natural Law works through us in life. It is advantageous to explore a few of the historical figures as well as the more recent figures whose lives have been undeniable demonstrations of the inexplicable and loving gift of Light.

MEDIUMSHIP AND TRANCE

All of the spiritual teachers and messengers that assist humanity in the physical realms have been adept at accessing the gift of communication from higher dimensions. Visionaries, shamans, and spiritually sensitive people are able to decondition the mind from learned cultural conventions and dissolve the boundaries of the mundane. Higher spiritual communications are received via clairaudience (clear hearing), clairvoyance (clear seeing), clairsentience (sympathetic pain), and automatic writing about what one sees, hears, and feels. Although the depth of reception and perception will vary, these abilities are inherent in all people. True clairvoyance is having the awareness of mind that perceives and understands the pure machinations of Universal Mind Principle. Only those that ardently practice resonating with the Presence of this spiritual principle can experience exactly what the Light of true love and knowledge is really like.

Mediumship and psychic abilities are not always the unfolding of the Universal Mind Principle. All psychic imagery, forms, shapes, and words that are received through mediumship are subject to interpretation by the personal mind of the individual. The human psyche influences all manner of thought forms. And people may be more submerged within their own chaotic thought turmoil than they know. In this study we begin by exploring how Spiritual Light aligns with the unique nature of the individual to communicate. As we explore the spiritual aspects that are reflected in the lives of those with strong capabilities, we can begin to understand the deeper nuances of how invisible frequencies manifest and permeate the worlds of the material, the ethereal, and our lives.

Authentic mediumship requires the stilling of the ego/mind in order to function without interfering with subtle vibratory spiritual energies. Trance is when the medium cannot recall the words that come through. Mediumship and trance have been an essential part of the seership that has existed in all spiritual religions. The term *spiritualist* means that the teachings are derived, or channeled, from personalities that are not manifest in a temporal body. The unmanifest personality uses the mind, eyes, ears, and vocal abilities of the spiritualist's body to communicate. Telepathic abilities and the ability to communicate effectively are valuable skills. Developing these skills is part of our challenge if we are to adapt, survive, and find real answers to modern dilemmas. Let us now explore a few of the more recent and extraordinary examples of human achievement in this area.

EDGAR CAYCE

The Association for Research and Enlightenment, in Virginia Beach, Virginia, established a posthumous library containing records of fourteen thousand readings given by the world-renowned Edgar Cayce (pronounced Kay-cee), known as the Sleeping Prophet. Cayce is perhaps the most sensitive psychic documented in the history of psychical research. The ARE center has kept the work of Edgar Cayce alive as one of the best-known clairvoyants in America. Cayce (1877–1945) was a pioneer in the development of holistic medicine and emphasized the important relationship between mind, body, and spirit. He did not indulge in alcohol, but he smoked cigarettes, which was said to be a factor in his death in January 1945.

Cayce was able to read the energy of people's auras, and he showed the sick how and why they were sick on both physical and psychological levels, as well as how to heal through natural means. Cayce was able to lose consciousness at will and enter a deep theta state accomplished in a reclining position that allowed him to fully relax into a trance, while his lifelong secretary, Gladys Davis, took notes. He described in stunning detail the erg of energy that began at his base chakra, working its way up the spine until a burst of light would flood his brain with expansive consciousness. In this altered state of consciousness, Cayce tuned in to the center of what he termed *Universal Intelligence* and peered into lost records of ancient civilizations, describing the precise location of the Dead Sea Scrolls. He also obtained helpful personal readings for those who sought his help, and he divined past and future information of earthshaking importance.

The erg of energy described by Cayce can be likened to the kundalini energy in yogic literature. The trance state assumed by Cayce awakened the "coiled serpent" energy that lies dormant at the base chakra of the body. This state of higher consciousness activates the entire ethereal chakra system coiling up the spinal column until a burst of light in the pineal and pituitary areas of the brain awakens higher frequencies of knowledge. Cayce proclaimed that life is a testing ground and learning process. "Death is a beginning," he said, "a passing in and a passing out. Not unlike the seasons and their changes. Don't worry so much where you live but how you live." These were wise words from Cayce.

It was Edgar Cayce who in 1920 described the electrochemical functions of the body in a trance state saying, "The human body is made up of electronic vibrations, with each atom and element of the body, each organ and organism, having its electronic unit of vibration necessary for the sustenance of and equilibrium in that particular organism. Each unit, then, being a cell or a unit of life in itself has the capacity of reproducing itself. When a force of any element or organ of the body becomes deficient in its ability to reproduce the equilibrium necessary for the sustenance of physical existence and its reproduction, that portion becomes deficient in electronic energy."

Interestingly, Cayce also described some new sources of energy that would supplant the poisonous gases of fossil fuels. He claimed that the principal energy source of the future would be water, broken down into its component parts, hydrogen and oxygen, then electrified to produce energy. He also described a process for harnessing energy through using the inward and outward movement of the tides. The sun was foreseen by Cayce to be used to both warm and power buildings. Cayce saw massive desalination of seawater to end water shortages. The discovery of new solar systems and encounters with extraterrestrial life forms were also included in Cayce's predictions.

A strong proponent of Divine Law and Natural Law, Edgar Cayce was optimistic—while deploring the dissension in organized religion as a disregard of the Law of Divine Influence, bringing chaos and destructive forces into human experience. "More wars, more blood has been shed over racial and religious differences than anything else, but these differences will soon be mended," he said.

Cayce also talked about the importance of the mental forces in relationship to spiritual awakening. In one reading, for example, he referenced "the hearts and minds of those that have set themselves in that position that they become channels through which spiritual, mental, and material things become one in the purpose and desire of that physical body." To Cayce, the individual was not only the physical presence of the body but also the spiritual essence carried over from previous existence. Cayce noted that something of the spirit invariably remained to shape the inclinations and aspect of the currently incarnated personality. He said, "It is a privilege to incarnate and to have another chance to live the right way. We must remember this and be mindful of our every word and thought."

He knew so well that what was inside of a person ruled what was outside. He advocated for living in the spirit of Truth, saying that the human spirit could turn things around. Cayce encouraged people to become aware of their relationship to the Universe and to rely upon the force within. "And that force was exemplified by what the psychic force did mean, has meant, and does mean in the world today; to reach a higher consciousness," he said.

Cayce stressed that people working together, for the same cause, could raise the energy and thought to a spiritual level. As to the changes that are coming, he said, "These will depend on what individuals and groups do about what they know." The Earth changes of the past were experienced, as Cayce noted, as an omen of our need for a greater global community. He foresaw a unity toward diverse people working together rather than becoming victims of their own self-indulgence. "There is an ideal, and that ideal must be in the spiritual life," he said. Free will to align with gratitude, or lack thereof, for the gift of life is a prominent feature in Cayce's work.

Edgar Cayce's prophecies were not written in stone. He explained that what he saw could be changed through free will, and ultimately Cayce predicted a spiritual renaissance for the regeneration of humanity. "Do not fear death, but conscience," he said. "For balance in the physical life is but a reflection of the necessary development in the spiritual life. If one will make an effort, the knowledge of how to use to spiritual advantage any and all conditions will be opened from within." Cayce noted that, "We become blinded by the needs we constantly magnify. Fear clutches our heart at the least sign of failure, and through lack of faith we lose our inner resolve."

Ultimately, Cayce's message for all time is that, "There is set for thee life and death, good and evil. As to what, as to which, as to where, as to how ye will choose, this is within one's own consciousness. Those who have faltered, gain new courage. Those who are disappointed and disheartened, gain a new concept of hope that springs eternally within the human breast. All knowledge that ye may have is within self. There is a longing for those experiences belonging to the Soul. For without spirituality the Earth may indeed be a hell. As never before Man is being called to stand forth and be counted on the side of creativity or destruction. The average person does not realize that choices made daily, by the moment, are part of this responsibility to choose this day what you will serve. It is the will, a divine heritage, which must be exercised daily. The pattern of the mind may be destructive. Only a strong will can turn a life from such a path. Only careful self-observation, the weighing of positives and of negatives in the smallest decisions will bring needed balance. Through Man recognizing himself as co-creator with God, can Man grasp the importance of his choice."

JEANE DIXON

In the 1960s, the late Jeane Dixon lived in Washington, D.C., and was known as one of two or three great and sensitive mediums of her time. She was highly respected because she never commercialized what she referred to as her God-given talent. It was well known that Jeane Dixon held a great deal of reverence for life, and this was reflected in the way that she lived. Jeane's diet was composed of mainly vegetables, fruits, and juices and almost no meat. She never smoked or drank alcohol to, in her words, "keep her channels clear." Jeane was a very religious woman of ritual, and before going to Mass each morning she stood at her bedroom window facing east while repeating the Twenty-Third Psalm and requesting that the power of Spirit guide her work each day.

Although Jeane Dixon's claim to fame was the eerie premonition that she received foretelling the death of America's late President John F. Kennedy, her reflections and insights are still very valid and timeless. Jeane said, "We are all put here to prove our own worth. We are all given tests for courage, love, faith, and endurance. No matter what our language or religion, there is the same Almighty Power above us. In each of us the Spirit is manifested in a particular way for a particular purpose that was designed for us. One person has the gift of wise speech, and another can put the deepest knowledge and beauty into writing and music. Another one has the gift of healing, and another the gift of prophecy that come through channels from another sphere."

In her time, those in Washington looked for a glimpse of the future from this devoutly religious woman who was determined to use her gift only for the benefit of others. In 1945 when President Franklin Delano Roosevelt asked Jeane how she felt about some decisions that he would have to make, she corrected him, saying, "It is not how I feel personally, it's what I get spiritually and psychically. Many of the things I get this way are not what people want to hear."

Those that worked closely with Jeane Dixon claimed that her recurring slogan was, "It's not what your country can do for you; it's what you can do for your country." Her slogan found its way into print in the *Army Journal* of 1946 and in only slightly revised form became the stirring rallying cry of John F. Kennedy's inaugural address in 1961.

Jeane was able to help people find their niche in life by touching their fingertips, which allowed her to discover latent talents that they could develop and utilize. She particularly tried to help the amputees and the wounded of the Second World War to realize that life was worth living.

The accuracy of her many forecasts forged an impressive chain of evidence. However, like all people she was not infallible and blamed herself for misinterpreting the symbols that she was privy to. As a deeply religious woman, Jeane tended to be overtly puritanical in deciphering some of her visions. Interestingly, much of the symbolism that Ms. Dixon observed was accomplished with the aid of a crystal ball. That this educated and sophisticated woman used a crystal ball seems inconceivable and conjures up visions of the gypsy fortune-teller. Those who were close to Jeane claimed that they were not able to see what Jeane saw in her crystal ball. She preferred to work with her crystal ball in the early hours of the morning when most people were asleep and the energy of the mental field was less chaotic.

In her prime, many people simply did not have the capacity to accept the precognitive talents of Jeane Dixon and her crystal ball. However, it is well known today that crystals make it possible for people to reach new levels of consciousness. Crystals can tune in to energy from other sources, as well as organize, magnify, focus, harmonize, and redirect energy. We have a crystalline structure of DNA, and our glands produce hormones that are crystal structures that receive and transmit energy. Energy that travels between two crystals has a timeless quality, and this is how Jeane Dixon received much, but not all, of her information.

Many people with unusual spiritual talents struggle with expressing the messages they receive. Jeane described how for several days before an important vision, she experienced an odd sensation of withdrawal. After the vision vanished, the sense of worldly detachment would remain for three more days. To receive information from people, Jeane could feel their vibrations; this was oftentimes very exhausting work. Sometimes people would question her pronouncements, and Jeane had to remind them that her visions were not her own thoughts. They came through channels from another sphere. "The will of humanity does not change the will of God," she said.

One night Jeane saw that her father was standing beside her bed as he so often did in her childhood. He had come to bid her goodbye . . . before the telegram of his death had been sent. He told her that she must go on, that sometimes she would seem very much alone, that she would have to work hard, but more tranquil days eventually lie ahead. In her life Jeane was dedicated to helping the less fortunate, but she herself never spoke of these works. She was not like those that do good works for charity and receive recognition for it. The only thanks that Jeane requested from those she helped was that they would in turn help someone else in need.

Vibrations were especially important to Jeane as a tool for reading people, and the ability to read good or bad vibrations seemed to be a determining factor in choosing whom she helped. This included lost or abandoned animals, as well as wayward young girls and immigrants. It was said of Jeane that she was an angel on Earth whose whole spirit was attuned to helping others. If only they had listened to what she told them, so much misery could have been avoided!

When Jeane Dixon was invited to appear on an NBC television program, she pointed out that she could not turn her spiritual gifts on and off at will. This was her way of saying that the spiritual is not the product of one's personal prerogatives but rather the outworking of that sublime partnership of humankind and the everlasting source of wisdom. Nevertheless, her visions as a seer did not fail her. This is who she was and where she stood in her spiritual development. She was a Light in the world. "Our lives take the same kind of beating as a ship on the seas," she said. "People can feel the storm within themselves."

An interesting light was shed on the ongoing controversy of Kennedy's time in office. Jeane claimed that the presidential victory was stolen from Nixon in the 1960 election, putting JFK in the presidential chair. Had he waited one more term, she claimed, those who would thwart his efforts would have fallen away. She described JFK as "a shining star that simply could not break through the dark clouds that surrounded him." The truth is—Jeane had many disturbing visions surrounding what Robert F. Kennedy called "the conspiracy of evil" revealed to the brothers within the American government. Robert Kennedy wrote a book called *The Enemy Within,* describing the struggle the two Kennedy brothers had with the arrogant military elite overstepping the president, the merging of the CIA with the Mafia, and a trigger-happy war establishment that justified their existence by creating a constant state of anxiety and animosity, a constructed paranoid reality, and reign of fear.

Kennedy's book was slated to become a Hollywood movie when the project was halted by the very forces in the government that interfered with many movements toward exposing the truth. What worried John F. Kennedy the most during his presidency were the secret machinations of his own small-minded, dysfunctional government. It took all of Kennedy's determination to secure success in his political achievements due to those in his government that would work against his great struggle for transparency. This struggle is a reflection of the fact that various arms of a government will work against the majority of people in order to serve the corporate elite. On November 12, 1963, President Kennedy commented to a Columbia University class, "The high office of president has been used to foment a plot to destroy America's freedom and before I leave office, I must inform the citizens of this plight." Jeane Dixon was cognitive of the dark side of government; the CIA death labs, planners of assassinations, Mafia plots, poison pills, and long-range rifle fire during public appearances.

It has been said that Jeane's visions shed light on the events of her time in the way of the Old Testament prophets. Jeane also had a precognitive vision of the untimely death of the great spiritual leader of India, Mahatma Gandhi, about six months before his assassination by a Hindu fanatic.

According to some, Jeane Dixon's precognitive powers came in on the highest channel of any seer recorded in the past three hundred years. She was an extraordinarily saintly woman that has no living peer. When Jeane was interviewed by a Pentagon official who brushed aside her explanation regarding the vision that she had surrounding Kennedy's assassination, insisting on knowing the "real source" of her information, Jeane replied, "My source is the same source which is available to all of us." Jeane also replied, "I ask God to show me anything which I should be able to tell others for the enlightenment and betterment of Mankind. I think that God is the best judge of what I should know."

In regard to religion Jeane said, "No soul should be tied to one church because no matter where we worship, the same almighty power guides each of us. Children belong to God and are entrusted to the parents. It is a parent's responsibility to see that the unique talents of the child given at conception are developed. God-given talents and gifts are best used only for good on this Earth."

Jeane described her visions as coming in a way where everything around her would change, including the air. "I seem no longer to be in the atmosphere. I feel peaceful and a love that is indescribable, I stand alone, and nothing worldly can touch me. I feel that I am looking down from a higher plane and wondering why others cannot see what I am seeing. A vision fills you! I can only describe it as my cup runneth over! I'm so filled with glory that I want to give everything to everyone. I feel I will never be tired again, because I'm so full of strength. At such a time I feel there is nothing in this world I will ever want for myself. Once you have had a vision like that nothing in this world can awe you. You feel that at last you can feel the word *Love*. You know what it is to truly worship God. You learn to develop the talent that is assigned to you, to do this work on Earth. When you do that simple thing you are thereafter filled with Love. You do it automatically. And you want everyone else to experience this Love you have felt."

Jeane Dixon was a very determined, dedicated, and active woman who cultivated the ability of great spiritual concentration. Her conviction exemplifies what all people are capable of.

BAIRD T. SPALDING

One fine day I was fortunate to find the most fascinating and rare old book in a used bookstore in San Francisco, called *The Life and Teaching of the Masters of the Far East,* by Baird T. Spalding. Mr. Spalding was one of eleven practical, scientifically trained metaphysical researchers who covered a large area of Tibet, India, Persia, and China on several lengthy expeditions in the 1800s. This team of both men and women, who spent the greater part of their lives in research work, arrived in the Far East as metaphysical skeptics and returned to America spiritually converted. Some of the research team later returned to the Far East to learn to perform the works and live the life of the very limited number of advanced masters, both male and female, that had guided their journey in the Far East.

The third and last of the group's expeditions took a few months short of four years, ending on the winter solstice of December 22, 1894. Baird T. Spalding published a series of five books describing this extraordinary experience, with the first release in 1924 by California Press in San Francisco. This first publication was the one that I discovered in the course of my research in the 1990s. It was quite old, and I was surprised and elated to locate the other four rare books through the library of California State University at Long Beach. These however, were of a later copyright, in 1955 by DeVorss & Co.

Originally born in India, Baird T. Spalding became legendary in the United States due to the living testimony to the Truth that he created by introducing the Western world to the knowledge that there exist rare few advanced masters who are devoted to assisting and guiding the destiny of humankind on Earth. His books were cherished from the early to mid-twentieth century and used by teachers and lecturers of Truth in order that the knowledge contained in them would benefit all.

Mr. Spalding passed away at age ninety-five near the spring equinox on March 18, 1953, in Tempe, Arizona. Those who knew Mr. Spalding personally have recorded a biographical sketch of his generous and impeccable nature. In light of his experiences with the masters of the Far East, and in reading the accounts of the research team, it is very believable when Mr. Spalding describes the ways in which one of the advanced masters he referred to as Emil demonstrated many extraordinary abilities during the expedition.

Emil possessed the real ability to travel from place to place in the invisible by heightening the frequency of his body and then reappearing by lowering the vibratory frequency of his body. Emil communicated effortlessly with wildlife and produced the material comforts that were required for himself and the expedition from spiritual Substance using the same vibratory methods. However, Emil did not take credit for these abilities for himself, saying, "This is not the mortal self that is able to do these things. It is a truer, deeper Self: God within me. The mortal self can do nothing. It is only when I get rid of the outer entirely and let the actual *I Am* speak and work through me. When I let the great love of God come forth I can do these things. When you let the love of God pour through you to all things, nothing fears you and no harm can befall you."

According to Spalding, the works of Emil and much more were accomplished without ostentation and in perfect childlike simplicity. As Spalding noted, "They know the power of love to protect them and they cultivate it until all nature is in love with them and befriends them. They can walk on water, go through fire, travel in the invisible." Spalding observed a striking resemblance between the life of Jesus and the advanced masters who guided the expedition in the Far East. These masters taught that humankind derives all daily supply direct from the Universal. Spalding stressed that these masters are few, and their lives are dedicated to reaching out into the invisible and helping all who are receptive to their teaching. They refer to their abilities as Christ Consciousness, the great liberator of humanity from material bondage and limitations. They claim that there is nothing mysterious about the works that they bring forth. The perfect ease and poise by which they accomplished their tasks surpassed any of the expedition's former experiences.

The members of the expedition were highly impressed as the masters swung into line with the rhythm and precision of music. They exhibited a fineness of character—always cool, collected, and a marvel of efficiency, always calm, accompanied by quiet precision of movement, with great power to think and execute with ease. Their claim is that the human spirit in the right estate knows no limit of time nor space and can accomplish any distance instantly. While in a manner of repose, some of the masters left the body where it lay inactive in order to greet another at an appointed place and time, fully developed and visible. Some of the researchers on the expedition also accomplished this Lightness of Being. The masters assured the expedition that there is no mystery to this and that all ordinary humans can develop these powers of Spirit.

The out-of-body experience seems to bear this out and serves as living proof of our multidimensional nature. When the master Emil produced ice from a bowl of water in front of those observing, he explained how he achieved this amazing feat: "I held the central atoms of the water in the Universal until they became formed, then lowered their vibrations until they became ice and all other particles formed around them, until the whole has become ice. One can apply this to the little glass, tub, pond, lake, sea, or whole mass of water on Earth by the authority of using a perfect law. What I express returns to me as truly as I express it. Consequently, I express only the good, and the good returns to me only as good. In the little room where you left me, I held my body in the Universal by raising its vibrations until it returned to the Universal where all substance exists. Then through the I Am Christ Consciousness, I hold my body in my mind until its vibrations are lowered and it takes form in this distant room where it can be seen. Where is the mystery? There is none: Heart, soul, strength, mind . . . the whole I/Spirit in action."

Emil went on to say, "Accept, allow this Holy Spirit to unite, adhere to the outer expression until you are able to say to the mountain of difficulties, 'Begone!' and it will be done. Call this the fourth dimension . . . God expression; you are individualities not personalities, you are free wills, not automatons." When we all know the Truth and it is properly interpreted, are we not all one with the Universal Mind Substance of the same source? Are we not one great family, no matter caste or creed? This is an unbroken ancestry reaching back to when life first appeared on this planet.

The advanced masters teach that disease is the absence of ease, meaning the sweet, joyous peace of the Spirit reflected through the mind and the body. Senile decay, which is a common experience of people, is but an expression that covers one's ignorance of the cause of certain diseased conditions of mind and body. Even accidents may be preventable by appropriate mental attitude. The youthful Spirit within is the only life that lives and loves eternally. Age is unspiritual, mortal, and unsatisfying. Thoughts of fear, pain, and grief create the decomposition of old age. Joy, love, and ideal thoughts create the beauty called youth. Age is but a shell, within lies the gem of reality—the jewel of a youthful Spirit. When we practice acquiring the pure consciousness of childhood, a spiritual joy body is brought forth, ever young and ever beautiful.

After all of his experiences in life, Baird T. Spalding believed that cultivating Christ Consciousness was the most important endeavor for all. He said, "The moment we say the words *I can't* we are betraying the true nature of humankind. It is the self that holds you stationary, not God. You are using God power in limitation if you remain where you are."

MARSHALL VIAN SUMMERS

The New Knowledge Library in Boulder, Colorado, has established a library of thousands of revelations received by Marshall Vian Summers, a modern-day spiritual messenger.

Summers's work has brought forth a profound body of spiritual revelations that are essential for the human family in understanding how to navigate the challenges of modern times. This body of work has been faithfully recorded in order to capture its purity and prevent alteration of this important new message. Although Summers is averse to the term *channel,* he does receive the information as a trance medium, or vessel, to communicate that which is beyond his own comprehension. He did not necessarily welcome the overwhelming task of transcribing the extraordinary body of information he has received; however, he was tested and chosen to mediate this modern gift of wisdom with the intention of inspiring unity, strength, clarity, purpose, and power during this important turning point in time.

What makes Summers's work fascinating and unique is that it is based on knowledge and wisdom from what is termed the *greater community,* and requires learning what is termed the *Way of Knowledge.* There is another very important and profound aspect of Summers's work called *The Allies of Humanity.*

Living the Way of Knowledge challenges the beliefs that drive what we think we know. Learning to open the mind is essential for grasping the messages contained in this evolutionary and award-winning work that has been heralded as the greatest modern spiritual revelation. The spiritual wisdom in this work teaches that knowledge is not only intuition, or certain kinds of urges, feelings, sensations, insights, recollections, or premonitions—it is a living spiritual Presence within you, the Mind behind the mind, the Spirit within the mind—a Spirit that is not an individual, but a Spirit that is flowing through you as an individual; it is a greater power expressing itself.

The New Message shares common ground with the spiritual insights of Edgar Cayce and Jeane Dixon; however, Summers's work goes far beyond that which has already been established. The New Message serves to illuminate the core truth regarding what is really happening in our times by way of the Allies of Humanity. The Allies of Humanity reveal in great detail how humanity is emerging as a race on the threshold of a universe of various intelligent life forms that have a fervent interest in bartering for resources. These insights offer new awareness toward inspiring insightful action in the face of the great changes that loom on our horizon. The New Message also deepens and renews interest in human cosmology as being essential for understanding the importance of establishing rules of engagement as we emerge into the greater community of worlds. Although the Allies of Humanity have a very important message, they will not describe themselves except to reveal that their home world is a free nation and they seek to promote freedom wherever they can. They see that despite our foolish activities, our spiritual power is still alive as a great promise.

The practical message here is the importance of understanding that in order to maintain freedom, humanity must become self-sufficient; unify to protect itself and the environment by creating peace; and discontinue projecting human problems, fantasies, and desires out into the Universe by satellite. The Allies of Humanity explain that humanity's misuse of the environment has attracted the attention of a collective of technologically advanced, but spiritually bankrupted, barterers who are much more adept at manipulating the mental environment than is humanity.

The allies explain that those intervening are not evil—they see humans as acting like parasites that destroy the host with their self-serving behavior. When people act like locusts consuming everything in sight, they leave a wasteland and then die out. This collective of unworldly alien barterers sees the Earth for what it really is—a green-blue jewel rich with biological diversity. Their attitude is "We're going to get in there and intervene if they can't use their world properly and preserve it. We'll save it for ourselves. The humans can work for us." The Allies of Humanity also teach that there are some people who are profiting greatly from and working to establish what is called the *alien intervention of Earth* because they think that alien races will save humanity from itself. These ignorant and greedy humans believe in the same perspective as do the alien races, and they intend to sell the human family down the river. The Allies of Humanity warn us that technologically advanced races are rarely spiritually advanced races. The *Allies of Humanity* books two and three are among the most important books on the planet for insight into an area that cries out for understanding.

The deeper aspect of Summers's work is the New Message, a spiritual treatise pointing out that those who have established peace within themselves are tapping into what is beyond the mind—spiritual guidance. Without the Spirit to guide the mind, it is prone to chaos and destruction, so the mind must follow the Spirit. Although it is difficult to fully define Spirit, Summers describes Spirit as the spark of awareness we are born with and will leave with.

Summers's work supports the idea that each person is here to experience and express a unique purpose. However, this purpose is not something the individual creates; it originates from one's innate spiritual knowledge, and to enter a greater state of existence one must do the work in cultivating wisdom and knowledge. Summers explains, "When you function with knowledge you become a Light in the Universe, you shine like a star and can enter the reality beyond the physical." The mind is the vehicle for communicating and navigating experiences, and Spirit gives a deeper confidence in choosing what and how we experience in life. Summers's work addresses the fact that 99 percent of our thoughts are adopted from what we identify with in our environment: family, school, social standards, religion, and politics.

Escaping the prison of the mind often requires an event that disrupts our self-obsessions. A change of reality that forces a deeper inquiry into what we are becoming is a promising opportunity to escape our antiquated beliefs, judgments, and expectations. We must view the coming challenges as great opportunities to exercise human strength and spiritual evolvement, rather than being led into technological enslavement.

The future requires an unprecedented and unfamiliar course of action for the human race as we emerge into the greater community of worlds, so there is an emphasis on preparing for these challenges in Summers's work. This is a body of work that is so prolific and imbued with such great love that it has the potential to help humanity redeem itself and change the course of the potential path of destruction of life on Earth.

There are few dedicated voices in the modern world that offer clarity and direction to an ambivalent and confused world population. Summers explains that there are three levels of existence: physical, mental, and spiritual. All must be valued; physical requires mental, mental requires spiritual. Each is a vehicle for the greater reality above it. This is how true integration occurs. This integration is important to build the strength and dedication that is required during the greatest transition humanity has ever faced.

This transition not only involves meeting the challenges of Earth's emergence into the greater community of worlds; other major issues to be determined are those surrounding global population, political challenges, restoration and protection of the environment, shrinking resources, and our ability to work together to unify, secure, and balance our world. This affords humanity a tremendous opportunity to advance beyond the imbalance that we have created and gain a vaster perspective and purpose in regard to how we choose to concentrate our energies. There is a warning of great turbulence in regard to those who will work against human evolvement by generating conflict and discord. Whether the result of this transition is constructive or devastating is up to us. The challenges ahead require a new approach and a new understanding that is imbued with hope. Preparing for this greater perspective represents the most vital education that can be fostered and extended to humanity today. To resolve the growing challenges of the world involves all aspects of learning.

The amazing body of work that Marshall Vian Summers has dedicated his life to bringing forth is geared to helping each individual play an important role in the evolution of our world, as a vehicle for creativity and creation. This is the highest expression of our minds and bodies—to be vehicles for the ineffable power that lives within us, which represents the essential and immortal aspect of the true Self. As Summers reveals in the New Message, "In the Universe, if you are to represent the Divine, you must become a representative that makes good things happen in the world. Advance here . . . and you will see that God is working within you in the world, and you will not hold God responsible for human error."

Exceptional individuals—creators, inventors, scientists, spiritual leaders—all have tremendous relationships behind them, both in the visible and invisible realms. Their ideas did not come solely from themselves. Great ideas are translated through a spiritual frequency of genius in a form that can be recognized and used by the temporal mind; after all, what is genius but a temporal mind that is connected to a greater spiritual wisdom? All minds must expand in scope and capacity to ascend the ladder of Consciousness.

In Universal Spirituality, technology is not the prize, nor money, nor power, domination or advantage. The prize is spiritual knowledge and wisdom as the greatest form of fulfillment. This is what is direly needed in the world right now. What we concentrate on today will bear fruit tomorrow. What we contribute to life today will determine the life of those to come. We must not sit back complacently thinking in error that the Divine will save us. We are here to anchor and maintain the essence of Divinity on Earth. The Way of Knowledge has been given to individuals everywhere, in all races, cultures, and worlds. This represents the work of the Divine throughout the Universe (or *One Verse*) that represents pure knowledge, pure spirituality.

Unlike the message from the advanced masters in Baird T. Spalding's work—that all of humanity may acquire self-mastery when the separation between matter and Spirit is unified—Summers claims that there are no masters in the world, only proficient students in the Way of Knowledge. Either way, it is evident that we have work to do in cultivating and bringing forth in ourselves the self-mastery or greater potential inherent within the human family.

WHAT IS SELF-MASTERY?

The advanced masters teach us that the divine purpose of the Law of Life is in working toward the refinement of one's nature until it is a complete and perfect expression of unity, or "at-one-ment" with the One Source. This requires the conscious intention of *willing* to come into harmony with Universal purpose. Self-mastery is the measure of humanity's moral nature and the indicator of spiritual development. It is a liberated religion that reveals itself through the inner nature of the individual.

Self-mastery can be achieved independent of the many forms of ceremony, temples, priests, and special traditions. The goal is one's own perfect adjustment between the physical necessities and the spiritual requirements of the ideal mortal existence as effected by higher Principle. Mastership is bringing to the surface the higher Self that is buried within. This is achieved through cultivating inner silence within all daily actions, which allows the Spiritual Mind to emerge.

There is no one who can teach you mastery, nor will anyone give you mastership—for these are already inherent within the individual. To advance, practice is required. We must live, think, act, and speak from the deepest side of our own nature. Your teacher and your master is your own Self—God within. Some may insist that it is necessary to practice religious rites and to find a teacher outside of yourself, but a true master will encourage you to find the teacher within. This is the main teaching that Jesus the Christ attempted to make clear. The ancient Greek concept of having a God within is referred as *entheos*. In many diverse cultures, healing has always been a process of cultivating higher consciousness and working in unity with the Inner Teacher.

This God/Mind is the only master we can ever find that leads to our ultimate connection with life. Once we have found the higher Self of God/Mind and have become that Self, then one is upon the path of self-mastery, which in time will manifest into becoming a powerful world helper. This humbling power is seated within the depth of the awakened consciousness. This is not a passive practice; it is a dynamic radiation of working with the inner life. People working together within this deep inner radiation spread a powerful frequency of peace and healing over the world. Merely relying upon the vibratory effect of chanting words in repetition does not assist the inner radiation of self-mastery. Rather, the power of self-mastery lies within the practice of constantly refining your own life by respecting and protecting the life all around you. Always work toward holding from condemnation those that cause injury. Free your mind of criticism of others, and bless them with the healing Light of universal life.

War is an unnatural, incompatible condition for those on the path of self-mastery. The Spiritual weapons at our disposal are compassion for those who worship sin, unfailing forgiveness, matchless goodwill, abounding Love, overcoming evil with good by willfully choosing to transmute darkness into Light, vanquishing hatred through Love, and overcoming fear with a courageous living faith in Spiritual Light. This practice is far from being passive; we always seek to approach every condition as an active inner religion that preserves inner calm.

Women stand equally with men in spiritual endowment, and men must not arrogantly seek to monopolize the ministry of spirituality. Spirit obliterates all religious discrimination based on racial distinction, cultural differences, social caste, or sexual orientation. The indwelling Spirit is the most powerful unifying influence in the world, and enduring human problems will be resolved by following the path of spiritual advancement. A new order of living flows through the lives of spiritually aligned people through self-evaluation combined with self-control, which in turn leads to the various levels of self-mastery.

According to the original records maintained by the Siddha masters that exemplify true mastery, or unity of body and mind with Spirit, we find specific traits that are helpful in defining one considered to be an advanced master. The term *master* always refers to self-mastery. For example, Jesus is an Advanced Master who continues to teach self-mastery through the integration of body and mind with Spirit as something not outside of self, but inward.

However, all advanced masters display the same traits and abilities shown in the works that Jesus performed. The advanced masters assure us that all of humanity is endowed with the same potential attributed to Jesus and there is no mystery involved in performing these works when humanity accepts its own origin in Divinity. Mastery is relative, and even advanced masters become students of the discovery of even greater mastery. Self-mastery is a form of self-transformation and rising to higher plateaus of consciousness that, in turn, enhance and contribute to the building blocks of life.

- A master worships the true Principle flowing through all humanity as being the indwelling divine God Principle of Light and Life. A master knows that alone one can do nothing. However, united with one's spiritual force, one is conscious of the good seeking to manifest itself. When one chooses to achieve in this way, one aligns with the Divine in oneself. With this heartfelt inner authority, one knowingly, in complete silence, welcomes forth the force within that has been termed Christ Consciousness. This acceptance accomplishes this intention instantly. Therefore, a master never goes back to asking in repetition because repetitive prayer engenders doubt.

- A true master is always in the present awareness of being. A master will not claim to be capable of achieving any more than what the ordinary person is capable of achieving. Therefore a master will never claim to be a master.

- A master works toward the proficient understanding of the vibratory frequencies of the Spiritual Aqua Substance, or unmanifest Substance, to bring forth assistance from the spiritual realm to the physical realm. Therefore, a master's life is a life of service.

- A master understands how to focus, concentrate, and direct vibratory frequencies that transmute Spirit to matter, and matter to Spirit. This is accomplished by working with the conscious processes of Mind to raise and lower vibratory frequencies. This is how Jesus fed the masses and walked on water. Therefore, the advanced master has no need to beg for food or money. An advanced master can produce a golden coin, food, drink, and the like from the unmanifest spiritual Substance at will. An advanced master is able to spiritualize the body in order to work and travel within the various realms without a conveyance or vehicle.

- A master communicates through mental telepathy, or thought transference, a subtle force termed *atma* by the advanced master—Soul conversing with Soul, using no other medium. Therefore, masters are always in touch with each other as well as those they serve through this profound form of mental telepathy.

- A master understands that burden does not exist for the true God/Mind. God/Mind within the human is the power to think rightly (right-use-ness) and directly through any condition. God/Mind is the focal point upon which every thought and act is centered. It is in this way that we bring forth the divine spiritual human through the direct, pure mirror of thought force. When we continually project our divine nature, our desires are conceived in divine order. A master is the bringer of Truth, and the Truth may be the bearer of both roses and thorns.

- Mastery does not require travel to a reality beyond our own; it requires *being* the reality, which in turn opens a new dimension of existence beyond the machinations of the digital and the mortal mind.

- This is the essence of mastership for all humanity—not anyone is excluded. Supporting the human form is a pure crystal, dazzling emanation of white Light. Pure white Light represents God/Life: the inclusion of Soul in man, woman, child, and all Souls.

WHEN SPIRIT SPEAKS

Recognition of the spiritual reality in life has always been universal. All manner of spiritual phenomena has been recorded and widely accepted historically for thousands of years. A few well-known and brilliant historical figures that have professed to have experienced one or more forms of powerful unexplained psychic phenomena include Socrates, Plato, Isaac Newton, Joan of Arc, Leonardo da Vinci, Helen Keller, Henry Ford, Thomas Edison, Nikola Tesla, Edgar Cayce, Jeane Dixon, Moses, Buddha, Muhammad, Jesus, and many more.

Interestingly even before the birth of Jesus, the Hindus, Buddhists, and Christians all recognized the eternal growth of the Soul through the process of reincarnation. It is reasonable to surmise that few Souls, if any, could possibly achieve self-mastery in one temporal lifetime. Through reincarnation the Soul develops a wide range of coping skills. We test and explore the Natural Laws of evolution, and we learn the self-mastery of evolved consciousness through the Law of Reincarnation. It was in 553 CE that the Second Council of Constantinople denounced reincarnation and the church rejected it, regardless of its empirical acceptance. Here we note another example of the power of organized religion to dictate religious doctrine as being factual, when in fact it is an untruth. Ironically, many saints possessed higher psychic abilities that were connected with reincarnation, and they also relied upon precognitive dreams as a valuable asset assisting the human experience.

Yet by the ninth century the Church felt threatened by the higher psychic abilities of the people and created an industry around accusing people with developed psychic abilities of witchcraft or sorcery and pronounced it a crime and a conspiracy against Christianity. The church's continuous quest for political domination led to the heartless and inhuman Inquisition of the fourteenth century. The church employed judges, jailors, exorcists, executioners, scribes, and woodchoppers to torture and murder more than four million women healers. At first, the spinsters and widows were targeted and their land and property confiscated—but with time everyone regardless of social position, age, or sex was fair game.

In the midst of this insanity, people feared for their very lives if they experienced precognitive dreams, clairvoyance, clairaudience, or any other valuable psychic ability because it was assumed that they were guilty of doing the devil's work. Consequently, the residue of these fears, the misinformation, confusion, misunderstanding, and lack of information remains today as we continue to suffer and search for answers to assist our authentic power.

The truth is—Spirit inhabits a different level of existence beyond that of embodiment. Precognition, premonitions, intuition, clairvoyance, out-of-body experiences, and experiencing oneself in other realms of existence are some of the ways in which Spirit speaks within the unique life of the individual. People remember hearing a friendly inner voice that does not belong to anyone in particular as a level of knowledge that is protective and well meaning. Metaphysically the faculty of hearing is activated as a means of communication, or clairaudience, between the celestial and the terrestrial realms; this is very similar to receiving an invisible telegram. We may not often have these experiences—but when we do, we know that they are important when they arrive.

Through personal experience and through listening to or reading about the spiritual life experiences of various individuals, it is truly inspiring to learn of the powerful ways that Spirit influences lives. Personal experiences that make an impact on how we think are invaluable for illustrating the myriad of ways that Spirit manifests through us. A variety of such examples is explored throughout this book—some being very original, others more common. However, none of these experiences are mundane.

In the Line of Duty

If we look and listen, we see and hear the media reporting many spiritual experiences of individuals. There are various accounts of police officers describing how they feel the hair prickle on the backs of their necks, or tingling sensations throughout their bodies during encounters with criminals who have harmed others. In other instances, the officers may not have located the lost child yet, but they somehow *know* that something very important is about to happen in the encounter; then they ultimately find a child that has been involuntarily imprisoned for many years, or they are able to assist in shedding light on a dark mystery.

The minds of these officers are deeply impacted by these hair-raising experiences that resonate with Truth and that guide them in their work. When a person recognizes the responsibility of honoring that which serves life, they are then able to understand and apply spiritual guidance for the benefit of all involved. It is a relationship of reciprocity between the individual's field of action and Divine Grace. It demonstrates the interdependent relationship between the physical body, the mortal mind, and the Spiritual Mind.

Let's Play Ball!

In his authorized biography *Willie Mays: The Life, The Legend,* the famous baseball player shared an amazing story describing how during the night preceding his big games he would see himself playing baseball in his dream; it was here that he had premonitions of exactly where to stand in the field to catch the ball for the next day's game, or the position that his body must be in to hit a home run. The humble Mr. Mays explained that even though he did not fully understand how he received the information, he simply *knew* how to play the next day's game. This was his way of saying that he trusted in and surrendered to the higher guidance that was within him.

This miraculous knowledge and his ability to follow the Inner

Teacher made it joyous for Willie Mays to execute the techniques of an extraordinary athlete, as well as becoming a great inspiration to his many fans. Willie Mays explained that he enjoyed playing baseball for the passion, not the money. So we observe with this insight that in the Universe there exists a pure guiding force that serves to support not only the evolution of life but also the genius of a talented baseball player.

When Spirit speaks to us, we do not always know how to respond because when we do not yet recognize the God/Mind within ourselves, it can be a flabbergasting and inexplicable experience. This alchemy of the Divine infuses our lives with a higher order of meaning, creativity, inspiration, wonder, and mystery. When we cultivate the ability to interpret and follow through with what we receive and do our part, we begin to understand how to work with and not against Natural Law. Our lives also become more balanced, joyful, and gratifying when we grow into this understanding.

Game Day!

In his enthralling book *Season of the Witch,* author David Talbot narrates a gripping tale of game day at Candlestick Park in San Francisco on January 10, 1982. On that day, the San Francisco 49ers and Dallas Cowboys played a game of football that was to be immortalized as one of the greatest battles in NFL history. Talbot described how on that Sunday game day the rain clouds had parted and bathed the stadium in a cathedral-like light, and he described how the high, soft last pass that was thrown by Joe Montana looked like a prayer.

In the frenzied last moments of the game, quarterback Joe Montana went into an altered state that he described as "a deeply tranquil zone." For a moment in time, Montana did not know where he was, or whom he was playing, and amid a roaring crowd of more than sixty-five thousand fans, he heard no noise. He saw colors and each player as a bright and vivid shape, the goal line . . . and silence. Then he threw the last pass in team member Dwight Clark's direction. When Clark soared higher in the air than he had ever been, making "the Catch" that won the game, the crowd exploded into a cacophonous frenzy. Montana's silent bell jar was suddenly shattered, and he knew that Clark had completed the miracle.

Joe Montana's experience is a good example of the advanced masters' description of how there is silence when the Holy Spirit fills the consciousness. When the 49ers and their genius coach Bill Walsh went on to win their first Super Bowl two weeks later at the Silverdome in Pontiac, Michigan, I was listening to the game while at work at the Opera Café across the street from Lincoln Center in New York City. If the 49ers were to win the Super Bowl, it would also open a window of time allowing me to break free from Manhattan and a toxic relationship. On game day—as I heard the sports commentator announce victory for the 49ers—I quit my job and packed my bags. As I forged a new career in San Francisco, I was privileged to meet and work with 49er legends Joe Montana, Ronnie Lott, and Jerry Rice on more than a few photo shoots. All good things are profoundly connected through Spirit, and yet, as John F. Kennedy liked to quote, "the Greeks defined *happiness* as the full use of your powers along the lines of excellence." This is the focus in life that is always required for all of us in order for miracles to occur.

A Sad Story

What happens when a person does not follow the Spiritual Light of the Inner Teacher? I took notice of a very sad story and publicly documented case in the December 2010 issue of *Vanity Fair* magazine. A married man was dabbling on the Internet with a woman who was actually an undercover agent posing to catch child predators. Although the man claimed he was only interested in a salacious encounter with the woman, the female agent insisted that the man meet up with her and her two young daughters. The man claimed he attempted to dodge the invitation to meet with the woman's young daughters, but after some coaxing he finally agreed to meet with all three.

Interestingly, the night before this meeting was to take place, the man fell asleep and had a vivid dream that depicted in no uncertain terms that the woman was an undercover agent! The dream was a warning—a big red flag that danger was ahead in regard to his interactions with her. The next day he e-mailed her explaining his dream, and the female agent responded to him in expletives: "That was one f——d-up dream," she said to him. Sadly, this man allowed the false ego to overrule the spiritual reality that attempted to guide him in his own dream the night before. He chose to meet with the undercover agent who was waiting . . . not with her daughters but to place him under arrest as an alleged child predator.

This unfortunate man was given a trial and spent time in prison. His marriage ended and he lost his home. The haunting and sad thing about this tale is that this man was most likely not a predator of children. He was dabbling in a dangerous area and was given a spiritual warning of the possible terrible consequences. When people are deliberately causing harm, they will most likely not be gifted with a spiritual warning; rather, people of evil intent are not warned and are eventually brought to justice. In this story, the man was charged with the crime, and yet he was worthy of a warning. The destruction of one's life is a very hard way to learn in hindsight that the warning was offered, and yet the man had not cultivated the ability to listen to or trust the Inner Teacher. This story exemplifies the manner in which people create their own misery and burdens by allowing the dispirited ego of the mortal mind to rule.

In modern times it is rare for a person to be educated from youth that following the nuances of spiritual Guidance is very important in life. The majority of people are carefully taught to look for their spiritual needs outside of the self and that Spirit and heaven are somewhere out of reach, far . . . far . . . away. However, actual experience disproves this belief. Many people have witnessed lifesaving knowledge through dreams and visions. Though these may occur rarely, they are precious, potent, and unforgettable experiences that expand our understanding of life's deeper reality.

A Lifesaving Dream

The following story is from a personal experience that made a powerful impact in my own life. While attending art college in San Francisco in my twenties, I had a very clear and vivid dream the night before our design class was to leave on a field trip. In the dream, our class was being transported from school to another location in a long white van that had no seats except for the driver's seat and one passenger seat in the front. The dream showed me that I was to be seated on the floor, with my back facing the rear doors of the van, as I was the last one crowded in before the doors were closed. Then, in the dream, the van sped down the freeway and those two white double doors flew open violently behind me, flapping wildly with the force of the wind. It was a very vivid, simple, yet powerful image that really got my attention, and the dream ended there.

The following day for the field trip, we were indeed transported in a white van with no seats save the two up front. Our class piled in, holding tea and crumpets for the morning trip. As the dream indicated the night before, I was the last one stuffed in, with my back to the doors. I made a keen mental note that I would *not* lean back near those doors! So, rather than relaxing back on the doors, I hunched forward, placing my elbows on my knees and calmly chatted with my classmates while enjoying my tea. We were speeding down the freeway, and sure enough, the doors of the van flew open suddenly, flapping wildly in the wind. Everyone sat in stunned silence as the driver quickly pulled over and made sure the doors were securely locked before continuing the trip. We all looked at each other, but so engrossed was I in my own thoughts, I did not share the dream I had the night before with my classmates . . . I was too stunned and amazed to speak about it.

We all arrived safely that day thanks to this most protective precognitive warning dream. Some dreams stand out more than others; they are very clear and powerful. This extraordinary dream was an unforgettable and life-altering experience averting what surely would have been a tragedy for all concerned that day. There was great potential for disaster on that trip. And I am deeply grateful for what came to me as an unforgettable experience of Divine intervention.

The Oracular Message

In times past, the art of following one's inner guidance was not only practiced, some of the stories survived and were documented, such as the following story of old that was reprinted in *The Complete Guide to Edible Wild Plants,* by Katie Letcher Lyle. The story was related thus. . . . In the *Aeneid* the hero Aeneas was given a puzzling oracular message to the effect that his wandering sailors would know their new homeland by this sign—they would consume their plates along with their food. One night on the shores of Latium (Italy), Aeneas glanced up and saw that his men were eating the vine leaves used to hold the roasted meat from the fire. He then realized that they had arrived at their new home.

In this simple story we are given an example of a more complicated sign for Aeneas to interpret, yet it is brimming with spiritual eloquence and creativity. It was an important moment for Aeneas to be able to guide the men in his charge to what would be their new home, assisted by his spiritual dream.

We see from these few real-life stories that when our perceptive abilities are developed properly, we gain the capacity to decipher what is important with a good deal of accuracy. It may be imagined that everything is a spiritually guided sign or that spiritual guidance is at our beck and call, fulfilling all demands and desires. This would be a complete misunderstanding. Spiritual guidance is always earned. When we are humble there is a great element of surprise, disbelief, awe, and responsibility that accompanies spiritual experiences.

SPIRIT KNOWS WHO YOU ARE

Spirituality is a deep and direct experience, an inner voice, an inner knowing, and an Inner Teacher. It assists in the exploration of the true nature of the Soul in order to be of service to the divine plan of evolution. This is defined as the nonmaterial transformative higher power at work within the realm of the material. It is a life force that attempts to compel intelligent life toward a higher conscious awakening.

The true nature of the higher Self is really without definition, and yet it defines itself through experience. In these stories we observe how the human journey is shaped by the ability to discern the Universal Truths from intellectual illusions. It matters not whether one believes or conversely does not believe in higher guiding forces . . . Spirit knows who you are and waits patiently for you to align with this valuable asset. When you find balance between your intellectual mind and the existing spiritual assets of your life then this unity becomes transformative. If you are offered repeated guidance and it falls on deaf ears, then Spirit lies dormant until the individual is ready to *wake up!* After all, you are an integral part of the process.

When we cultivate this understanding, there is an automatic movement away from fear, from depression, and from the accompanying attachments of self-destruction. It is time to measure where we have placed ourselves relative to the scale of spiritual maturity in order to comprehend the possible scenarios for the future. The quality of life for all who dwell here is cradled precariously within the capable hands, hearts, minds, and spirits of the human family. Let us not squander this greatest opportunity.

When life becomes too difficult, tiring, confusing, chaotic, fearful, and lonely, it is possible to begin to build a bridge that connects the secular with the spiritual. It is time to go deeper within the self. Take time to nurture your inner being. Clear the mental clutter from the mind. What does this feel like to you? A peaceful mind and open heart is a good place to start. This is where the answers are that give us the strength to go forward in life.

The use of affirmations and prayer for spiritual alignment are best when they are tailored to one's present situation. It is not the words that give the affirmation power; rather, it is the intension, feeling, and emotion backing the words that is powerful. Words not lived into being are merely benign, impotent utterances. A creative fluidity of mind will emerge when we align with the perfect unity of expression that brings balance to all things.

Self-awareness in its highest, most pure form emanates from the inner Light. This is the higher Self of pure consciousness that has been referred to as pure ego. Pure ego is the spiritual "I Am," the inner Light that endures beyond the life of the physical body. Pure ego exists free of the constant sorrows, manipulations, judgments, and desires that are attributed to the false ego of the material realm. Perhaps this is why people that have out-of-body experiences always offer the description, *I Am* right above my body looking down, or why don't they see me, *I Am* right here! Pure ego is the spiritual aspect of the Self that knows it exists as an extension of Creation—the real I Am that does not die. It is a clear discernment of the mind that teaches us how to fulfill the tasks of living in accordance with the inner Light, or Creation's will.

THREE SIMPLE SPIRITUAL PRACTICES

Busy people may easily begin to engrave spirituality into their life processes through gratitude, which is at the root of spirituality. By entraining the mind with gratitude, we begin to develop simple spiritual values in daily life. Here are three simple ways you can cultivate gratitude:

1. At meal times place both hands upon your plate and say silently or aloud: "I/We give thanks to all those who helped bring me/us this food. Amen."
2. The cleansing and life-giving properties of water are often taken for granted. Before, during, or after a shower or bath, thank the water spirit for the gift of cleansing and purifying the body.
3. Learn to ask Spirit for protection to help you achieve your goals in life. Before embarking on a journey, travel, or drive in the car, ask silently or aloud for Spirit to guide you on a safe trip.

SIMPLE MASTER AFFIRMATIONS

The natural ebb and flow of our biological lives will bring both lack and abundance. In times of lack, if we believe we are not prosperous and abundant, we build thought forms of lack. We have isolated ourselves from the flow of abundance that forms during times of change and transition. There must be an effort to consciously release the personal sense of limitation that we ourselves have built. The following statement opens all avenues of expression and closes none. It recognizes the presence of Spirit and the conscious unity of the self with the Source. This is the teaching of the advanced masters—no limitation exists regarding the power of conscious alignment. This is the simple affirmation:

I Am Abundance.

Consider saying this silently to yourself in times of financial challenge or in passing a homeless person in need. This may inspire the offering of a few coins, a warm cup of soup, a warm smile, or whatever feels appropriate. Sometimes even the smallest gestures of caring can give people the strength to go forward in life.

Happiness, prosperity, and abundance are innate to those who understand knowledge and gratitude. Use of the following affirmations will vitalize one's energy body with a new awareness of knowledge, gratitude, and harmony. These are the simple affirmations:

I Am Knowledge.
I Am Grateful.
I Am Harmony.

Consider using the first statement, "I Am Knowledge," when you wish to know something or are in a dilemma or when something does not feel right; be patient until you know. The second statement, "I Am Grateful," is useful to acknowledge the support of Spirit moving through one's life; always count your blessings! The third statement, "I Am Harmony," is very effective to call upon when feeling angry, upset, or confused.

Spirit, or Principle, is harmonious and flows in alliance with definite Laws with which people can learn to work. The significance of spiritual Principle is lost when religious theory is emphasized rather than spiritual practice. The Principle itself dwells within the Soul and is for humanity to use. Replace worshipping the idol by replacing it with the indwelling Spirit through the use of the following affirmation:

I Am Spirit.

This may seem extreme or even sacrilegious to some. The statement "I Am Spirit" simply acknowledges the pure golden flame, or indwelling Presence of God, residing in the Soul of one's complete body form—the God Within. These statements were attributed to Jesus as a way for humanity to express the higher Self. The affirmation "I Am Spirit," meaning that God lives within us and expresses through us, is the tenet that the people held against Jesus. The people perceived this statement as being sacrilegious, and yet it is the essence of what Jesus the Advanced Master came to teach.

When one is alight with a joyous love of life and exists to impart this joy to every Soul, one finds this to be both a challenge and a great privilege. This endows one with the healing power and wisdom of a flowering master. This is the affirmation:

I Am Love.

This is always useful in every moment and especially when prayers are answered.

In moments of sadness, darkness, fear, depression, and similar feelings, consider the following affirmation:

I Am Light's purest intention.

This is very effective and is a special prayer from the spiritual teacher Kuthumi.

RECIPES FOR ALIGNMENT

✳ Affirmation for Alignment ✳

I am ready to learn. I trust in Spirit to guide me now. I willfully choose to align with what is beyond my physical boundaries and barriers. I may have been inattentive for a long time, and I am now opening my heart and mind in reverence of Spirit's great and guiding Light. I am grateful for all that I may give and for all that I may receive. I am open to spiritual direction toward the benefit of inner vision, which is my lifeline to my true work in the world. I align my body, my heart, and my mind with the spiritual assets that eternally abide with me and help me to know the Truth. I am in deep gratitude for this profound gift of love. Thank you.

✳ Daily Affirmation ✳

I surrender to the loving guidance and direction of the higher Mind of Creation. Thank you for this day that I may be of service to the Light within me, with all of my heart and devotion, that I will know my way in life through alignment with the Higher Realms of Wisdom and Love. Thank you.

✳ Spirit and Matter Exercise

Imagine that you are holding the energy that represents your material life in your left hand. And then imagine holding that which represents your spiritual life in your right hand.

With your left hand, set your material life down in front of you, and throw all worry away.

Hold spiritual consciousness in your right hand, and rub both hands together focusing on the fingertips; rub for thirty seconds. When you stop rubbing you will feel a palpable ball of energy in your hands. Close your eyes, and press this ball of energy into your heart. This energy is difficult to describe in words, so just feel it.

Choose up to five words to describe what you feel. Trust this supportive, uncontrived, silent, effortless energy as a resonant spiritual template for the frequency of your pure consciousness in the physical. Now pick up the material life that you left in front of you and move forward, creating balance from this integrated understanding of unity.

✳ Prayer of Power ✳

My thoughts turn now to the suffering Souls in crisis. May all suffering be healed through the invocation of the Light of Divine Love, Harmony, and Balance. My thoughts turn now to deception and ignorance. May deception and ignorance be transmuted through the invocation of the Light of Divine Knowledge and Wisdom. May my work in the world align with the highest Law of Love.

TESTIMONIALS

Our brain acts as a filter, screening out what it doesn't consider significant. A certain key must be in place before our brain can say Aha! and recognize something. And of course, what we recognize has real consequences. The larger principle is that what we experience is determined by what we are able to perceive. It leads me to believe that we should be willing to accept other people's experiences, for instance, of telepathy or precognition . . . or at least consider that they have validity even though we do not share them.

ANDREW WEIL

Spiritual enlightenment filters through us in an unlimited variety of ways: through a small, still inner voice; through animals and nature; through a friend, a stranger, or a family member; through oracular dreams and precognitive visions; through symbols and numbers; through feelings, thoughts, emotions, and sensations; or through what is simply an intuitive hunch. Spiritual prescience can be very subtle or quite powerful, so it is not always easy to distinguish that which is merely a projection of one's own mind and imagination from pure unadulterated intuition as we hurry about in day-to-day living.

Listening to intuition requires vigilance, patience, faith, stillness, openness, and awareness. And once we experience the value in accepting and understanding these powers as a living Truth, then we begin

147

to recognize this phenomenon in the stories and experiences of others. Observable in all genres of life, we see that all perceived boundaries between race, gender, age, religion, culture, belief systems, and intellectual capacity have no bearing upon whether Spirit speaks through mortal beings. Not everyone can relate to experiences of spiritual guidance in life. In some there may be a deficiency in awareness or perhaps physiological difficulty in reception of these finer energies. People have varying degrees of perception.

There is scientific evidence that certain habits and lifestyles are not conducive to cultivating spiritual relationships. Let us take heed of the fact that the biological brain plays an important role in our perceptive abilities, and our bodies are sensitive sensory instruments. Some people claim that their lifestyle does not affect their ability to receive guidance, and others claim that they are much more cognizant of their dreams and finer perceptions after quitting lifelong habits that are destructive to the brain and body—such as the daily ingestion of drugs, alcohol, and junk foods. We don't have to be perfect, and we are all unique in our physiological makeup. However, when there is little connection to spiritual progress, it is incumbent upon that individual to ask why and do the work required to assist a greater awakening.

The following stories are in-depth testimonials of the collective experiences and individual impressions of how spirit illuminates the human journey in life. These testimonials further describe the way that inner knowing works, the way that Spirit works, and the way that Truth reveals itself through individual experience. They also exemplify the ways in which inner guidance protects and inspires. The intention in offering these expressions is to better assist us in embracing the unnameable and help us to get to the essence of a multidimensionality within us that cannot be cataloged or quantified.

Those who are prone to identify with only the manifestations of the material world will hopefully be inspired by those who have experienced the realities of the Spirit. It is a reality that truly reveals the living presence of the Divine within personal experience. It is a profound reality that is intended to bring out the best in humanity. These testimonials also illustrate how spiritual experiences hold the keys to understanding our lives.

Many people have well-documented, life-altering out-of-body experiences during surgery or during traumatic events. These testimonials are always profound and unique to the nature of the individual in relation to what is learned. Personal accounts of these extraordinary occurrences never fail to fascinate the reader. It is no secret that there has always been controversy surrounding the phenomenon of multidimensional experiences.

There have always been the unbelievers and the hyperrational scientific intellectuals who attempt to devalue what for some people are the most powerful, transformative, and sacred experiences of their lives. In truth, there is really no one who can denigrate the authentic spiritual experiences of the individual. It would be difficult to translate a spiritual experience without understanding how transformative and mind opening this can be, so we will begin with two testimonials from my own life experience.

A CHILD'S STORY OF SPIRIT

A long time ago, as a wee youth of perhaps six . . . Spirit first came a-calling. It happened in the magical neighborhood of my mother's youth, outside of the humble clapboard house of soft pink trim and gray shingles that Grandmother Stella and Papa Mike lived in. The day was fine enough, so we played in the long front yard, as many young ones will do. It was earnest play, and my hair was clasped tightly with a favorite barrette to keep the long hair away from my eyes. I remember the barrette well as a simple white bar studded with four tightly closed rosebuds of pink, yellow, orange, and blue.

Suddenly a gathering of storm clouds arrived and, in passing, gently dropped a few very large raindrops on the sidewalk in front of me, and some landed on my head. I felt movement through my hair and on the top of my head. Raindrops had fallen into my hair, I reasoned with myself . . . and I brushed them away with my fingers, thinking no more of it. But the raindrops were not finished with me, and I felt a stirring in my hair like that of a large spider or the touch of someone's fingers lightly combing through my hair. The touch did not let up until, alarmed, I reached up to the area where I felt the barrette. I quickly pulled it out and looking at it . . . I was astonished to see that the little rosebuds that had been so tightly closed . . . had fully bloomed.

This was a miracle! I thought, so I ran inside to show my mother and grandmother the fully opened rosettes. They looked at the miraculous barrette cradled in my small hand and then at each other, not knowing what to say or how to respond. Of course they did not believe me! They did not see the transformation—and really, how could they? Perhaps they did not realize the rosettes had been tightly closed before the raindrops opened them. Nevertheless, I was disappointed with their lack of enthusiasm, and I went back outside to play. However, I never forgot the day that my barrette bloomed. Looking back, I know that Spirit had decided to introduce itself to the child in a most delightful, playful, and gentle way. And yet it was so powerful, magical, and real . . . that it was never to be forgotten. This was my first introduction to the magic of life.

BEYOND THE BODY

It was during my twenties, when many young people are in full tilt survival mode that I was gifted with a profound life-altering experience, one that was so unforgettable that the memory of it would support and uplift me throughout my life.

I had been working a full-time job by day and attending a few art college classes in the evenings. During the final exams the workload was so overwhelming that there was little time to catch up on sleep. My body and mind became so fatigued that I was unable to sleep for several nights. By the third night I finally fell into a very deep sleep. During this exhausted slumber I was suddenly lifted up and out of my body. I experienced myself as being lighter than air and acutely cognizant that my full conscious awareness was hovering at the top of the tall ceiling of the old carriage house built in 1908 that I lived in on Henry Street in San Francisco. I had been living in this historic building for less than a year and had a few strange experiences in the front, right-side apartment.

On this particular night, my Soul would be propelled toward new heights, and wonders were revealed unimagined by the intellect. My eyes were opened so wide that I saw far beyond the veil of death. The most profound essence of the out-of-body state that I was experiencing was that my whole being was in the most rarified and acute state of joy, freedom, peace, and wholeness that I have ever known. Every vestige of limitation had disappeared, as though my consciousness was held in a boundless space. I entered a dimension of Divine Peace where my consciousness was energized with the ecstasy of being everything and everywhere at once. I was free from all negative conditions, enjoying a glorious state of superconsciousness in a state of pure radiant joy.

Few words could describe this powerful experience of awakening to heaven by *being* the great Universal Mind Substance and the Law of Love that unites life as one. It is this Oneness that dissolved all of my fears of aloneness, death, and separation. The doors to the threshold of Spiritual Light were opened so wide that I could realize the totality of my being. It was an awakening from illusion to a rightful heritage of Divine consciousness.

This was such a profound and intoxicatingly ecstatic state that I felt the omnipresence of the vastness of Creation throughout my consciousness as the purest quality of life. It felt like a communion with the Creator energy, a feeling of pure consciousness through actual experience. The most succinct description of this state in words would be a total stillness that is vibrantly alive with a profound quietude of serene joy.

This aspect of pure consciousness is the greatest of all experiences. The original core energy of who and what we really are ignites the flowering process of thought, much like the energy of the sun draws the essence of the seed upward toward the Light. Meanwhile, I could see that my body lay well below me on the bed in a state of limbo, but I was completely unconcerned with my biological body. My location had little to do with the physical body; my consciousness was not locked within my biological brain. I learned that consciousness at a higher, more potent frequency creates another dimension.

It was as though I was being guided out of my body, and if given a choice, I would have continued onward and upward, enveloped as I was within the higher resonance of a Universal Soul force that is beyond words. Then—just as suddenly—I descended and my consciousness returned to the density of my body of flesh and bone. It was an experience of quality, not quantity, and I knew that I had experienced the most profound clarity of self-awareness possible in my life! Such clarity established incontestably that we exist as multidimensional energies beyond the dense and heavy frequencies of a physical body. What we truly are eclipses our physical form, our troubled minds, and our ego-driven desires and intellects.

Is what we experience beyond the body directly related to individual consciousness? We have all heard stories of people leaving their bodies and having very dark and frightening experiences. Dark thoughts do mirror the energetic quality of personal frequencies of conscious awareness, or mind. When those who experience a frightening darkness return to their bodies, they are inspired to seek a more fruitful path of inquiry and alter their state of consciousness through transformation by transmuting the negative energies in their lives to positive vectors of Light. These experiences of dark and light are blessings that allow people to see and experience what they are creating through what they align with. This also demonstrates that there is no hiding behind unspoken thoughts. Even though we may not actually say what we think with the intention of being polite, the dissonant frequencies remain alive as a frequency in the psyche. We may oftentimes hear people say, "I just want to run and hide." Truly, we cannot run or hide from our own self-created frequencies.

There is nothing that can compare to having a life-altering spiritual experience and once we have one or two, we begin to look for all the ways that Light weaves its way throughout the world that surrounds us. I began to record the multitude of ways that the Spiritual Light expresses itself through others. I noticed that many creative and artistic people work in sync with and are very connected to the Spiritual Light within the Self. Sometimes they would share their experiences when they were being interviewed on radio, television, or in books. It is important that people have the courage to share these spiritual experiences to benefit others.

In the true testimonials throughout this book, it appears that what people are really talking about is nothing less than their authentic religious experiences. And it becomes evident that one's allegiance to Creation requires a fresh personal engagement of an extraordinary kind. Awareness of this engagement helps us to identify over time that which is Light driven and, in contrast, that which is driven by the darker desires of our own mortal minds.

LIFE

After my nighttime sojourn on Henry Street, it was fascinating to read a most interesting out-of-body testimonial in the autobiography *Life*, by Keith Richards, guitarist for the Rolling Stones. Mr. Richards described his out-of-body experience during a car accident. At the time, his girl-friend, who was seven months pregnant with his first son, was in the pas-senger seat when a hydraulic fault in the car caused it to roll over three times, then into a hedge. At this point, Richards recounted, "My body left the car, I watched it all happen from twelve to fifteen feet above. Believe me, you can leave your body," Richards explained. "I'd been trying all my life, but this was the first real experience of it. I watched that thing roll over in slow motion three times, very dispassionate, very cool about it. I was an observer. No emotion involved." Richards wondered if his girl-friend was also watching from above, and suddenly, after the car stopped rolling, he found himself back behind the steering wheel of the car.

What an extraordinary experience this must have been for Mr. Richards, and he lived to tell his story! In reading this book it is obvious that spirituality is woven throughout this artist's life. Richards explained that the inspiration for his songs emanate from the heart, yet songs must be written down right away or they will be lost. Mr. Richards explains that "great songs write themselves, you're just the conveyor, the skill is not to interfere with it too much, ignore intelli-gence, ignore everything; just follow where it takes you. You really have no say in it, and suddenly there it is." It is not surprising that Keith Richards is decidedly antitechnology; he says that "everyone has been led by the nose and gotten carried away with it." However, he feels that people are slowly swimming away from technology because it does not compare to *feeling* life, the enthusiasm and spirit of the Soul, and feeling is everything. Simply stated, what we are really cultivating is how to be a medium in life for a greater power and reality. This will harmonize our goals and bring us into right relationship through the process of cultivating self-mastery.

I DREAM MY MUSIC

In a 2011 television interview with Tavis Smiley, the musician Lenny Kravitz stated, "My music is dreamt. I dream my music, and I wake up and play it on the tape recorder before it goes onto the album. I spend a lot of time alone, but I'm not lonely. I spend a lot of time communicating with God, and I thank God for giving me this life and this talent."

We appreciate the beauty of spending time alone and being with Self when we are connected to our spiritual power. When the spiritual connection to life is dormant, one is uncomfortable being alone. When one is spiritually engaged, the "awful" silence of being alone is transmuted into a creative opportunity for self-expansion, and in this self-expansion is the still, small voice of our own abilities. Tapping in to these abilities requires a modicum of both inner and outer stillness.

I CHANNEL MY MUSIC

The comedian, actor, musician Steve Martin shared in a 2011 interview with Charlie Rose that the songs he writes for banjo are "channeled." This statement can be perceived in several ways; however, it appears to indicate that Mr. Martin feels that his work comes through him as a creative endeavor, and not from the ego/mind; rather he taps into the pure ego of creativity and serves as a kind of bridge between his physical body and the creative Spiritual Light.

UNFORGETTABLE

In her autobiography, the talented singer Natalie Cole described the magical connection between herself and her late father, the unforgettable singer Nat King Cole. She explained that her late father, knowing of her love for butterflies, communicated his presence and love by way of butterflies that would float across the stage while she was performing her songs.

In this story, we see that simplicity inspires that which is more complex, and that which is complex may express itself through that which is simple. In Natalie Cole's experience, the simplicity of the butterfly expresses the complexity of the deeper mystery of love between her and her father in relation to the deeper realms of existence.

Oftentimes multidimensional realities are perceived from a very young age. If the childhood is traumatic and we are vulnerable, we may hear inner words of encouragement and see uplifting images. This is when the child realizes that he or she is not alone and that there is a greater reality that abides with him or her that is pure, loving, and supportive. Once a child latches on to this guiding force, a trust forms that serves that individual throughout life. Trusting in this presence, we learn to meet adversity with strength and rise to the many challenges in the world with strength and integrity. In this way we become better equipped to contribute to the needs of others through the ability to maintain personal balance.

A MARCH FOR PEACE

Leymah Gbowee, the author of *Mighty Be Our Powers,* is one of three women that received the Nobel Peace Prize in 2011. She was called by her inner voice to make a stand for peace due to the widespread violence and suffering of women and children in Africa. In a Free Speech Radio interview with Amy Goodman on *Democracy Now!* Gbowee explained that she had a dream, and a voice said, "Leymah, gather the women together and march for peace!" Gbowee went on to say that as she went forward, following the direction in her dream, she was greatly challenged by her mission. She expressed how tempting it was to give up on this demanding mission of Light—but through perseverance, strength, courage, and dedication she followed through. And her life was transformed in the process, and much good was achieved through her strength and brave, valiant efforts.

PRINCESS DIANA

One afternoon, Mr. Edward Williams of the South Wales town of Mountain Ash, Mid Glamorgan, went cold with fear after receiving a psychic vision that the beloved Diana, Princess of Wales was in grave danger. Several days before the fatal car crash that would take Diana's Earthly life, Mr. Williams was out hiking alone when everything around him became blurred and was replaced by shadowy figures. In the middle of this obscured vision was the sad face of Princess Diana. The vision was a chilling omen that haunted the psychic enough to file a police report. The officer taking the report knew Mr. Williams had correctly predicted that the pope and Ronald Reagan would both be victims of assassination attempts. Unfortunately, the report languished on the desk of the chief of police until it was too late to warn Princess Diana; consequently, her extraordinary work in the world as the Queen of Hearts was cut short in her prime at the young age of thirty-six.

GOD IS WITHIN

Glenda B. a singer and performer, recalled that when she was only four years old, she insisted that her parents begin taking her to church.

I just loved Jesus and was attracted by the rituals of the church. I wanted to be a nun! I was a real fan of religion until I was about thirteen years old. One day I was alone in church waiting for my mother to pick me up. She was late, and I sat in church full of angst, as many thirteen-year-olds are at such a tender age.

I don't remember the cause of such angst, but I was pleading desperately to God for help. I felt so alone—so quiet, so open, in a kind of meditation, pleading to God for help on my knees, as tears rolled gently down my cheeks. All of this intense pleading energy was directed outside of myself as though I were a frustrated victim needing to be saved from my angst. I thought I was suffering alone as I looked at Jesus on the cross . . . when, although there was no one else in the church, I heard a male voice

as though sitting right next to me, whisper gently into my right ear saying,
"God is not outside of you; God is within."

It was then that my consciousness opened in a new way, and this
experience awakened the realization that I was attempting to follow a
spiritual path that was not really serving me. I changed my way of thinking,
and since then I practice cultivating my inner guidance rather than pleading
outwardly for God to help me; rather, I have faith in what God has put
inside of me. I have this deep desire to share my talents as my gifts to the
world. I have learned that when you are not following your intuition, you
get taken advantage of. This was an experience that transformed my view
of reality.

Considered to be a pioneer in uncovering the mysteries of human life
in the spirit world, Michael Newton, PhD, is a master hypnotherapist,
holding a doctorate in counseling psychology. In his fascinating book
Journey of Souls, he asserts that sometimes our teachers from the spirit
world offer hints when it is to our benefit or when it is time for the individual to know things. True knowledge remains hidden until it is given
to those who are worthy of it. National surveys by psychologists indicate
that one in ten people admit to hearing inner voices that are positive and
instructional in nature. These voices are not hallucinations associated
with the mentally ill; they are guiding voices of genuine integrity. People
may also find that friends or even strangers relay helpful messages at critical moments in time. Feelings and emotions that calm and offer support
and reassurance also help us to know that we are not alone in crisis.

A STILL, SMALL VOICE

Jim B. is an eighty-year-old gold miner in Northern California who
related the following two accounts in a narrative to the author.

STORY ONE
Go into Your Room

I believe my inner guidance comes from the Lord. When I was nine years
old, just before the Navy closed down the antiaircraft training center near

our home in Montara, California, I was home from school sick with the flu. I got out of bed around 10:00 a.m. to get a bowl of cereal. Right over the kitchen table there was a skylight, and I poured my cereal and sat down at the table under the skylight to eat, when to my surprise a small, still voice inside of me said, "Go into your room, you will be more comfortable there." Well, okay, I thought . . . and I picked up my bowl, went into my room, and sat down. Not more than a few seconds later there was this loud Crash! Then, the sound of glass falling: tinkle, tinkle, tinkle. My mother screamed my name, thinking that I was still at the kitchen table. She did not see me go into my room. I ran out to see what had happened. And I saw that the nose, the propeller, and the engine of a navy target drone had crashed down through the skylight over our kitchen table. The wings were still hanging out on the rooftop to keep the plane from falling all the way through the roof.

Well, analyzing that situation—normally it's a radio-controlled target drone that the navy flew out over the ocean in front of the gunnery range there. If they didn't shoot it down within an hour it would be flown back inland to a field where it parachuted down to be reflown. The parachute opened too soon, or too late, or the wind caught it just right on this particular day, and it came right down through the skylight. It could have landed off to the side of the house or a hundred feet away, but only God knew that the drone was going to parachute through that skylight, and that I was underneath the skylight at the kitchen table. This was a guardian angel that talked to me. In the Bible it tells about a still, small voice, and that's what I heard—a still, small voice in my head. It was not like I imagined it. Somebody said hello in order to protect me, and I will never forget that for the rest of my life.

Take the Money

When I was thirty-five or thirty-six I was into building Harley chopper motorcycles. This one guy gained my confidence after I worked on his motorcycle—chrome and paint and stuff. He asked me how much I wanted for my Harley chopper. Well, I said, "$2,800." He said that he had a deal cooking to raise the money and he would get back to me. About a week *later he came over with an offer to make a trade for the motorcycle. He suggested that I could make several hundred dollars more from the trade, and so I was tempted by this idea. I chronicled this in my journal, and while he was telling me this and we were going over the figures and he was kind of conning me into this, an inner voice said to me, "Take the money; take the $2,800." Well, I didn't listen to the voice this time and made the trade rather than accept the money.*

The next day I rode my chopper over to his place. He wasn't there, so his pretty girlfriend gave me a ride back to my place in his Corvette. Now, a couple of days later, my house was vandalized and broken into, and . . . guess what's missing? The traded items were gone, and so I figured it out right away. It didn't take Sherlock Holmes to figure out I had been conned by this guy. So I called up the police, and they listened to my story. An officer finally came over and did a preliminary investigation. They asked me to come in to the police station the next morning. I went in and I think there were six detectives at the table. Well, I learned the guy whom I had been dealing with was an ex–San Mateo County police officer, a dirty police officer. On one particular case, he had allegedly siphoned off part of the bust. He was living in an upscale apartment with a lovely girlfriend, a Corvette, and a new motorcycle—on cop pay—very suspicious. So these detectives wanted him! They gave me immunity, and they had my chopper impounded.

The trial went forward, but it boiled down to insufficient evidence, and he walked away from the whole thing. We met up again in the elevator after court, and he informed me that his lawyer cost him $10,000. I never got my chopper back because the pink slip was signed. Unfortunately, the evidence was not enough for a conviction or for me to get my bike back.

After Jim related these two stories occurring at different times in his life, it is interesting to note that when he was a child he did not question or hesitate to follow the inner voice that guided and protected him in his youth. However, in adulthood the ego/mind was an overriding factor in his decision not to listen to the Wisdom of the inner voice. The results were less than desirable in the end.

EVERYTHING WILL BE ALL RIGHT

Kyle S. is an artist and designer who related the following two accounts in a narrative to the author.

Kyle's recollection is that this occurred when he was about twelve or thirteen. It was the beginning of autumn, and he was going back to school, which he dreaded. He walked out the front door of his childhood home heading for school and had just stepped onto the driveway to walk to the sidewalk when this inner voice spoke to him. It said, "Everything will be all right. Go inside, stay there, and when you turn forty, everything will be okay." Kyle continued walking to school and kept remembering the voice all day long by repeating what the voice had said. What he thought the inner voice meant was that he was to protect that part of himself that was being tormented, tortured, teased, and humiliated because he was considered to be effeminate; he was called "hawk nose," the n-word lips, and "ostrich neck" and basically did not fit in to the idea of what everyone thought a boy should be. Kyle did indeed follow his inner voice and stay in this protected place very deep inside of himself until he was around forty.

Through many years of therapy, Kyle emerged as a full human being and did indeed begin to experience himself more comfortably at around age forty. This was Kyle's first introduction to listening to an inner voice. It was a gentle, male voice. It was a voice that came from within. It wasn't influenced by anything outside of himself.

Kyle thought many times about this experience over the years. He had seen and heard of children being humiliated, tortured, and teased for being homosexual, effeminate, or not like other people—for being different. Kyle also saw that some people who have been tormented have been so possessed by the desire for revenge that they have harmed and killed people; they have gunned down children in schools. Kyle learned to always look into himself whenever he heard of someone doing something like that . . . and he asked himself if that was how he felt back when he was being tormented. The answer was no. He only wanted his tormentors to stop and wished the humiliation would cease. Kyle could not change for others; he was simply who he was.

The inner voice that spoke that day on the driveway in front of Kyle's childhood home essentially guided him into a place of protection when he experienced bullying. He was subjected to things like three or four guys holding him down and having his pants torn off and thrown up into a tree or over a telephone pole where he couldn't retrieve them. Kyle suffered two broken violins as a violin student. He was constantly being humiliated in and out of school. Sometimes books would be thrown across the room, and Kyle would be hit and harmed—a combination of emotional and physical torture. At one point he felt as if he was going to war every morning because when he got up he didn't know what he was going to have to endure that day. Again, the stress did not make him want to retaliate, kill, or harm. Because of this inner voice, Kyle felt protected. His body took the brunt of some things, but his soul and inner being and core were protected.

DON'T DO IT!

Kyle also shared this more specific experience.

He attended Catholic high school and told me of his first-period class, a music appreciation class. Each morning this beautiful Latina girl named Angela would come into class. She sat in front of Kyle and would dump out her makeup bag on her desk, prop up her little mirror, and take out her black eyeliner pencil. Kyle watched her pull the lower lid of her eye down and run the pencil on the inside of the lid; then she closed her eye and pulled the outside of her eye tightly so she could move the pencil along the top lid, and then smudge it with her finger. Kyle would catch a glimpse of her in the mirror and thought this way of accenting the eyes was so beautiful! One afternoon when Kyle went home and his mother wasn't home, he tried her brown eye pencil on his eyes. It was not as heavy as Angela's, and Kyle thought it looked really great. So he ventured to school wearing the subtle eye pencil around his eyes for several weeks. Eventually, one day a girl named Teri said, "You're wearing eye makeup! Your eyes have eyeliner. . . . I know you're wearing eye makeup and I'm going to tell!" A few days later Kyle woke up in the morning, and the inner voice spoke, "Don't put the eyeliner on today. Don't do it!" Kyle followed this advice and went to school.

Halfway through the day Kyle got a note that the dean of boy students wanted to see him in his office. Kyle entered the dean's office, noticing the dean was a little uncomfortable. He cleared his throat and said, "Kyle, there's a rumor going around school that you're wearing eye make-up. Is this true?" Kyle looked up at him and said, "No, Father, it isn't true." "May I see for myself?" the dean asked. "Certainly," Kyle replied. From under his brown Franciscan habit he pulled out a handkerchief and came over and rubbed Kyle's eyes, first the left one, and then the right one. He looked at the handkerchief and saw that there was nothing on it. Kyle looked up at him and asked, "Is there anything else, Father?"

While walking down the corridor to return to class Kyle looked up to heaven, to God, to whatever was above, and said, "Yes!" It was one of the first times that Kyle really understood that the Higher Power of God—whoever He/ She, It, or They may be—was on his side, and he has never thought differently since then.

What Kyle learned through these two experiences was to listen to the inner voice of his Spiritual Teacher when it came, specifically remembering to watch out for red flags. Kyle didn't fully grasp what this meant until he did a visualization and actually saw a line—like a line on the horizon. He described brown below the line and blue above it, almost like the Earth and the sky. He saw a tiny red flag out on the horizon line. From then on, anytime danger or fear engulfed him, this was the image in his head. The red flag appeared to protect, guide, or warn him, and Kyle would pay attention to what kind of red flag it was. Was it a little thing poking its head up, or was it a humongous flag the size of China waving all over the place. Kyle learned to pay attention to any red flag no matter how small and learned to pay attention to the things he felt and thought, no matter how minuscule, because they all meant something important. Whatever we're thinking, whatever is on our radar comes to us for some reason.

Ever since his initial connection with the inner voice on the driveway, he has felt protected—be it Angels, Souls, family members who have passed on—whatever it is allows Kyle to know he is protected, watched, cared for, and not alone. Kyle feels that behind each individual human being there are thousands and thousands of people who all participated in our being who we are today. We may not be able to see them, but they are there in Spirit. Kyle didn't need religion to validate or invalidate his experiences. Experience is part of the Knowing system, rather than the belief system. Knowing is inalterable. Belief is what can be changed.

At different times in life we have more education, which may change our belief system, but what you *know* is what you know without question. Nobody else needs to agree with it, and nobody else has to support it or acknowledge it. Kyle's understanding of Knowing as unalterable and belief as something that can be changed aligns with the teachings of Elisabeth Kübler-Ross, whose work emphasized that we are spiritual beings experiencing a physical reality. The Soul knows what it needs. We don't know what we need, but the Soul knows. The protective system that each one of us has within ourselves is touched and tapped into by the ability to connect inwardly and listen.

There are mental disorders that people have in which they hear voices all the time. That is not what the spiritual voice is. People that do not have mental disorders may sometimes hear a voice in a soothing tone, a comforting manner, to protect, to give information and support. The problem with people diagnosed with mental illness is that they cannot turn off the entities, or voices that may be tormenting them. The spiritual voices that come to us are a part of our lives and come to us in different ways because each individual has his or her own mechanism for understanding. Each one of us has our own protective system. Every one of us has a different experience. So none of us can say that you must do it this way . . . or you must do it that way, because you must do it your own way—not the way anybody else does it.

THE SPIRIT INTERVENES

Marianne S. is a married Danish housewife and mother of two boys. She related the following three accounts to the author.

Look!

Some time ago we planned a trip to Los Angeles from San Diego around Christmastime. My husband Tom, the kids, the dogs, and I were returning home, and I had too much champagne to drink at a family reunion. It was a two-hour drive back to San Diego. Tom was driving, and it was late at night. I was sitting in the front seat and I was huddled up in the fetal position because I didn't feel good at all! I was trying not to throw up. The kids were asleep in the back of the car, the dogs were asleep a little farther back in the car, and I fell deeply asleep.

We were on the freeway for a while, and then in the last twenty minutes of our trip before arriving home we were driving on the frontage road. You could go 45 miles per hour on that road. We were almost home and I was facing Tom, sleeping, and suddenly I heard a voice . . . it was a most beautiful female voice. In a beautiful, singsong way and very lovingly and patiently the voice said, "Ma-a-r-i-a-n-n-e, wake up!" So I opened my eyes and kind of looked over my shoulder and thought, whatever—and I went back to sleep. As soon as I closed my eyes, again this very patient voice said, "Ma-r-i-a-n-n-e, look! Look, Marianne, look!!!" Then I opened my eyes and looked at Tom . . . and I saw that Tom had fallen asleep behind the wheel—then I looked at the road, and saw that our car was heading straight toward these huge transformers in the neighborhood with a cement wall in front. With horror I yelled, "Tom!" He was startled awake and at the last second was able to steer the car back onto the road.

If it had not been for the voice that would not let me sleep, we would all have been dead. Yet I was so confused by this inexplicable experience for days. I thought, what was that? I had never experienced it before. Something saved our lives. It was just out of this world. So that was the moment I moved more into meditation and exploring my own spirituality. I went from being an uninspired atheist to exploring my spirituality.

I'm Going Home

After thinking about it, I realized that I have had other spiritual experiences, but they have been different. There was a time in 2001 when I went for kayaking lessons with my son Brian. It was a three-day weekend. The first practice day was in a pool. It was learning how to right yourself in a kayak; meaning that when the boat flips upside down, you use the paddle in a way that rights the boat back up to the surface. I did great in the pool, practicing this maneuver. The next day we practiced in a lake, and the third day we practiced in a river. We were with a group of nine people and three instructors.

Everyone had made a mistake by flipping over and managed to get back up, usually with help. After a while, they managed to do it without help. So then the instructors looked at me and said, "Marianne, you haven't flipped over yet." They encouraged me to flip over while we were practicing in the lake, which would be good practice before we got to the river. "All right," I said, and I flipped over. I was upside down, and I was very contained. I felt like I knew what I was doing; I positioned my paddle correctly to flip back up again, but I used too much force! I came up for a breath of air and then flipped right over again. I was okay because I had some oxygen in my lungs. I told myself to concentrate and not execute the movement too hard. I did it again, and I couldn't believe it . . . this time, I stuck the vertical side of the paddle in the water and cut right through the water, so there was no resistance to flip me over. I was wasting all of my energy, and I could not come up, so I stayed under water. I thought, "Oh no, no, no! Concentrate, Marianne, this is not good." I tried to right myself once more, and it didn't work again! I was getting very tired! At that point my lungs were bursting. I was so confused and felt for the string to release my body from the kayak skirt. I couldn't feel it. I let go of my paddle, and it was like I came out of the womb. I tried to swim up to the surface, but I was only able to get one corner of my mouth up to the surface to get a tiny breath, and then I went back down. Then suddenly, I stopped struggling and just hung upside down under the water. I saw the reflection of the trees in the water and thought . . . this is so beautiful! This is so great. It's okay . . . I'm going to die.

I felt this incredible warm feeling that embraced me under the water, and I had a smile on my face. As I smiled under water, I was thinking, I'm going home. I didn't even know what home meant. It was such a wonderful, warm, incredible feeling. I was okay. I didn't think about my kids, I didn't think about Tom; I was giving up my life, and I was so welcoming of it. I was so happy!

The next moment, I was suddenly out of the water. I came up somehow, and I was just sitting up in the kayak. I have no idea how it happened. I didn't have my paddle. The other kayaks were alongside mine, but I pushed them away. I came back up all by myself, and they looked at me, and the instructor said, "My God, I've never seen anybody have so much strength in the waist to be able to flip back up to the surface without a paddle!" I too was wondering how the kayak raised up to the surface! They erroneously thought that I was this super athletic person that was able to achieve that amazing feat! I have no idea how I got up, and I was totally stunned. I got out of the boat and out of the water, but I had the feeling that, wow, there is some Divine hand that was showing me that it's not my time. I still have work to do . . . and it was just unbelievable!

I have written my stories down because at times when I'm in doubt, or when meditation doesn't work out, or I'm starting to question why—then I reread my stories, and I realize that's why. There's really something more at work in life, and I need to fight for it during my meditation to attain whatever it is. So far it has no name.

STORY THREE

Scream!

There was another incident when I was younger, in my twenties, but I did not yet recognize how spirituality worked in my life. I was living in Israel on a kibbutz at the time. The kibbutz was right in the middle of Arab territory. This is what the Jews do; they sculpt out land in Arabic territories with the intention of slowly taking over the area, to make their presence known. This was at a kibbutz near Tel Aviv. While I was there a girlfriend of mine came to visit me from Holland for an adventure. I had been exploring on the weekends, but always in a group. Now all of a sudden, I was in charge. So I really wanted to think about what I wanted to do for my friend's visit. In the kibbutz, my favorite place to work was collecting eggs from thousands of chickens. This was a big building, and right next to the building was a big grain silo that was very tall with a tiny ladder that led to the very top. No one in the kibbutz wanted to go up there because there had been a suicide hanging at the top. My girlfriend came to visit, and we climbed this tower the first day.

The next day was Yom Kippur, a holy day of remembrance. No buses would be running. The only thing we could do was to hike. From the tower, we had seen a lake far away. It was a big body of water. We decided to hike there the next day. I was an inexperienced, twenty-year-old hiker from a cement city. We had one little bottle of water in our backpacks. It was hot. We went through orchards and into the territory outside of the kibbutz, into Arab lands. I thought it was just fine. Everyone was at home anyway because it was a holy day. On our way we found a small puppy in a shed and we decided to take it with us to the lake. We ended up at the lake deadly tired, hours later. In those times we always wanted to have a tan, so we lay down in our bikinis by the lake. The only living creature we had seen that day was the dog. We were by the lake and fell asleep sunbathing. I woke up first. The sun was already going down. When the sun goes down, the Arabs are done with their day of holiday rest. I heard a jeep. I woke up my girlfriend and said, "Oh shit! A jeep! We need to hide . . . it's Arabs!" We quickly went and hid near some bushes. I said to my friend, "We are in deep shit! We need to go all the way back to the kibbutz. The Arabs are going to be out!"

We avoided the main road and went through agricultural lands. We were badly scratched up. We had to go over barbed wire fences . . . and we had the puppy, too. At one point we passed closely by these three Arab guys and an irrigation faucet. We were so very thirsty, we had no choice but to go nearer to these three guys than was prudent to get water. This is water that hasn't been cleaned, hasn't been treated—but we were so desperately thirsty. By this time it was pitch black, and we were stumbling along. We came up a hill and saw all of the lights of the kibbutz. We were so happy to see that we were close—and perhaps out of danger!

On the left side was a cotton field that belonged to the Arabs, and on the right side was an almond grove that also belonged to the Arabs. Very far away we saw truck lights in front of the kibbutz. We thought we should be very careful. I explained to my friend that if the people in the truck were Arabs then we were dead. Unbeknownst to us while we were walking back, everybody at the kibbutz was looking for us. Three women had been killed in a nearby town earlier that year. To our horror, the truck came our way. We hid ourselves in the brush, but the puppy freaked out because of the lights, and it slipped out of my hands. I tried to reach for the puppy to make sure it wouldn't get run over. The truck stopped.

There were three Arab guys just staring at us. I looked at my girlfriend and said, "Run!" We ran behind the truck. The three guys were stunned. While we were running we heard the engine power down. I saw a foot lift off the brake pedal. I heard them running toward us, but we couldn't see anything. This friend and I had taken self-defense karate for two years. We knew that you should not be attacked from behind. We decided to keep our backpacks as defense as we had been trained to do. The backpack can be a weapon that you can swing in front of you, but you have to face your attacker. We could see their faces reflected in the lights from the kibbutz. One of the guys was huge. He had huge hands, and he went for me. There was another very tall guy who went for my girlfriend. The third one was a little guy who we could tell didn't really agree with the whole thing. He didn't really do anything to facilitate the attack. As my attacker lunged towards me, I went into self-defense mode. I went for his crotch area and he in turn grabbed me by my long hair and pulled his fist back, ready to punch me in the face. I thought . . . oh, my God, I'm dead.

Those two years of karate lessons weren't working out that well! Then the smallest guy grabbed my attacker's elbow and said, "No!" Nevertheless, we continued fighting ,and I told myself not to fall down. My girlfriend was managing to stay up. I was fighting and fighting with all my might, and I was getting so exhausted, so tired. He finally managed to kick my legs, and I fell down. I fell on my back, and then he grabbed my hands and leaned on me. His intention was to rape me. I thought that I was going to be raped and then killed, because those are the horror stories I had heard—they rape and they kill. I started spitting in his face. I thought to myself, "Is this it? Is this how I'm going to go?" Then suddenly, an inner voice told me, "Scream!!! Scream like a lunatic!" I didn't do anything at first. I wondered, "Am I hearing this right?" That voice didn't have any gender. It wasn't a male or a female voice.

Then I screamed at the top of my lungs. It was like a sound from the bowels of the earth that rose out of my stomach. It was so loud! The guy I was fighting with looked at me; my friend's attacker stopped. Everyone looked at me. I realized that what I was doing was powerful, and I kept doing it. This unearthly voice was coming from deep within my body. My friend saw their reaction and the result it had, so she started to scream, too. These guys looked at me, and I knew a little bit of Arabic . . . they said the devil was in me. "The devil is in her!" I realized that they were afraid of me, so I kept screaming. To our amazement, the men ran back to their truck and took off.

This is a very weird and painful story, but while it was happening I really thought, "This is it." I thought it was the end of my life because I had no energy to fight left in me. I was twenty years old. At that point, I did not realize that the voice that guided me to scream was a Divine intervention. There is another dimension that intervened and helped us out of that life-threatening situation. The otherworldly voice that I heard was so alien, inexplicable, and profound to me that I did not even share what really happened with my girlfriend because I thought that she would think that I was crazy.

Thankfully, we returned to the kibbutz. Our friends there were upset with us. Some of the men attempted to find the Arabs that had attacked us. Ultimately, it would only have complicated the already tense situation. I felt it best that the conflict should just end . . . because it was already enough for me that I had experienced my first miracle—a miracle that graced the day with wisdom and love from a mystical dimension.

Although shocking, the gravity of Marianne's story was made clearer to me after reading Helen Winternitz's book *A Season of Stones: Living in a Palestinian Village.* Her up close and personal experience revealed that the core of Palestinian settlements had been bought before the war that created Israel in 1948. Soon after the war, the Israeli military government began confiscating Palestinian territory and enlarging its toehold on the West Bank. From then on, the Israelis took much land, settling to the north, south, east, and west until they controlled half of the West Bank's land, squeezing Palestinians and Israelis closer and closer in an unwelcome embrace. Palestinians felt the land was theirs, just as it had been the land of their ancestors. The Israelis felt they were enacting a Biblical promise in the Book of Genesis that their God pledged to the descendants of their forefather Abraham, who passed on the entitlement to the Jews. They also believed that the land, which was under the hegemony of King David two thousand years before, was still Jewish land.

The Palestinians were losing within a system of land tenure that was convoluted, confusing, and easily manipulated, never having an official state to provide protection for their land. Palestinians are kept unarmed by strict Israeli policy—acting as a harsh, circumscribing surrogate government. The Palestinians are surrounded, outgunned, outmaneuvered, invaded, and seemingly helpless. These are feelings that when tempered hard enough and long enough turn to anger and rage. To add insult to injury, Washington, D.C., provides roughly $3 billion annually in aid to keep Israel as an ally in the Middle East. This information is lodged deeply in the Palestinians' collective mind. War is damaging not only to precious resources but also to the nature and character of entire nations of people who become traumatized. This criminal competition for power and influence has nothing to do with true spirituality.

On a lighter note, the Sufis, the mystics of Islam, demonstrate an easygoing attitude regarding daily affairs. Mystics are not concerned with religious tradition and beliefs. They are more open to the mystery of unlimited Creation through spiritual contemplation and experience.

Perhaps the most unsettling practice discovered by Ms. Winternitz's experiences in the Middle East is that creativity and the freedom to choose is stifled by the belief that people who do not follow the tradition of religion, who can think for themselves, and who know how to tap into the power of inner knowing are considered to be a threat. Yet it is a truth that our connection to God depends on that spark of Spirit that God has put within us to follow, regardless of what we may be led to believe. Our beliefs can both help us and hinder us from discovering the power and the presence of higher guiding forces.

Interestingly, although alcohol is prohibited in the Muslim countries, use of the hemp plant as a narcotic is an old and common tradition. Hashish may be found in many markets and is procured to produce a self-inflicted inebriation of the body and mind. This state of annihilation of the faculty of thinking produces a kind of slumber of the Soul. Scientific studies on the effects of narcotics have determined that mental faculties are greatly reduced in people who regularly use these drugs. During the Crusades the Syrian warriors used a mind-altering drug distilled from hemp called *hashshasheen,* a name derived from the word assassin, meaning "to confuse and disarm their enemies."

I WON BIG!

Paul E. was a lobby guard in an upscale business building in a large city. He related the following account in a narrative to the author.

When Paul's father passed away, Paul was in a state of mourning and profound openness. He felt that there was very little that was inspiring and little to look forward to. One day during this difficult time, Paul was watching *The Price Is Right* on television, when a very strong feeling that he could be a contestant on the show washed over him. This feeling was strong enough that he acted on it and a total of three times went through the application process to appear as a contestant on the show. The third time, they chose Paul to appear, and Paul won $25,000 and a new car!

Paul felt that this experience was given to him to show that life can be exciting, magical, and blessed. The feeling of "knowing" in regard to his experience with *The Price Is Right* seemed like a surreal mixture of worlds: material and spiritual. Paul had always believed that we live in a multidimensional state, and that faith without action is dead. "When you have strong feelings of being guided and you don't follow those feelings, then that is being alone," he said.

HALL STREET

The poet, singer, songwriter Patti Smith wrote beautifully in her memoir *Just Kids* of "listening to a silence that would take a lifetime to express, a different kind of prayer, a silent one, requiring more listening than speaking." She explained, "It's the artist's responsibility to balance mystical communication and the labor of creation." This describes her intimate relationship with the spiritual forces that guide her in her creative life. In the same book, Ms. Smith shared a precognitive vision that also revealed her deep connection to Spirit as follows: "One night at Hall Street I stood at the entrance of our bedroom while Robert [Mapplethorpe] slept and had a vision of him stretched out on a rack, his white shirt crumbling as he turned to dust before my eyes. He woke up and felt my horror. 'What did you see?' he cried. 'Nothing,' I answered, turning away, choosing not to accept what I had seen. Though I would someday hold his ashes in my hands."

Patti Smith's story is an outstanding example of the power and the truth of spiritual communion. What was being communicated was very upsetting, shocking, and uncomfortable. The spiritual message is not always pleasant, yet it is the truth. The truth can be a very difficult thing to accept at times. The truth may be revealed when a correction is in order. We are being warned and prepared to act or not to act on something and to focus on what we may not be aware of. Ms. Smith's vision was actualized when her dear friend Robert Mapplethorpe succumbed at a young age to AIDS. If she had been able to communicate what she saw to him, which would have been difficult because her vision was very abstract, perhaps his choices would have been different . . . and perhaps not. People cannot always be saved from themselves, but we can try if we are taught to trust in, express, and communicate our premonitions and inner guidance when appropriate.

GOOD VIBRATIONS

The Louvre Museum in Paris, France, houses many letters and drawings created by the brilliant artist, inventor, and scientist Leonardo da Vinci (1452–1519). It was in one of these letters that he recounted having been scolded for falling asleep on the scaffold while painting the ceiling in the Vatican. They called his attention to it, and he replied, "While I am asleep I am doing more work than while I am awake." Da Vinci claimed that while asleep he saw everything right before him that he was to paint, even the exact colors that he was to use; then he would awaken and render in the material realm what he absorbed in the spiritual realm. He said, "Everything that I see is an exact resemblance, and the vibrations of that which I put on the walls are the vibrations that I pick up, and I can manifest those and bring them forth with perfect ease after I see them in my sleep." Leonardo da Vinci's ingenuity and ability to capture motion and expression set him apart from other artists of his time. He applied thin layers of paint on top of others, creating a realistic effect, and applied a dark glaze around his figures that softened and blurred the periphery. He constantly pushed the limitations of his capabilities and brought about a golden age in Italian art.

BECOMING A KEYHOLE

The iconic American artist Andrew Wyeth said, "To know a thing spiritually, one must live around it, in it, and be a part of it." He described his artistic process as becoming a keyhole by suppressing what he called the altered ego and not placing too many restrictions on the creative process. "Feel an intuitive rightness about the subject," he said, "something akin to revelation, as the potential of wider meaning. One's system becomes so altered that the voice goes up a pitch, goose pimples appear, or hair stands up on the back of the neck. One exists in a charged and ominous atmosphere where time and self-awareness is suspended. Emotionally we are brought to the very edge of our subterranean and hidden selves, the enigma of existence. The genesis and happenstance of such moments suggest the compelling importance in understanding the artistic, creative process."

Through these few examples it becomes evident that what we concentrate our minds on helps us to open to the greater variety of Spiritual Intelligence that is available in life. If we really think about it, we actually achieve nothing alone; indeed we are not alone. Just as deep sea divers and mountain climbers implement the buddy system, so too are we all immersed within a spiritual buddy system that guides life through and toward the beauty of the next great discovery.

THE ALCHEMY OF DESTINY

In the core of our Being we are singular and unified;
At the surface of our interactions with the world,
we are multiple and dispersed.
In transformation we seek to recover that unity.

RALPH METZNER

One definition of *alchemy* is the knowledge of how to keep all things in life in creative balance through transmutation. That which we aspire toward must be undertaken with a quiet passion day by day. Willpower and ardent desire to align with Spirit combined with persistence is the starting point of self-mastery. It is important to establish that all things do not contain Spirit. Some things are void of Spirit. No experience that influences us through higher spiritual forces can be harmful.

There is a silent and supportive power that literally embraces sentient life and imparts hope in the face of discouragement. Destructive emotions will generate a dissonant frequency that destroys one's sense of justice and fairness if not controlled through the chemistry of the mind. Thought backed by a strong desire tends to transmute itself into its physical equivalent.

Spiritually inspired directives may be nebulous, ephemeral, and abstract. It is important to treat them with respect: write them down and act upon them as soon as possible. The creative faculty is awakened in proportion to its development through use and the habit of persistence, just as any muscle in the body is strengthened through persistent use.

The Creative Mind Principle is not something that we possess; rather more correctly, we are imbued with the cells that receive and project the frequencies of the Divine Mind Principle. The human intelligence can be transmuted into the Divine Intelligence. It is a matter of choosing to serve Divine Intelligence. Therefore, the creative faculty is only a potential power. We must use creative knowledge as it is acquired and persistently breathe it into being. However, it cannot be forced; it is a matter of aligning with the flow of Spiritual Intelligence.

The advanced masters teach that God is the power that is generated and exhilarated by the driving force of our own thought action. Thought is the most potent force in the Universe. However, just thinking about something will not accomplish the thing. It is true that the higher power of thought is within and all about us, but Spiritual Intelligence remains inactive until we consciously choose to align with it, tap into it, and know that its Truth is revealed through experience. Through our thoughts and actions, we may choose to amplify, project, and bring forth the force of good in the world. It is in this way that our daily lives become a living prayer that manifests quite naturally. However, God cannot control our thoughts and actions; it is we who have dominion over our own conscious frequencies.

The process of education emerges through experience. The word *educate* is derived from the Latin word *educo,* meaning "to educe, to draw out, and develop from within." For some people this is a journey that is too frightening to undertake. No one should allow fear to block the Soulful journey because our power ends where our fear begins. Every adversity, every heartbreak, every failure carries with it the seed of an equivalent or greater benefit. The educated man or woman is not necessarily one who has obtained specialized schooling, but one who has developed the faculties of the mind through consciously working with the wisdom of Divine Mind Principle. The great contributions of Thomas Edison and Henry Ford demonstrate this is true. Thomas Edison, the inventor of the lightbulb among other things, had only three months of general schooling during his entire lifetime. Henry Ford, the inventor of the Model T automobile, had less than an eighth-grade education.

There is one weakness in people for which there is no remedy—lack of ambition. Some people claim that ambition is dangerous, destructive, and unspiritual. This is true when ambition is misguided and improperly implemented. Self-discipline requires a healthy dose of ambition. A person who has the ambition to study and create in his or her spare time has those qualities that inspire leadership. Both success and failure are largely the result of habit.

We observe that many people are becoming more sensitive to the invisible energies of the unseen worlds. Those who have experiences that are out of the ordinary are beginning to accept them as a very real phenomenon that is not smoke and mirrors, but a bona fide extension of existence. The path of material existence follows established Natural Laws in harmony with the Universal Intelligence of Creation. And here we see that humanity's inherited systems of religious belief are not a total replacement for the constantly changing experiences of the individual life.

As a general rule people are not taught that they exist on more than one level of consciousness or that what they have within them is the seed of the miraculous that operates on a very personal level. It is ultimately incumbent upon the individual to cultivate this awareness in life through experience. It is not sufficient just to talk about it; we also have to awaken and implement our understanding of enlightenment. When the inner voice speaks and we have intuition or other signs that guide us in our lives, it is part of the multidimensional reality of being alive. We are conditioned to believe that masters, mystics, and mystery or anything that is out of the ordinary is witchcraft, evil, invalid, or impossible. Consequently, we are led away from our inner power—encouraged to look elsewhere.

The advanced spiritual masters are exceptional teachers who encourage humanity and all intelligent, sentient life to strike out into the secret labyrinths of experience that underlie all of the outer forms of religion. Humanity has arrived at a new epoch in time that requires a refamiliarization with the interior domain of the Spirit. Our focus or lack of focus on this deeper domain will determine human destiny as a whole. There has never been a better time for syncretism of the pantheon of religious belief systems. In truth all religions emanate from one universal Source. And yet we see that true religion is a very personal journey requiring the skills of the alchemist—transmuting darkness into Light and awakening the slumbering self to know the ever presence of enlightenment.

The journey of the Soul lifts us out of our linear mind space into the vastness of heart space. This is a clearer state of consciousness that resonates with Love—the underlying foundation backing life. We are not responsible for changing others; we can only work toward mastering the potential of our own consciousness. The unfolding outer life of a person is a reflection of the person's inner life. From a very young age the imprint of the Soul is evident from observing the manner in which one relates to others and to the environment. We meet ourselves on a potentially perilous journey of refinement in a world in shameless competition for our bodies and minds. Family influences, culture, and tradition all play key roles in the education and the persona of the individual. Yet what is considered to be the fate of the individual may be attributed to the affinity that one has for inner vision.

We don't have to dissect every aspect of how and why we exist in order to appreciate the miracle of life. We can experience all that is needed in the natural stages and steps that we take along the way. Ultimately we are to choose what capacities we will develop within the Laws of Existence.

We are powerless in attempting to change others. Real power lies in the ability to change oneself. In monitoring the context of one's thoughts it is easier to discern what thoughts are prevailing in the mind—the impulses, desires, fears, and avoidances that drive the mental processes, all creating frequencies of energy. We must ask ourselves, how much of this energy is illusory and propelled by our own invention?

Objectivity regarding our lives opens the door to feeling what is really there. Being open to performing a routine self-inspection allows for negative self-generated energies to be discovered and transmuted, which in turn allows more peace, creativity, and self-confidence to prevail. The tools in this chapter are designed to help reorient one's focus by uncovering that which obstructs and holds back the progress of balancing and harmonizing one's life.

We are cultivating a greater degree of purity of both the body and the mental processes that in turn will support a greater degree of telepathy, clairvoyance, precognition, and psychic healing. Difficult childhood experiences can be a catalyst for helping to develop impeccable strength of character. Conversely, the individual may remain crippled from past abusive circumstances because of the manner in which the experience is held in the mind. A great deal of mental pain and suffering may be released through transmutation. Transmutation is the process of identifying, recognizing, and working through disharmony step-by-step. It is a way of challenging one's growth in order to graduate to a higher stage of mental development.

It matters not what conditions prevail in life; we always have options. It is possible to gauge our progress through conscious observation—in other words, by being aware of how spiritually conscious or unconscious we are and, in turn, what we experience because of it. Our experiences may then be interpreted truthfully or falsely. We may fall prey to the propensity to blame others for our dissatisfactions in life, which delays progress and obscures the truth. We may seek to distract ourselves from that which is unpleasant or uncomfortable when these are the very beacons that require a deeper contemplation and inquiry.

Emotions that are linked to trauma can choke the natural flow of the mind, and progress may be thwarted until the hope for transformation and transmutation has been lost. So our job is to maintain a courageous consciousness in order to address that which presents itself. If a person cultivates the courage to look within, then life opens to the freedom of a greater adventure. The difficulties will be surmounted, and the path of life becomes unencumbered through the realization that the path resides within us. Spalding said in his lectures, "The moment you look 'without' for the master, you forget about the master within, and humanity has made the greatest mistake by looking for God elsewhere, because you are looking for that which is right within you."

When we unify the seen and the unseen worlds and cultivate a higher frequency of consciousness, it acts as a kind of *divine tuning fork* that produces the geometric access codes that sustain the Universe as a whole. When we vibrate with the destructive low frequencies of entropy and refuse to make the physical and mental adjustments necessary to resonate with the *divine tuning fork,* no entity can penetrate the veils of the higher dimensions of Light, regardless of one's perceived cunning or power. Cultivating a higher resonance creates a *geometric frequency key* that penetrates ignorance. A *frequency key* also protects and guarantees the purity of the higher dimensions.

There is a lack of awareness regarding the destructive effects that lower frequency thoughts, words, deeds, and emotions have upon us and the surrounding environment. Spoken or unspoken thought, be it for good or ill, carries with it a corresponding effect upon the physical, mental, and spiritual planes. Negative attitudes are indeed one of the most damaging environmental contaminants. These contaminants cause people to waste precious time destroying the beauty and the innocence of natural relationships in life.

Thoughts, spoken words, and emotions are all varying energy potentials of Light. How can one express beauty, purity, youth, perfection, abundance, and divinity until one sees, hears, feels, and knows them by bringing them forth in word, thought, and deed? Through cultivating these expressions we are worshipping them, actualizing them, and impressing them into consciousness. The process is the same with destructive and negative thoughts and words. All is reflected back to the source from which the vibratory images have been established. Mastery requires first forgiving and then forgetting the untruths that are suffered through ignorance. We must simply break the shell of ignorance that we have allowed ourselves to be encased in. The individual has the power to do this completely. There is no limit to love, forgiveness, or Divine Mind. The moment we have forgiven, we are right back to Universal Mind Principle, or Absolute Truth. Yet how far will we wander to avoid the Truth?

ADDICTION TO DISTRACTION

One day while lunching in San Francisco I overheard a conversation that two men were having at a nearby table. One man confided to the other that he required a great deal of distraction in his life. "I need the distraction in my life, I have to have it!" he exclaimed emphatically.

Distraction is a preeminent condition of our age that many people struggle with. It is reasonable to enjoy a certain amount of distraction in one's life. However, addiction to distraction creates an obstruction to the deeper self. It is a form of self-avoidance and a denial of how one is really feeling about life. Constant distraction helps people to avoid difficult realities and maintain self-deceptions. It is difficult to enjoy a moment of peaceful insight when there is an impenetrable wall of distraction driven by an erratic state of mind. If we cultivate the courage to simply *be* with the experience, however unpleasant, it enhances the clarity and deeper understanding of life's lessons in a constructive manner.

Some people are so accustomed to noise and distraction that the subtle path of the Soul passes unnoticed. The mind becomes entrained and addicted to stress and the need to fill each day with methodical busyness and empty moments. Regular peaceful interludes sharpen and balance the mind, as well as maintaining flexibility in one's perceptions, so it is imperative to avoid the things that hold one back and waste life's energy. The power of spiritual insight is what gives people strength in challenging times; even though our thoughts and emotions may become contaminated, we can heal ourselves. If we do not, lessons crystallize in the body to create illness and burnout. Time, energy, and attention are necessary for learning greater things if we are to escape the shadow of these times and mend our world.

When people are afraid to be alone, they are not connected to their Soul and thus to who they really are—which is an extraordinary spiritual being creatively expressing in a temporal world. Taking the time to be with a deeper awareness of who we really are and what we are feeling is a form of self-realization. Self-realization establishes what action we must take. Is there something in our awareness that is recurring and attempting to get our attention in the silence beyond the distraction? Without this deeper connection, life tilts toward becoming more chaotic and self-destructive. The habit of self-avoidance through the overuse of drugs and alcohol also masks the important issues that tug at the core of one's being. When people are afraid to feel, it is because the personal mind is not engaged with the Spiritual Mind. Here the Universal Mind Principle is not being honored.

Honoring and implementing our spirituality assists us in surmounting the difficulties and challenges of life in the physical. In a material world we can become disillusioned by the overwhelming array of things to do, places to go, and people to see. The handheld digital devices that people are obsessed with also attempt to capture minds and sway attentions away from the deeper processes of thought.

Amidst our distractions, can we rescue a world in decline? If our obsession with distraction and technology surpasses our quest for spiritual evolution, the demand for materialistic possessions will be all consuming. How will we balance busyness with quietness and sustained concentration? Will productivity prove to be constructive or destructive? Do our activities propel us toward spiritual advancement, or do they hinder our progress? Devastating mistakes are made when people are distracted for too long.

In an increasingly technological society, people are becoming less aware of the interior energies that move them from Light to dark and dark to Light, so deciphering these energies is an exercise in self-awareness. It is you who is in command of your own thought processes. No one else can do this for you.

PSYCHIC CLEANSING

To enjoy good health, to bring true happiness to one's family, to bring peace to all, one must first discipline and control one's own mind. If a man can control his mind he can find the way to Enlightenment, and all wisdom and virtue will naturally come to him.

BUDDHA

Disposing of both physical and psychic waste is important. Mental poisons can burden and harm a person just as insidiously as accumulated body waste.

From the time of birth the brain files emotions, thoughts, and experiences in memory like a computer stores data. Memory is stored in brain and body cells as well as the magnetic auric field around the body. Blockages and weakness in bodily organs, meridians, and chakras also play a role in determining the stability of the mental processes, control of the emotions, and the ability to release ingrained thought patterns. Achieving a more balanced perception of our thoughts and emotions allows the body and the mind to merge more naturally with the spiritual nature. Maintaining a vigilant awareness of our thoughts and emotions provides a path to self-evaluation. Self-evaluation is an essential step for determining a constructive way forward for the individual.

Self-evaluation is a cathartic process of elimination that fosters a deeper recognition of the seeds that one must plant and the weeds that one must overturn and eliminate. Through achieving a greater understanding of the resonance of our emotions and thought patterns we can clarify which strengths create bridges and which limitations create barriers.

The fallible and imperfect personality expresses the imbalance, or the weeds. The spiritual, or the Soul force, expresses the seeds that are representative of higher actions. Because the energy that follows every thought and action creates a frequency that radiates out upon other people, the environment, and one's self, our evolutionary process encompasses a call to replace our weeds with seeds by balancing the body and the mind with spiritual consciousness. Now is the time for the human family to become very involved and evolved in achieving this!

Transforming the world requires personal transformation. When enough people begin to concentrate upon the higher duties that make life more meaningful, a more divine world will emerge. A profound understanding of the Universal Law of Cause and Effect will take center stage, and the human race will outshine the darkness of the past and shine a great Light on the present and the future.

DARKNESS

Darkness and Light both represent the Universal and Natural Laws of nature. They work together in order to evolve and facilitate the cycles of material life. Darkness, death, decay, entropy, and destruction are not evil. They are a natural function of third-dimensional creation of energy and the destruction of energy. The mental processes may become limited through identifying with the forces of entropy, death, and decay. The mind processes, develops, and maintains the ever-present threat of death, religious dogma, military dogma, and survival. Heaven and hell are human inventions that exist in the mental environment that is created through the Law of Chaos, otherwise known as free will.

It is free will that also transforms or transmutes self-generated hells into self-generated heavens by voluntarily changing the mind's direction. Through acknowledging the presence of dissonant lower frequencies in the human mind, we are in a position to transmute this energy into something more constructive and useful for both the bodily environment and the mental environment. When we align with the One Mind Principle of higher intelligence, the mind and body will triumph over entropy and death by consciously resonating with the forces of Light that open channels and gateways to higher dimensions.

The following quote by Carl Jung is very inspiring: "I am not what has happened to me, I am what I choose to become." It takes courage to acknowledge and to heal what we perceive as the darkness in our lives. Just as the organs of the body suffer from toxins that constipate proper function, the mental processes can become encrusted in the mud of self-pity, unworthiness, selfishness, blame, victim consciousness, and self-destruction. Our lives are infused with a full spectrum of thoughts and emotions that require deeper inquiry, contemplation, and transmutation. A natural antidote for generally unpleasant or hellish experiences is a process of inner purification, a housecleaning of sorts. To change old habits to new habits requires the will to transform and transmute one's illusions.

Science has determined that 80 percent of the brain's cells consist of astrocyte cells that produce electricity and vitality for the body. Astrocyte cells generate a pulsed electromagnetic field. When the whole energy field is unified and unblocked, there is an enhancement of the auric membrane that expands to accommodate rarefied energy frequencies. This molecular action is a catalyst to the chemical actions that help repair damaged cells and harmonizes the physical and mental states of being.

Just as the heart pumps blood and the lungs breathe air, the brain is the organ of organization that correlates data and secretes thought. Any organ of the body, including the brain, when out of harmony manifests a characteristic disorder, and that disorder involves every part of the body that is dependent on the proper functioning of all organs. The atom itself, the cells of the body, the organs, and the tissues all have the ability to harmonize. Physical and mental balance requires constant adjustment in constructive thought, word, action, and deed. When the body and mind are balanced, the capacity to discern true love is greatly enhanced. It is here that we realize that we find Love by becoming Love.

Very few people take the time to delve deep enough into the work of self-evaluation to transform daily living. The old adage, "We all know a fool when we see one, but not when we are one," illustrates how tricky it can be to become aware that we are in danger of committing unexpected acts of folly and error based on our own mental machinations.

We all make mistakes, and there are no guarantees that the road to glory will not be rocky. Even when we are adept at being inner directed, life's tests and challenges are sure to stretch our abilities to the tipping point. Recalling the challenges of the great spiritual teachers throughout history helps us to be more compassionate with ourselves and with others as we strive to grow, learn, and improve on all levels of existence. Conversely, one may choose to court the darkness that accompanies treacherous behavior and worship mental poisons and destructive habits that erode the spirit until the abyss becomes intolerable, or one's life ends of its own accord.

THE PLANES OF DARKNESS AND LIGHT

There is ample evidence through empirical experience and research that demonstrates that when we are depressed, tired, worried, fearful, anxious, or sad the functioning of our immune system diminishes. Conversely, when we are hopeful, loving, happy, or positive our immunity increases. This helps to explain why both adults and children tend to get sick when they are under stress. Likewise, it has been established that immunity is also connected to self-esteem. Part of immunity is the ability to discern what is true from what is not true in order to create a defense on every level, including disease fighting.

This is why it is important to understand the real impact that our minds have. When thoughts evoke emotions that create energy in the physical, mental, and spiritual realms we engage in a reciprocal relationship that is delicately balanced by the purity or the lack of purity in perception. Thoughts are very long wavelengths of electromagnetic frequency that can influence vast areas in the material and the nonmaterial realms of intention.

Free will allows us the freedom to choose to resonate with the progressive kingdom of Light and life or a mental domain of darkness, confusion, despair, and depravity. Experience bears witness to the fact that divine warnings may oftentimes be useless in dealing with conditioned or embittered human nature, and conversely, we know that cultivating the Inner Teacher develops nobleness of character. When we see nobleness of character in others we are inspired by those fellow human beings. It is through noble and exemplary examples that great changes begin to transform one's disposition and the mental reactions to life's challenges.

THE LADDER OF CONSCIOUSNESS

When we draw from the perfect principle of Universal Consciousness, we may find answers to the questions that we seek without going from one lesson of study to another. The lessons bring us to the attitude of understanding from which we can step forth into the Light of Universal Mind Principle. Thought exists as a frequency on a magnetic band of energy, and similar to a radio, the frequency that you resonate with determines your aptitude for real Intelligence. The higher frequencies allow for fuller brain capacity and a deeper resonance with the language of Light.

The depth and quality of one's daily thoughts have a resonant, cumulative effect that reflects varying wavelengths, creating energy fields of various qualities of resonance. For example, higher thought forms resonate with geometric energy constructs of Light, intelligence, and cellular integrity. Conversely, lower thought forms mirror, accelerate, and generate distortions that siphon energy from the mechanism of consciousness that has the effect of disintegrating cellular integrity.

Consciousness is ongoing and eternal. When consciousness is raised, the entity that created it ascends through the spiral of frequencies into the next higher dimension of thought. Fine-tuning the consciousness is a daily contemplation in gaining control of one's reactionary ego/mind through self-evaluation. It is a great challenge to discipline the intellect with the intention of achieving a nonpolarized geometry of mind. There are no halfway measures between the polarity of dark and Light. There is only one plane of cellular integrity . . . Light. It is the responsibility of the individual to willingly transmute the quality of one's consciousness toward transformation and to maintain it.

Once during a meditation, two very distinct planes of existence came into my perception. The planes were not horizontal but vertical,

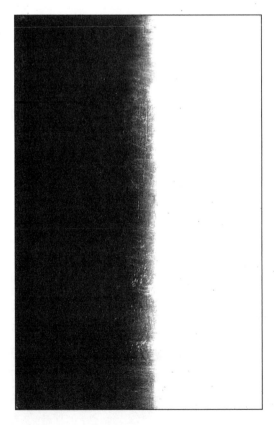

Figure 5.1. Painting of darkness to Light, the magnetic planes of thought and being

with the left side being deep black, and in the center to the right side blazed a magnificent golden Light. The two planes exhibited a strong contrast to each other. The black plane was rich, like cultured compost waiting for the seed. The golden plane was radiant with nurturing rays of warmth and life. The dark plane was silent, and the Light plane was gently undulating with live breaths of soft, warm Light. The magnetic planes of dark and Light are clarified in the most basic way by figure 5.1, made from my memory of the image. I feel that these two planes depict the magnetic planes of thought and being.

THE DAKOTA

On the night of December 8, 1980, I was living in New York City on West 70th Street, two blocks from the Dakota building, where John Lennon, the famous Beatle, and his wife Yoko Ono lived. The two artists were returning home to the Dakota that night after a recording session, when out of the dark John Hinkley Jr. emerged and brutally shot the peace-loving member of the Beatles three times in the chest. The shocking and sad story that John Lennon had died at the age of forty by an act of violence was announced on the 11:00 p.m. news that night.

The next day was overcast and gray. I set off on my bicycle for a dental appointment that required crossing into Central Park via 72nd Street—the site of the Dakota building. I encountered a police barricade with a large crowd of people who had gathered to mourn the death of John Lennon. I observed that both sides of the sidewalk were impassable, entangled with people. The peace officer guarding the road kindly allowed me to ride past the barricade through to the center of the road, where I was suddenly sandwiched between crowds of grieving people. The desolation and heartache emanating from the people was a heavy and palpable frequency that hung in the air like a sodden blanket of sorrow. I felt the heavy energy of anguish lift as soon as I rode past the crowd and entered the verdant, natural green setting of Central Park.

I will never forget that moment as being a potent living demonstration of the power of thought and emotion. When extreme fear or grief is created en masse, it is felt like an atomic detonation in the various levels of existence. Thoughts, emotions, words, and deeds create ramifications that we do not always understand; yet we are continually projecting and receiving the vibrations of these energies. We produce frequencies that are released into the ether beyond the material. It is here that we comprehend that the invisible or spiritual energy of mind surrounds and exists above and beyond the material. People are unprepared for death and loss. When a loved one passes, prayer vigils are powerful enough to raise the discarnate spirit up into the Light. When people cannot let go of grief, it hinders the progress of the loved one who has passed.

If we could see the effect that our minds have upon our auras, it would be easier to learn how to adjust our behavior to gain control over our conscious emanations. This would be a very important step toward self-mastery because, of all the barriers to development, we are oftentimes our own greatest enemy. Our own attitudes, misconceptions, and prejudices can be significant obstacles standing in the way of navigating the mental and physical planes of existence. It is the continual work in striving toward self-mastery that ignites both individual and social change.

LET'S JUST CALL YOU AURA

As a young adult, when I was not very familiar with the nuances of the human aura, I attended a social event where I met a young man about my age, and we introduced ourselves to each other. When I told him my name, he said, "Let's just call you Aura." I then asked him what he meant, and he just grinned at me with wise amusement.

Auras have always been a form of fascination for people. Ancient depictions of the four types of auras—Nimbus, Halo, Aureola, and Glory—are recorded in the sacred books of every civilization. The first two surround the head, Aureola surrounds the entire body, and Glory connects all three auric energy fields into one. The energy fields of the aura are composed of prana, a Sanskrit word for "wheel of Light." Prana is not negative or positive; it is a pure, flexible energy of holographic light that underlies biological life. The bioplasmic structure of prana remains even when a part of the body is missing, which is why amputees feel that a missing limb is still attached after being cut away. The Soul cannot enter the body without prana. As the Soul enters the body, the information stored in that Soul is transferred through the seven layers of the aura (the areas where the aura appears in the body), which influences the creation of the biological body. The chakra system is also connected to the aura. Magnetic spiral energy centers in the hands, and feet are extensions of these spiritual fields that respond fluidly to the energies we experience in the physical, mental, emotional, and spiritual realms on a daily basis.

It would be quite some time before a deeper understanding of the field of energy that emanates from all things would become part of my studies. Eventually seeing auras emanating from certain people and things at certain times confirmed the importance of understanding the aura energies as being a direct link to the relationship between the body, mind, and spirit.

My experience in seeing auras differs from the experiences of other people that have written about this enigmatic energy field. In fact, it seems there are no two accounts that are alike. This leads me to believe that the type of effect we see is for the purpose of learning at our current level. I have seen the steely white aura surrounding a pine tree as being similar to the aura emanating from my own hand. I have clearly seen a strong violet-colored band emanate from an author when we clapped for him to show our appreciation after a speech. I have seen beautiful teal blue hues emanating from teachers on highly spiritual missions.

The energy emanating from the human body is an electromagnetic field that vibrates and fluctuates at different frequency levels. This frequency is a direct reflection of one's inner state of being that manifests in various aura colors that depict one's mental, emotional, physical, chemical, spiritual, hormonal, and genetic disposition. Up to seven layers or dimensions in the aura have been observed—as well as spiral energy cones, also referred to as chakras, that serve as a protective mechanism for incoming and outgoing energy exchange. These energy vortices symmetrically surround the aura and function similar to respiration organs that rhythmically breathe in and breathe out circulating energies. This process is likely a part of the step-down hierarchy of existence. In the waking hours, the colors of the aura are subject to endless variation reflecting both positive and negative levels of consciousness, feelings,

and emotions that predominate in the aura. During sleep, the aura emanates a semitransparent pearly or milky field, with radiant opalescent
hues. The aura is the ethereal body double, or vital body, that shrinks
and expands and sparkles with energy particles that resemble steam or
heat rising from the body. The aura is the human energy field that may
be seen escaping from the physical body during sleep and times of stress.

The particle/wave phenomenon is a process of creation that is cat-
alyzed by a fundamental frequency of light and life that is endowed
with electromagnetism permeating every living cell, which functions
similar to a battery. This electrical system is subtly reflected in the
aura, which is a photographable and measurable electromagnetic field.
Through the human energy field of the aura, particles of pranic breath
are drawn into the body, and with each exhale, minute energy particles
are released by the subtle body that remain in the atmosphere for a long
time. Interestingly, these particles leave a scent behind that is detectable
by dogs, cats, and other animals.

The human aura is the holographic magnetic garment of Light emanating from the combined frequencies of an individual's body, mind, and
Soul. In fact, the holographic aura may very well be part of the so-called
missing link between man and ape. There is enough evidence to suggest that human beings were originally holographically projected onto
Earth rather than evolving from the ape. We experience the holographic
overlay of existence when we dream at night. In dreams we see everything around us as a holographic projection, or image of thought, that
appears just as real as when we are awake in a physical state of consciousness. Creation is facilitated through living holograms—synchronized,
undulating, alive, kaleidoscopes of pulsating color and form, all throb-
bing with the energy of life, curling, connecting, and interacting.

Edgar Cayce stated that the aura is a holographic image of the
Akashic Record. The Akashic Record is similar to a cosmic library containing the "Book of You" and a record of every cosmic being. The aura
has also been referred to as the L-field, which some scientists claim controls and regulates the physical manifestation of the body. The strongest frequencies of the aura run along the chakra points of the spinal
column up to the medulla oblongata in the brain. More advanced aura

readers have reported seeing a green line between the upper and lower halves of the aura. Well-balanced people reflect symmetry between the upper and lower halves of the aura. Since 1999, author Kala Ambrose has observed never-before-seen crystalline structures forming in the auric fields of people. Kala feels that this indicates that our energy bodies are being expanded to accommodate more Light and energy. She describes new energy cords in the solar plexus and heart and above the head. The cords grow to form a grid system around the individual that she calls a "higher conscious grid." This phenomenon is seen in those who emit the strongest energy from their heart chakra. These structures breathe, glow, and pulse with vibrant new colors not seen in the third dimension. Since 2006 Kala has also observed a virtual evolution of our Light bodies.

When the energy cones of the chakras become integrated we are able to assume a role of leadership without projecting superiority over others. Emotions, thoughts, impressions, words, and actions amplify the traits that are wrought into the aura's vibratory patina. The finer energies of the aura can also be felt. The aura expands and sparkles, or contracts and darkens, given that a simple change in thought will immediately alter the color, emanation, and magnetic affinity of the aura. The aura expands in sunlight and shrinks while indoors. In ancient Egypt the human aura was so valued and well understood that individuals were encouraged to choose colors for their attire that harmonized with the dominant color in their aura.

Although the light of the aura is a cosmic force field of protection, it can be weakened and carelessly forced open by undesirable manipulations, harrowing experiences, surgery, drugs, alcohol abuse, smoking, dissonant radiations, deep-seated fears, and other insecurities of the mind. The aura may become damaged through stress, emotional pain, illness, and extreme hardship. A generous person's aura is large with pastel colors, and the aura of a miserly person is small, murky, and muddied. A compressed aura around the body may be reflected in the persona and facial features as a hardened or stiff look. The auras of people living together in long-term relationships begin to blend as people adopt each other's behaviors and characteristics.

Sleep recharges the aura with prana—the energy or Spirit of life—as the aura is the result of prana. World cultures have different names for prana; in China it is called *chi,* in Japan it is called *ki,* and in Egypt it is called *ka.* Sunlight and natural surroundings such as plants and animals; the energy and sounds of nature; fresh air and water; natural foods; cloud watching; medicinal herbs; and swimming in clean rivers, lakes, and oceans are some of the wonderful things that strengthen pranic energy in the aura. The Earth itself is a living, breathing vessel of sustaining pranic energy, which explains why it is very restorative to sit or lie under a large tree for several hours. The Earth is an abundant reservoir of pranic energy. There is also a definite energy exchange through showing affection; kissing and lovemaking, where the auras blend together, which changes the pranic energy in either a positive or a negative way.

Through the misuse of free will, the vibratory rate of human atoms may decrease to the point that the aura resonates as dark and sullen and the body and mind amplify darkness, blinding one from the creative potential of Light. This is why it is difficult to be in the company of a depressed person for any amount of time; it feels like having the life sucked out of you. A sluggish, cloudy aura may indicate poor nutrition, lack of sleep, stress, or smoking in the home. Drug addicts, alcoholics, and mentally ill individuals exhibit gray clouds of astral mucus in the aura. Astral entities attached to the aura will appear as black or gray spheres. People who feel inferior, incompetent, unworthy, and undeserving exhibit a collapsed aura. Deeply hurt individuals build a prickly shell around the aura that prevents intimacy. Spiritual guides, Angels, and Divine Teachers will appear as small white orbs or spiral Light energies near the head area of one's aura. Pregnant women display pastel auras; singers and musicians may display strong colorful auras when they perform.

The Laws of Creation both preserve and destroy. It is possible for those who cultivate the frequency of destruction to be consumed by their own identity—a free-will destiny determined by their own consciousness. When we choose to shape our consciousness in harmonious accord with Natural Laws the vibration of the aura increases, expands, and becomes stronger. The aura is a kind of unique fingerprint of the history of the Soul of a living plant, animal, or person.

Our minds and emotions create vibrations that correlate with all the colors of the rainbow and beyond. Beams of light are generated by the pineal gland in the brain and appear around the human head area only when the person is spiritually healthy. The halo surrounding the crown area of the head is a familiar symbol of the spiritually advanced individual in religious paintings. The beams of Light represent the connection one has between the mind and the heart consciousness. The

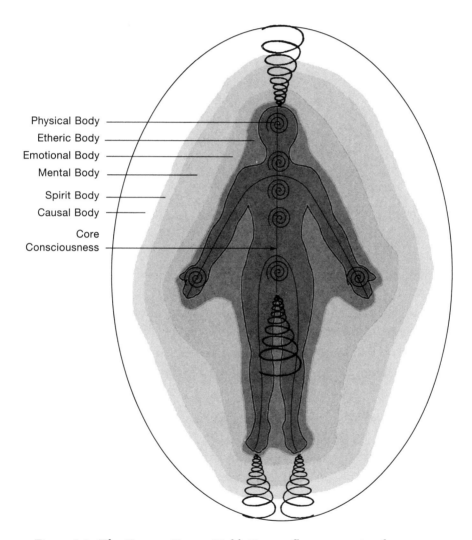

Figure 5.2. The Human Energy Field. Energy flow emanating from our core light is regulated by the sixteen major chakras, nine of which are shown here, shaped like spiral energy cones that function like valves along the spine from the brain to the hands and feet and beyond.

Maya believed that changing consciousness effectively changes one's reality. Erase the false belief, and the sickness vanishes.

From the shoulders of the body upward, auras of frequency and color are reflective of one's thoughts, emotions, and brain health. From the shoulders to the knees, the emotions extend downward to express a greater range of feeling in the body, particularly the stomach area, which is the most sensitive organ affected by thoughts and emotions. Colors below the feet reflect old energy affecting the individual's unconscious mind. A child's aura represents potential, and in old age the aura is the record of the life lived. Spiritual balance and imbalance, mental and emotional stability and turmoil, as well as bodily strengths and diseases will all be reflected in the aura color at the site of the affected part of the body. This all changes and fluctuates as the balance of the individual grows better or worse.

The science of iridology is a quick and helpful way of determining the spiritual level of a person by observing the clarity and the sparkle of the whole eye. Interestingly, when the eyes appear cloudy or veiled, this indicates that both the mental and spiritual potency of the individual is diminished or compromised.

One's ability to read the aura of another is not necessarily an indication of advanced spiritual development. Those seeing the aura of another are reading it through their own aura field, so one's own thoughts and emotions may color what is seen. In fact, there are many different factors at play in interpreting what exactly one sees in auras. To be accurate, one must also be able to read the complete life record (the Akashic Record), to correctly determine the aura value of an individual. Incorrect readings of the aura are harmful when qualities are discerned that do not exist. The state of a person's ever-fluctuating consciousness must be regarded as both the greatest asset and the greatest weakness affecting the aura energies. The Light-flooded aura is definitive of a Soul that is aligned with the root of its Spiritual essence.

The foundational essence of the aura is a crystal stream of white Light that is a tangible manifestation in the material world through the Law of Love. The aura is literally a broadcasting station for the energies of Light. We become enlightened when mental stillness is combined with higher knowledge that is broadcast and lived into the world. Those who understand the meaning of life know that there is no difference between the Divine Nature of God and the Divine Nature of God in the Self. When humanity's divine nature is properly understood, then we can begin the process of correctly weaving the sacred tapestry of life's true manifestation through understanding the aura. Below are a few basic interpretations of colors in the aura.

COLOR VARIATIONS IN THE AURA

White

The color white contains all colors. White in the aura is the foundational color of protection in all auras. White can range from cloudy white to brilliant to golden white. The white light may be indicative of purity, enlightenment, integration, balance, and selfless service in life. All colors reflect variants of higher to lower frequencies. A true saint, or great Soul, emanates with a pearly white light two feet all around the body, originating from the spiral design of the flower of life above the head area. Pale ethereal hues mixing with white in the aura indicate increased spirituality in the person. Cheerful, generous individuals with loving, bighearted natures radiate with expansive dilutions of white, such as pastel pink, pastel yellow, pale blue, and soft green. White in the aura also reflects peace-loving ideals and is seen in those who strive to make the world a better place. Balls of white light around people's bodies are sometimes visible in photographs as being inner teachers, deities, angelic beings, guardian angels, or loved ones. Dull white may indicate shyness, nervousness, muscle tension, foggy perception, high metabolism, and distraction. Silver and gold are variations of white and are seen in those who excel at taking on challenges and ideas on a large scale and actualizing them in the world, whether the projects are practical or impractical. True Gold represents Spiritual Royalty and Divinity. Any muddying of the colors are emanations of imperfect thoughts, feelings, and illness mingling with the pure colors released through the prism of the Law of Divine Light.

Yellow

Pure yellow may be reflective of personal power, intuitive intelligence, creativity, logic, intellect, and a perceptive, thoughtful, forgiving, optimistic outlook on life. Pale yellow and golden yellow hues indicate Cosmic Intelligence, knowledge, or Christ light in the mind of the person. Dull yellow may indicate worry, anxiety, emotional repression, stubbornness, and opposition to change. Muddied yellow indicates selfish intellectualism, cowardice, impracticality, withdrawal, false ego, lack of self-esteem, and lack of confidence, self-righteousness, and imbalance between heart and head. Yellow also reflects the health of the adrenal glands, an emotional center. Yellowish green may indicate artistic creativity, sympathy, empathy, or jealousy, dishonesty, and greed. Yellow relates to the spleen and life force energy.

Green

Green hues resonate with abundance, growth, renewal, universal healing and supply, empathy, generousness, and a loving, open heart. Green is neutralizing and calming and is seen in those who have an affinity for nature. Nature is creative genius in action. Vibrant greens are also seen in healers and those who are loving, kind, and compassionate. When people are successful at increasing the vitality of plants, they are said to have a green thumb. Chartreuse green and dark greens may resonate in the aura as exhaustion, deception, physical discomfort, distrust, spite, jealousy, selfishness, envy, or resentment. Green relates to the thymus gland and the immune system.

Orange

Orange reflects healing and the balanced emotions of a social personality that is creative, organized, healthy, energetic, sensitive, compassionate, selfless, and competent. Various orange tones may indicate the dreamer, the victim, the healer, childlike fragility, the addictive personality, or the artistic personality. Muddy or dull orange may be seen when there is a lack of emotional control, or overindulgence, or when one is irritable, inflexible, or undersexed. Orange mixed with dirty brown indicates a greedy, selfish nature where the aura is contracted and channeled into a narrow focus in which circulation is curtailed. Here, there is neither a cleansing of toxic energies nor input from universal energies; the aura is encrusted with the mud of confining boundaries, loneliness, and helplessness. Orange is also related to the health of the adrenal glands.

Pastel Pink

Pastel pink calms aggressiveness and anger. In the aura pink indicates opening the heart or being bighearted. Universal or Divine Love resonates with pink and may be seen in those who enjoy planning and dreaming of family and financial success. Pink houses have always had the effect of making me feel joyful, so I feel that pink also resonates with joy. Rose pink reflects love and happiness, while cerise pink resonates with passion. Pale cloudy pink in the aura may indicate weakness and anemia.

True Red

True red resonates with the vitality of the life force, new life, courage, and ambition. Deep reds reflect passion with a strong carnal connection to the body, the health of the blood, exiting physical work, materialism, a forceful personality, survival instincts, strong will or conviction, loyalty, motivation, generosity, abundance, playfulness, and sexuality. Clear red reflects friendliness, while magenta is a cheerful emanation. Dull brownish red reflects lack of vitality or self-centeredness. Fiery red resonates with irritability and anxiety. Crimson flashes or reddish-black streaks reflect the frequency of emotional outbursts, brutality, manipulation, emotional illness, anger, or self-defeat. Maroon red may indicate poor health, negativity, pain, and impurity. Red is the emotional color relating to the health of the reproductive system.

Blue

Blue of the ocean and royal blue is seen in those who are devoted to working with religious teachings. It is also seen in those who enjoy freedom, variety, communication, clarity, certainty, creativity, faith, trust, and practicality. Blue may also indicate arrogance, indecision, male energy, immaturity, melancholy, and judgment. Indigo blues may be seen in those who are wise with strong intuition and a personal awareness of the higher work of the Divine in the higher Self and in life. The lower aspect of indigo reflects a person that is too self-sufficient. The vibrancy and strength of the blues are altered when sadness sets in and we literally "feel blue." Blue relates to the health of the thyroid and metabolism.

True Violet

True violet is rarely seen in the aura, as it is the color of the Spiritually adept. Violet hues, especially ultraviolet, carry the essence of the visionary, psychic, creative, Spiritual truths, and indicate Spiritual transmutation and the buoyancy of being imbued with the Holy Spirit. Light, clear violet in the aura focuses clear thinking in the mind, has a calming effect, and opens the mind to abstract ideas and the power of Wisdom and Truth. Lavender-purple colors above the head always reflect Spiritual aspirations in the individual as being distinct from religious devotion. Violet may indicate charisma, clairvoyance, protection, mediumship, and therapeutic healing. Deep violet black resonates in the aura as self-righteous justification, self-importance, superiority, or heart and stomach trouble. Violet also relates to the health of the pineal and pituitary glands in the brain.

Brown

Brown in the aura may be associated with the Earthy personality of being grounded and practical. Brown may also reflect a somber nature, lower astral energies, declining health, or dependency on pharmaceutical drugs or may indicate being stuck in the mud of self-pity, confusion, mental illness, indecision, sloth, laziness, depression, negativity, and suppressed feelings. Suppressed feelings accumulate and cause a blockage of energy flow in one's being. Reinterpreting what we believe has happened to us releases the energy. It is here that we learn the intention of managing our own energy. People that decrease the vitality in plants are said to have a brown thumb. Brown in the aura is present in everyone by degrees, as it is also reflective of the instinctual human condition of selfishness in one form or another.

Black

Black is the total absence of color. In the aura, black may indicate negative or dark thoughts, dismal feelings, evil, degeneration, or disease. Creating destruction sets the frequency for self-destruction. Black also denotes the mystery of the unknown. The unknown and the unexpected are always at play in the game of life, as there is no single mind that can know all things. The unknown is to be given as much respect as that which is known—they are polar opposites that create balance. Black hovering in the aura may indicate the impending death of a loved one. A complete lack of color in the aura indicates the impending death of the individual. Gray in the aura indicates poor health, brain weakness, depression, and fear.

STRENGTHENING THE AURA

It is important to develop the habit of counteracting the shadow of negative influences that discolor the aura using basic techniques of self-mastery. The cleansing of undesirable conditions in the aura need not be a lengthy process. Discarding unworthy emotions and thoughts and making a sincere effort to correct errors will do much to purify the aura. The fundamental exercise for protecting oneself from destructive forces is through the internal reality of Light. Turning one's thoughts toward projecting a glowing cocoon of Light as a shield around the body and breathing the transmuting color of violet into your being as a protective meditation is also effective in assisting the purification of your aura.

Ultraviolet light is the spiritual carrier wave of sacred geometry that unites spirit to matter; has the ability to penetrate all material objects; and carries energy, information, and consciousness to and from any physical or spiritual location. In your meditation, imagine yourself as a flower unfolding the dominion of what Hildegard of Bingen termed *veriditas*. *Veriditas* is a Latin word for greenness and the ability to heal, grow, and birth. Dormant powers require exercise. We think ideas into thought forms that give substance to materialization. Remember that Light is the organism through which thought works and moves into form.

Auric Shields

- Protect the aura by minimizing various dissonant frequencies of radiation around the body.
- Do not allow your attention to rest on your imagined imperfections; this is a misappropriation of energy.
- Do not allow yourself lengthy concentration on negative qualities, conditions, deep-seated fears, and insecurities.
- Allow yourself to become aware of the ingrained patterns of your thoughts; identify what must be learned and what must be unlearned.
- Loosen the ties that bind you to the egocentricities enmeshed in the vain aspects of the mind. These are patterns that weave self-made prison walls of limitation.
- Earth is a schoolroom where self-mastery requires mastering one's own consciousness. Become aware that one's thoughts and actions impinge upon others and influence the experience of life, sapping the strength and weakening the action of Light in the aura.
- The key to self-mastery lies within the understanding that one is an emanation of Light that acts as a divine magnet to increase the flow of perfection into one's aura and then into the world. Work in pure silence and deep peace at being fully present. Go beyond duality, and work as a unit of wholeness: body, mind, and spirit.
- When discordant energies arise, create an alliance with the forces of Divine Light and knowledge. Building the aura requires that one becomes strong through aligning with the stillness that underlies all activity.
- Initiate and intensify your contact with Angelic Hosts as a means of fortifying your aura. Invite higher beings of Light to guide and assist you on your journey in the spirit of Oneness.
- Do not ignore the negative influences that hover in the atmosphere seeking to destroy the peace, power, purity, and unity of the home, the Self, and the human family.
- Offering oneself as a spiritual devotee in service to the higher good for all is a calling of considerable magnitude. The higher frequency of Light, Power, Beauty, Love, and interplanetary life does not enter the mortal mind unbidden.

- Strengthen spiritual reserves by practicing purposeful meditation. This will assist the conveyance of Truth in everyday situations. Meditate on the unfolding kingdom that is within you. Take responsibility for learning to modulate your own frequency. Be a keeper of Light regardless of the impediments that attempt to block the flow of vital life forces. Remember, we are ultimately the makers of our own destinies.

- Remember that thoughts create strong feelings, emotions, ideas, patterns, and habits that form energy vortices of pranic/auric substance that may fluctuate as semipermanent energies or remain long after the one who has created the energy has left. To neutralize your environment from thought vortices that linger—purify the area often with beeswax candles, ceremonial sage, prayer, and natural sounds such as singing, rattles, drums, and bells until the offending energy is cleared.

THE ASTRAL PLANE OF EARTH

The astral energies are described as the desire sheath that directs the physical body to satisfy basic survival instincts. The five senses—thirst, hunger, temperature, pain, and pleasure—are all part of the astral body. The astral body is also the emotional vehicle of an individual; it is a subtle extension of the physical body and is linked to the mind, so it is not subject to gravity. It is a mobile consciousness that has been recognized for explaining the near-death experience. The astral body is an ethereal energy system that can leave the body, interact with the inhabitants of the astral realm, and eject the consciousness from the body to protect a person from mental trauma.

Because the energetic substance of the astral realm is imbued with magnetic thoughts and emotions and the desire aspects of the human personality, the astral plane is considered to be the most dangerous plane of nature. The astral plane is the plane of emotions and illusions. The astral plane and the fourth dimension are magnetically charged mental realms where various thoughts either increase or impair the progression of the higher Self; these can include self-deception, delusions of grandeur, self-pity, criticism, mischievous intentions, suspicion, hypermateriality, lewd behavior, hope, fear, love, hate, suffering, joy, and more. In life we either move forward or slide backward, and the goals we fail to achieve are lost destinies. A spiritual garden, like a physical garden, requires constant and loving attention to flower and bring forth the fruits of Spirit.

People who are lost and confused, ignorant, malicious, or suffer from depression, addiction, or other mentally weakened states have torn or collapsed auras and may be susceptible to astral possession. For example, the addictive personality cannot continue the habit of addiction after death and the astral entity may attempt to attach itself to a living person to continue to enjoy the perceived pleasures of the addiction. Lower astral entities may become attracted to a loving, generous living personality and attempt to insert psychic hooks or tentacles that suck the energy from the unsuspecting victim's auric field.

In all cases of psychic intrusion from those who are dead or alive, the following simple prayer is effective to cut the ties when feeling ungrounded and drained:

I am cleansed of dark energies, I am Light, I am love,
all is healed and forgiven.

The biological brain has limited consciousness locked into a temporal reality of fixed space and time. Earth's time frame is also a locked vantage point—a physical perspective of reality. The body is equipped with an autonomic nervous system that functions similar to the mechanism of autopilot. This sophisticated biological autopilot mode allows the consciousness to ascend into the astral body each night for various learning excursions in the astral realm. While experiencing in the astral realm we learn that our thoughts, feelings, and emotions manifest instantly without the time lag that we experience in the physical realm. The astral plane and the fourth dimension are also where the process of evolution unfolds as repetitive rebirths into the physical plane. Each new life of learning for the Soul is called reincarnation.

The astral body is a different level of vibratory manifestation that is spatially superimposed over the physical form. The three frequency levels that overlay the body in the third dimension are the physical, ethereal, and astral bodies—all operating with varying degrees of energetic expression. The ethereal overlay is the domain of the aura.

When we experience in higher realms, we move into regions of consciousness that may be more challenging to perceive and understand. The astral plane embodies both higher and lower levels of thought frequencies. When we are experiencing on the astral plane through our dreams, we are visitors and will meet discarnate local inhabitants of the astral plane. The discarnate personality that is emotionally charged with the frequency of the astral realm can become trapped or frozen in a certain frequency until the thought form of the individual changes.

Frozen Consciousness

One night while asleep, I was offered a lesson in frozen consciousness. In this dream, I found myself in a tall building high in the sky with a group of people who were very frightened. "There is no way out!" said the woman near me, and before I had a chance to respond or help, I melted away from the scene because I did not believe that there was no way out. I simply changed my mind, and I was gone. The scene was energized by a group of minds frozen with fear and trapped in the fourth-dimensional astral plane. It was apparent that those minds were literally frozen with the limitation of fear.

The Fourth and Fifth Dimensions

Physical death and the release of one's beliefs, thought forms, and energy field into the astral plane will not guarantee salvation. A properly conducted Earth life will naturally form a corresponding resonating Light body; the frequency level of the Light body is the key that opens the gates to the higher frequency of the fifth dimension. The fifth dimension reflects the pure expression of the Soul, free from the illusions of the astral plane. Because so few people are educated in the art of self-mastery as a way to live, very few are able to resonate beyond the threshold of the fourth dimension into the fifth dimension of Absolute Truth, where one merges completely with pure Universal Awareness and Enlightenment. The fourth dimension reflects the mirror image of the Earth plane and is the astral body of Earth and all life on it, only on a much larger scale and a faster time frame of experience. The varying degrees of good and evil exist in the fourth dimension of space/time, including cosmic wars. The gift of free will is extended into the fourth dimension as we continue to learn and work out the responsibilities of co-creation and consciousness.

THE ETHEREAL CHAKRA SYSTEM

The origin of the chakra (pronounced chuck-ra) system can be traced to the Tantric period of yoga philosophy from around 500 to 1300 CE. *Chakra* means "wheel," and the pranic force flows through the conelike valves at the meridian points of the body, forming spinning wheels of Light that work together in two currents of frequency. The two currents that pass through the chakras and glands form the figure-eight patterns so familiar to the spiral shape of DNA. These two basic currents flow up and down in opposite directions as they circulate and energize the spinning currents of life and consciousness throughout the body and mind. When our frequency is in alignment with the vitality of Light, the thymus gland will activate and cooperate with the other glands—including the adrenals, pituitary, and pineal glands.

The Hypothalamus and Pituitary Gland

If we think of food and any other substance that goes into the body as the cement that holds the bricks of a house together, it is logical that when the cement is of high quality and balanced well, the bricks are held strongly in place. If the cement has too much sand and gravel, the brick walls are weak and will crumble with too much stress. So too can this concept be applied to the ways in which we manage mental stress.

The hypothalamus, referred to as the brain's brain, balances all body functions—body temperature, metabolism, sleep, growth, hunger, thirst, blood chemistry, and respiration—and sends signals to the pituitary to activate hormones. The hypothalamus reacts in particular to stress. In the science of iridology, the hypothalamus is known as the ego pressure (the degree of tension or relaxation) part of the brain, and it includes the pituitary gland as one of its structures. The pituitary gland is located near the brow chakra, which is connected to the left eye and governs the lower half of the brain. This area of the brain serves as a kind of bridge between mind and body, stimulating the endocrine glands and adrenaline. This is the part of the brain where thoughts are translated into physiological changes in the body. Here is where stressful thoughts and vibratory toxins can lead to blood pressure problems and stomach and bowel disorders. Toxic conditions can create high blood pressure and when ego pressure problems are added, a heart attack or a stroke is more likely than when a relaxed attitude of life prevails.

It is the degree of activity of the two glands held within the brain—pituitary and pineal—that is an important key to spiritual progress. The protection of these glands has been provided for by the blood-brain barrier. Only very tiny molecules are able to pass through this barrier. Unfortunately, much of what people eat is processed, and many products, including technology, cosmetics, and toothpaste, are designed to cross-penetrate this blood-brain barrier. This is causing great damage to the blood-brain barrier, the human brain, and the body.

The Glandular System

Metabolism, or the rate of energy use in the body, is controlled by the glandular system, along with growth, blood sugar balance, reproduction, and the rhythmic cycles in the body. The pineal, pituitary, thyroid, parathyroid, thymus, mammary, pancreas, adrenals, ovaries, testes, and uterus are all part of the endocrine and exocrine system of glands and ducts that secrete hormones and work together with the nervous system.

Although the way in which hormones affect the body are not fully understood, we do know that the hormones are crystals. Bernard Jensen's work in iridology suggests that perhaps these crystals control the vibratory rate in the body like a radio uses crystal to keep the channel tuned. The pure white aura Light of life is also crystalline. This cyclic hormonal tune that we dance to has a great effect on both personality and behavior throughout the various stages of our lives. So the main point of learning more about and improving the balance of the glandular system is seated in understanding the effects that are driven by these forces, as well as by the positive and negative thoughts that heal or hinder one's physical, mental, and spiritual vitality.

In tandem with the body's glandular system, the brain may be likened to a radio that both transmits and receives vibratory energies. Some of these signals are self-perpetuated and repetitious. They are driven by learned behavior and the nature of the individual, such as personal ideas, gender, beliefs, and cultural conditioning. Other frequencies are pure reality driven by Natural Law, higher or lower realms of influence, and experiences that defy definition. Unseen spiritual forces function within a transition zone between spiritual reality and physical reality. This transition zone is called "the wilderness." It is the area between a life of assumption and a life of true experience. The wilderness is what keeps life interesting, fresh, and challenging; it gives us a broader perspective. It inspires us to become more adaptable in regard to the precepts of inherited philosophy and theology.

The total focused human awareness may be observed as a matrix, or pattern, of frequency—for that is what we are in reality. Each cell contains an electrical charge; if the charges could be seen, they would appear as a pattern of Light surrounded by a finer thought energy that is emitted as these ethereal energies pass outward from the being. Since all of Creation in its basic form is thought, then it may be concluded that every cell of the human body thinks. This is how "feeling" is experienced. It is how a deep realization can cause goose bumps; for the entirety of the body has agreed simultaneously on a new concept of truth, and the conscious mind has opened to receive this information.

The thought function is not confined to the brain. It is the totality of the human that participates in the thinking process. Feeling is a combination of thought processes by the cells of the body utilizing the pathways of the nervous system. The analogy of a television, or cell phone without wires, can also be applied to the body as having similar and far more refined capabilities. What is called intuition is an example of this refined capability. It is a Knowingness that takes place on a cellular level and registers in the awareness at varying degrees of understanding tailored to the belief system of the individual.

The brain is designed to participate in a multitude of processes. It houses the most vulnerable and finely tuned of the endocrine glands. The precious secretions of the pituitary and pineal glands are the drives of the human body and mind awareness. The brain is the switching station for the receiving and transmitting of the thinking process. The combined thought process of the whole body is gathered and focused through the brain mechanism so that it may be exchanged both ways—between Spirit and matter, and matter and Spirit.

However, Spirit must pass through the belief system stored in the finer energies of the aura that surround the body and hold the belief patterns of not only the individual's experiences, but also the belief patterns of the entire planet. One function of the brain is to register and read this information upon request. Thus, when certain parts of the brain are stimulated, it reads not itself, but the stored data that is within the surrounding fine energy. Each human being carries its entire history of existence stored in the incredibly intelligent energy that surrounds it.

This is one reason that the human race as it currently exists on Earth encounters difficulty entering the higher dimensions, for higher beings are able to read the finer surrounding energy and know all there is regarding every thought and intention. This is a source of both intuition and telepathy. We practice talking across great distances with the assistance of telephones. There are spiritual Beings, however, who communicate over great distances without any mechanical devices whatsoever. Intuition and telepathy are recognized as established facts. There is great power contained in mental telepathy and intuition. It has been described as God speaking to God. Yet we have capacities far beyond our imagination. We are wired to be the passive receivers of spiritual messages through clairvoyance, clairaudience, clairsentience, sympathetic pain and sensation, symbolic imagery, telepathy, extrasensory perception, telekinesis, telethesia (mind reading), precognition, and oracular dreams. There are some who may feel that such a statement is sacrilegious. Sacrilegious or not, it is important that the human family maintain a connection to higher influences at all times if we are to nurture diversity and advance forward.

Words, thoughts, and emotions have power that commits us to a corresponding frequency, so we must command them carefully. They are forces in and of themselves and when they are concentrated on, we will be held accountable for them. The stronger our focus of mind, the deeper will be our insights, vision, and comprehension. The mind is really in service to the Spirit as a window rather than a wall. We must assume an observer position—which is much more educational than is being in need of constantly controlling everything and everyone.

To live creatively requires flexibility and awareness of negative and positive influences of the mind and emotions. When the mind gets stuck in negativity, we have the option of changing course and transmuting the energy of lower vibratory thoughts and emotions to higher ones. There is power that comes with the self-awareness to transmute vibratory energies. Understand the thought patterns that dominate your mind and you will find clarity in your role, as well as your responsibility for what is experienced.

TRANSMUTATION

One Law of the transformation of consciousness lies in the process of understanding transmutation. When destructive thoughts and emotions are present in the mind they may be transmuted through the simple process of changing the thought forms to a more harmonious frequency. The definition of the word *transmute* is "the changing or transferring of one element or form into another." For example, the emotion of jealousy is transmuted through acknowledging the discomfort that it causes, and then simply refusing to resonate with the negative energy of discomfort.

Transmutation is also the power to create through utilizing the Spiritual Aqua Substance to consolidate energy from a vaporous condition into form. Divine Mind Substance contains all elements, and all elements may be brought forth, or may also be dissolved into this aqua condition. Thought is the most potent agency in the Universe, and thought is the mediator between Divine Mind and every ailment and discord in the world. When disharmony arises, work to establish constructive thought currents and you will find support from the same unfailing stream of Love that holds the Earth in balance. Practice this process every day until it becomes second nature. There is no one else that can control your thoughts; they are for you to control.

People have many foolish attachments because emotions are born the moment we feel connected to something. Memories and emotions connected to relationships, family, past loves, and other experiences can be difficult to release. What is forgiveness but release in order to be open to life in the moment? It is important not to allow yourself to become discouraged when feeling blocked from the process of harmonizing the consciousness. Contemplate if you are resonating with thoughts of anger, fear, self-pity, anxiety, manipulation, greed, lust, revenge, or limitation. Ask yourself questions, and allow them time to be answered by your higher Self.

Remove the mental cause of suffering through understanding that all life is electrical energy, and the atoms, cells, organs, and tissues all have consciousness; then radiate Light into the dark concept of suffering. The greatest degree of human suffering originates in the mind—the games people play, mental contests, and ignorance. Gaining control over the mind allows for adjustment of behavior. It requires honesty and courage to make constant adjustments in our lives. The truth can be a bitter pill that people refuse to swallow. If someone in your life has the courage to speak the truth, it can ignite a transformation if you can receive it. Conversely, if you cannot humble yourself and accept the truth, the possibility for transformation is blocked, the mind remains unreceptive to transformation, and the opportunity for expansive consciousness is lost. Blocks dissolve when we transmute negative energies and allow our genius to blossom. Consciousness forms a hierarchical system. Like music, each dimension of consciousness reflects a range of frequency. Contemplate the genius of the Soul as a microcosm of Divine Laws. Breathe into the beauty of Soul Life, and it will reflect back to you a thousandfold. Spending time with wonderful people is a rare privilege in life, and this includes your higher Self.

The following lists and recipes are designed to help you take inventory of where you are in your physical and mental frequency, so that you can gauge where you are now and where you wish to go.

RECIPE FOR PSYCHIC CLEANSING

When we are aware of weak areas in our thoughts, words, and deeds, it is necessary to conquer all adverse frequencies through strengthening our Spiritual power. The ability to bring forth Divine Principle pays great dividends as one gains a greater understanding of Divine Law. The following charts are useful to clarify and determine the quality of thought patterns and the resonant range of emotions that form the greater balance or imbalance in one's life. The charts are tools that assist with identifying personal thought patterns, opinions, judgments, and the various vibratory forces that are rooted around and within the individual. Daily deep reflection in this area will help pinpoint adverse emotions and in turn will assist the process of reversing negativity. Centering conscious awareness in a deeper Spiritual union of thanksgiving, gratitude, and constructive thoughts will support the greater purpose, talents, and journey of the accomplished individual.

People develop deeply engrained mental and emotional patterns that block energy in the body and mind. There is a requickening that takes place when a space in the energy field is cleared of negative emotions. It takes patience and perseverance to clear the field of consciousness of useless weeds that are difficult to uproot. Yet when the field of consciousness is reseeded, the indestructible Soul, hidden within the perishable Earthly body, sprouts forth, yielding the fruits of more meaningful activities, fulfillment, and the sensation of being profoundly touched deep inside. It is liberation through harmonization of the mental processes with the power of Spirit. The essence of this harmonization is produced electromagnetically.

Thoughts that generate a pulsed electromagnetic field, producing electricity or vitality, create a magnetic resonance of Light. When the brain's pulsed frequency matches the tissues and organs of the body, and when they are in resonance, there is an enhancement of molecular action, which is a catalyst for health and well-being. Spiritual prescience is activated when the individual is open and ready to align with the higher purpose of connecting with it. Here the natural flow of communication that manifests through the inner being is enhanced.

Conversely, the downward spiral of sickness and disease is also greatly affected by one's vibratory level. This process helps to illustrate how the spiral is a living thread that can lead us to different levels of vision and energy. It is at this point that we find our inquiry moving inward and detecting the symbiosis between mind and matter. All life has an electric, and therefore magnetic, potential. The paradoxical dual polarity of magnetic energy linking the unconscious processes to awareness of them at the conscious level is a primary step toward self-development. Spiritual attainment has purpose when it is grounded in matter, in who we are, and what we work toward or away from in a conscious manner.

✳ The Recipe

1. Make a list of the important relationships and events in your life. List them in chronological order from childhood up to the present time.

2. Refer to the Emotional Balance List of Seeds below. Choose the words that best describe your feelings regarding each relationship and event, one by one, or write your own descriptive words next to the name or event.

3. Next, refer to the Emotional Balance List of Weeds, and choose the words that best describe your feelings regarding each relationship and event, one by one, or write your own descriptive words next to the name or event.

4. When your list is complete, start from the top and note the overall resonant energy that the words create in describing each person and event. Write out how you are feeling about the person or event next to the name. Note the areas that require more healing and release of ingrained negative thought patterns. Then forgive yourself and the other people; bless all individuals and events, and hold gratitude for what that experience, person, or thing has taught you. Just this process alone may trigger very strong emotions and therefore may take a great deal of time: days, weeks, months, or years. Be patient, have courage, and persevere.

5. The intention here is to revisit and explore what has been buried in the psyche, release it, bless it, forgive it, thank it for teaching you, and walk away in peace. Retaining ill feelings in one's heart and mind regarding another person or experience creates obstructions, impedes progress, and creates a paralyzing anger that manifests in unexpected ways, such as depression and lack of joy in life, or obsessive behavior. What holds one back is not something to be maintained!

6. The ladder of consciousness is an energetic scale of darkness to light and is useful for calculating the overall energetic quality that you feel describes your

life. Write the words that best describe your overall thoughts and emotions using the Emotional Balance Charts, as each day passes. This process of self-acknowledgment will reveal the overall resonance or Soul connection to self.

7. Finally, the Aspects of the Mind chart is useful for determining your overall focus.

8. For a deeper and more dedicated journey of self-acknowledgment, consider undertaking the *Steps to Knowledge,* a book by Marshall Vian Summers. The book outlines one step for each day of the year, and it is very cathartic and transformative.

Emotional Balance Chart: Seeds

The emotional balance chart of seeds depicts the higher mental environment with aspects of Spiritual Intelligence, presence, and stillness. These habits seed life with the Light of Inner Knowing. This is a foundation in life that is fully supported.

Abstinence	Accomplishment	Advancement
Affirmation	Assistance	Assurance
Awareness	Beneficial	Blessings
Clarity	Comfort	Compassion
Confidence	Consciousness	Contemplation
Cooperation	Courage	Creativity
Devotion	Direction	Discernment
Efficacy	Energy	Environmental Reverence
Expectation	Giving	Grace
Gratitude	Happiness	Harmony
Honesty	Honor	Humility
Independence	Inspiration	Integrity
Intelligence	Intuition	Joy
Justice	Kindness	Life
Light	Love	Maturity
Meaning	Objectivity	Peace
Permanence	Presence	Purpose
Renewal	Respect	Restoration
Reverence	Reward	Security
Sexual Healing	Success	Symbolic Dreams

Thoughtfulness	Truth	Understanding
Universal	Value	Victory
Warning Dreams	Well-being	Wisdom

Emotional Balance Chart: Weeds

The emotional balance list of weeds is useful for depicting mental poisons, a hellish mental environment without Spiritual prescience. Generally speaking, these are aspects of the false ego that are self-imposed. Only our thoughts are in alignment, or in opposition, to the very highest of attainments. The lower the frequency of thought, the more difficult it is for the mind to concentrate. Mental clutter adds another ingredient to this already difficult situation.

Abuse	Addiction	Alienation
Ambivalence	Anger	Apathy
Arrogance	Bitterness	Blame
Burden	Codependence	Compulsion
Condemnation	Confusion	Control
Corruption	Cruelty	Cynicism
Darkness	Death	Denial
Denigration of Men, Women, and Children	Deviousness	Disappointment
Discordant Thinking	Discouragement	Disharmony
Dishonesty	Disrespect	Dissonance
Divisiveness	Entitlement	Envy
Error	Failure	Fanatical
Force	Frustration	Greed
Grudges	Guilt	Habitual Judgments
Harshness	Ignorance	Illusion
Immaturity	Inadequacy	Ingratitude
Inhumanity	Insecurity	Intolerance
Irreverence	Jealousy	Lack of Expectation
Limitation	Lust	Misguided Ambitions
Mistakes	Nastiness	Negativity
Obsessive	Obstacles	Obstinacy
Possessiveness	Prejudice	Profligacy

Rejection	Sacrifice	Sadness
Sadomasochism	Scandal	Separation
Sexual Divisiveness	Suffering	Suicide
Suspicion	Torture	Unconsciousness
Undue Fear	Unnatural	Usury
Victim Mentality	Violence	War

Aspects of the Mind Chart

Aspects of the Ego/Mind	*Aspects of the God/Mind*
Lower Self	Higher Self
Finite	Infinite
Fallible	Infallible
Separate	One
Individual	All-Encompassing
Imaginative	Creative
Self-Serving	Serving All
Free Will (Limited)	Universal Law
Fear	Love
Distraction	Stillness
Closed	Open
Physical Energies	Ethereal Energies
Student	Master
Mental Energy	Spiritual Energy
Intellect	Knowledge
Ego	Humility
Illusion	Truth

MEDITATION AND CONTEMPLATION

It is in solitude that merits accumulate.

PIERRE DE LA CALLE

It is a very high art to focus a thought in silence without attempting to manipulate it with busy distractions and daily worries. The essence of consciousness unfolds within the silence. In silence there is an awakening to the simplicity of spiritual illumination. Humility and simplicity require opening to listen to the breath of the Soul. Yet to meditate is to receive the resonant frequencies set forth by directing contemplation. Contemplating that which is to be meditated upon is a self-clarifying looping process. Therefore, meditating upon nothing is self-canceling and may result in prohibiting higher communication. There is no frequency that supports nothing.

All thought forms resonate with an inherent frequency. The looping process ensures that messages are received on the same wavelength as the thought form that is contemplated. Therefore, contemplating the highest frequency thought forms will generate messages on a high frequency of consciousness. Contemplate the willful intent to resonate with the Cosmic matrix of Intelligence and Knowledge. Seed the field by cultivating the habit of perfection as your real Self. Then see this perfection as emanating forth from the very center of every cell, fiber, tissue, muscle, and organ of your body. Bring forth this inner Light as your divine right. When practiced properly, meditation and contemplation will circulate a relaxing, peaceful, healing Light imbued with solutions to seemingly irresolvable difficulties and perplexities. In fact, extensive research confirms that increasing the number of people meditating with a positive, peaceful attitude in a city or town improves quality of life and actually reduces crime.

As you practice this technique of love, reverence, and devotion, it becomes a natural habit, and in a short time your body will resonate with Light. Contemplate God as being the Creative Principle flowing through you. Through conscious direction our bodies are transmuted from a lower to a higher condition. In this way there is no separation. Enlightened teachers and higher influences can only dwell near you when there is a frequency of harmony and stillness of mind surrounding you. It is the sincere wish of higher Divine Intelligences to exalt the individual and to germinate the seeds of Light that live within the Soul. Ideally, one learns to live and breathe within the scope of the eternal wisdom of the Soul as easily as breathing in and out.

Meditation is not the invention of any one personage or school. It is an ageless experience that has been discovered and explored in every period and culture that we know of. The more complex a meditation is, the less useful it is. All methods of meditation are fundamentally the same regardless of where they were developed. Meditation is achieved at the point where mind and Spirit converge. The clairvoyant Edgar Cayce succinctly described the essence of meditation as "listening with the subdued ego." Meditation simply helps us to comprehend a new way of perceiving reality by paying careful attention to one's total being as something of real value. Ultimately, the goal in meditation is to achieve union with the Soul and to perceive God as energy, through consciousness as Love. This is the higher Self: Self-realization equals God-realization. This does not require religion or belief in an ideology; it is a tool for expressing the authentic spiritual nature of life.

In meditation we seek respite from the relentless din of the false ego and to restore the pure awareness that lies quietly beneath the clatter of thoughts, emotions, and impulses that permeate our lives. For this reason, meditation will be different for everyone. It is not necessary to labor in formal schools of Zen or in yoga meditation to tap into the subtle alpha rhythms that fluctuate throughout our systems during meditation. Children and adults naturally gravitate to meditation through daydreaming, or even a quiet drive in the car.

People who recognize the value in these altered states of deeper introspection naturally become more adept at discerning the various cerebral wave patterns. Reading these patterns helps us to engage in the breadth and range between the spiritual and the bodily systems. As a reminder, beta brain wave activity is alert, an active state; alpha brain wave activity is relaxation, passive awareness: theta is deep tranquillity to unconsciousness; delta may be ecstatic states and Spiritual guidance. Meditation and contemplation increase the electrical energy in the brain and heighten certain forms of sensitivity, such as telepathy. It creates an opening for the seeking mind to receive Cosmic Intelligence and learn from conscious observation rather than cultural conditioning.

In meditation as well as in life, the mind must be both passive and active. In meditation a variety of sensations may be experienced. Some of the signals of transcending the veil of space and time may be a feeling of falling, rushes of energy in the musculature, tingling, quavers, sudden shifts in orientation, a feeling of floating, lights in your field of vision, and ecstatic revelations to the connection of all life. All resonances with Divine Forces are uplifting.

There is not a more important journey than the exploration of the power of one's own consciousness. The goal in meditation is to release personal, mental, and physical hyperactivity and create an unobstructed, clear, unbiased channel that allows the mind to both receive and transmit spiritually illuminated thoughts and feelings. For example, the intention of thoughts and feelings may be shaped and focused on praying for the highest good for all, healing all dispirited egos, healing the planet, neutralizing those who impose suffering on others, the best guidance on beginning your day, or insight into translating last night's dream. Each day of practice builds the intention. It may take a day, a week, a month, a year, or more to achieve results on a particular focus of mind in meditation. Meditation may also contain prayers to uplift those who have passed from the realm of Earth, are suffering from illness, or need spiritual support.

So meditation is not the erasure of thought; rather it is the contemplation of a higher order of thought. We study the self by understanding that the whole of the atomic universe is within us, and we must go beyond the limitation of the surface mind. People become impatient and bored with meditation when they are in anticipation and expectation of something to happen. They are waiting for whatever it is the surface mind thinks will eventually arrive—if only they wait long enough. Consequently, nothing of importance happens because the first step is to still the thoughts that evoke limited rationale. When the mechanism of the mind attempts to continuously provoke the movement of thought, there will never be stillness enough for the Higher Realms to influence thought patterns. The Soul whispers and the mind roars, so stilling the mind can be a challenge. Here are some basic tips for successful meditation:

- Meditate in a quiet place alone, not with a group of people. Silence the surface mind.
- Close the eyes, and focus them upon the area of the third eye, located between the eyebrows. This area is linked to intuition (pituitary and pineal glands). Do not open to any random thought

form; align with your heart and not your mind. Your life force and stream of consciousness constitute a temple that must be protected just as one's home and belongings are protected. Visualize the expansive and ethereal multidimensional energy fields of the body (see figure 5.2 on page 193).

- Contemplate resonating with a high frequency thought form; radiate love out to everyone (love is the highest frequency thought form you can have). When you send out love to those who would do you harm, the energy they release reflects back to them. What we do to others, we do to ourselves. Ask to manifest health (not be healed from disease). Ask to express harmony and realize abundance (not be delivered from misery). Fill your thoughts with the Light of Christ Consciousness. It is a sacred process of allowing God/Mind to manifest through thought forms and thereby becoming manifest. Meditate on a high frequency channel of thought, then radiate with it. Just thinking a thing does not accomplish the thing; it must be given conscious expression. Otherwise it is possible to enter into a meditative reception of lower frequency thought forms.

- Ask the expansive "flower of becoming" that is within to teach the intellect. The "I Am Consciousness" expands and awakens through the reflective power of Light from the depths of one's own being. Life is a gift of grace from the celestial powers, and the language of life is Light. It is through the deep longing of heart Light that we strive to understand the aims of human evolution and discover the meaning of our own destiny. There exists a guiding Light that bestows the gift of inner knowing, which acts as a balsam, inspiring hope and healing to the aspiring Soul in meditation. High frequency energies are received through resonance in the glands and through the ethereal chakra energy systems of the body and mind.

Meridians

Most of the primary meridians or energy pathways terminate at the fingertips and toes. In meditation, stimulating and working with the fingertips alone can effectively awaken the major energy pathways of body and mind. The following suggestions balance and increase psychic sensitivity and improve well-being.

Meditation Preparation

Before meditation, rub your hands together briskly for twenty to thirty seconds, paying attention to the fingertips. After doing this, the energy in the hands should be palpable and strong enough to feel a small ball of energy that will be about the size of a small, delicate balloon. Feel this ball as though you were actually holding it in your hands. It is real, ethereal energy. This energy can be pressed over your heart or throat area. Then use your first finger and middle finger to massage the area between your eyebrows in a clockwise motion. This is particularly helpful to release stress and balance the energy in the mind. Balancing the energies in the right and the left hemispheres of the brain helps to settle the mind and the body for the stillness that is essential for deeper meditation.

It has been established that the body senses and the sixth chakra in the brain serve to connect matter and Spirit. The psychic ability of human beings has long been referred to as the sixth sense, or the mind's eye, due to the corollary between the sixth chakra and pineal gland and what is often referred to as intuition. The pineal gland is connected to the right eye and governs the upper half of the brain, expressing as the crown chakra of intuition. Everyone has intuitive psychic abilities in varying degrees. However, the pineal gland can become calcified due to certain environmental conditions such as fluoride, aspartame, and other chemicals that permeate the blood-brain barrier. Microwave frequencies from cell phones and rigid thinking will also greatly impede the function of the pineal gland. The mind must be kept fresh and pliable, think clearly and freely, rethink and recreate its thoughts, be open and accessible. Otherwise the mind will calcify; become hard, brittle, and impenetrable; and will defend its point of view without regard to reality or changing circumstances. This imperils, imprisons, isolates, and denies people the power of self-mastery. Stand within the prison of the mind, and it will seemingly engulf you. Stand with Universal Intelligence, and you will be able to see through the prison of the mind to properly direct and use thought.

With the development and overuse of modern means of

communication and transportation, we have essentially discarded the use of the sixth sense. When the sixth sense is not used or exercised it becomes dormant, in the same way that the muscles in the body and brain become flabby and dull from a state of disuse. The pineal gland in the center of the head is a very important key assisting the intuition of the third eye. The pineal gland in the brain is literally structured like an inner eye with light receptive cells and a vitreous, gel-like substance forming a structure similar to a lens. A study conducted by Jimo Borjigin, PhD, at the University of Michigan revealed that the pineal gland in a rat's brain produces the molecule DMT, a molecule that is present in many life forms. DMT has been referred to as the "spirit molecule" that induces intensely spiritual experiences.

The pineal gland also performs other functions that support reproduction and the immune system, as well as producing melatonin needed for sleep and restoration. However, the pineal has empirically been revered as the mind's eye to the deeper nature of consciousness. When the eyes are closed, the mind's eye is our alternative field of vision, and we may see images there. Therefore, when the eyes are closed in meditation, the focus is in the area of the third eye between the eyebrows. Beautiful color fields and various images may sometimes be seen in this alternate field of vision. It can be very energizing, inspiring, and sometimes shocking. When we resonate at the level of consciousness associated with the pineal, we are preparing to ascend to the next level of awareness.

Biochemicals

The pineal and the pituitary are ductless glands that are part of a special biocrystalline network of structures throughout the body that are associated with the phenomenon of Light. The pineal is located at the base of the brain's third ventricle and is a sensitive scanner that perceives vibratory rates. The pineal is one of the glands that regulate hormones, and it is also influenced by the cycles of day and night. Dark thoughts and emotions elicit potent biochemicals that have a direct effect on these sensitive glands. Conversely, when thoughts and emotions resonate with compassion and love, the pineal releases powerful hormones that flood the system and support healing.

When the Light capacity of the pineal membrane expands, so does our ability to resonate with higher dimensions of Mind. The pineal is a tuning mechanism that will contract and expand similar to the pupil of an eye. Light results in expansion; Dark results in contraction. Creativity is facilitated through the higher function of the mind. Self-mastery embodies monitoring the matrix of thought forms and becoming sensitized to a point where we instantly detect which thought forms are limiting and which thought forms are expansive.

Exercising the expansiveness of the pineal by raising the level of consciousness forms the first "veil of Light" around one's being. Here, we learn to create in a manner that reflects the attributes of the Infinite Mind. In this way our path begins to merge as one with Creation, and we are well on our way to self-mastery. In meditation, cultivate the flowering of your most precious form of power: your Mind.

The mental faculties of the individual are often overburdened, stressed, undernourished, and cluttered with concerns. This causes the spiritual consciousness to be weakened and diminished. If you are feeling stressed, chaotic, or anxious and inflexible, the energy vortex of the third eye (pineal) may be blocked or out of balance. When the ethereal electromagnetic energy field of the third eye is balanced, it is easier to achieve quietude.

The color vibration of the third eye is indigo blue. When stress is an issue it is very effective to work with this area. To help balance this energy, use an indigo-colored crystal such as lapis lazuli or hawk's-eye. First, clean the stone or crystal in warm water for one minute, dry it, and with your breath, ask for assistance in balancing your mind's eye. Place the stone between your eyes. Crystals and precious stones are used as tuning forks in radios, computers, and other technologies to magnify, focus, harmonize, and redirect energies. They are a miraculous tool for clearing and balancing energy in the body and mind.

Good quality essential oils such as lavender and peppermint may also be used. Place the oil on your left middle finger, press gently onto your forehead between your eyes, and massage in a clockwise circular motion. Allow your right palm to lie open, facing up, and continue massaging until you are completely relaxed. This is very effective because we are electromagnetic beings that are balanced by a healing touch. When pain is present anywhere in the body, touch it—stroke the area or massage it with aromatic oils. This manner of self-nurturing can be very effective before meditation.

Conscious mental receptivity in meditation will be greatly improved by physically relaxing muscle tensions in the body from the top, starting with the forehead and working down the body in the following order—forehead, eyes, mouth, neck, shoulders, arms, elbows, hands, legs, knees, feet.

Mental states associated with physical tension will substantially reduce the capacity to decompress. Clear the mind of thoughts that are stressful, release them, and allow your energy to become as still as a calm body of water. Connect with your authentic state of being. This openness is a place of unconditional acceptance, a neutral, benign state in which the delicate sensors allow us to attune to the finer undulating energy waves of the pituitary gland and become more receptive.

SILENCE

In the end, it's not going to matter how many breaths you took, but how many moments took your breath away.

SHING XIONG

The master, Emil, brought the group to a special temple and said, "This is called the Temple of Silence, the Place of Power. Silence is power, for when we reach the place of silence in mind we have reached the place of power—where all is one." Emil explained that diffused power is noise; concentrated power is silence. When the concentration is drawn to the center we have brought all of our force into one point of force, we have contacted God in the silence and become one with all power. The heritage of man is thus . . . I plus God equals One.

"One way to be with power is to consciously contact it from silence within. This cannot be done in the without. This power is for us to use at all times. Then humanity will understand who it is, and let go of self-delusions and vanities and realize that only the humble can perceive the Truth. This is a powerful inner relationship to Truth that speaks in the still, small voice deep in our own Souls. Learn to think things through and allow old ideas to drop away and new ideas to be adjusted. Take perplexing questions into this silent hour. The real gate to heaven is through one's own consciousness. It is through the symbol of Jacob's ladder that equals God's ideas descending from Spirit to form and ascending again.

"The wonderful law of expression whereby ideas conceived in the Divine Mind come forth into expression and manifest as form. All form may be transformed or changed in form, through a change in consciousness in regard to it. The 'I Am' in each Soul is the door through which the Life-Power Substance comes forth into expression by consciousness. God is within Soul as power, substance, and intelligence, or in spiritual terms, Wisdom, Love, and Truth. When we see that Spirit is all and that form is constantly being expressed from Spirit, then will we understand that which is born of Spirit, is Spirit. The gift that silence has to offer us is that by contacting the God/Mind, we can think with the God/Mind and know our true expression as we are in reality, rather than as we have thought ourselves to be."

Emil went on to say, "The mind of God floods consciousness as sunshine floods a darkened room. The infusion of the Universal Mind into the personal mind is like the entrance of the vastness of the outside air into the impurity of that which has long been held in some closed compartment. Blending the greater with the lesser through which the lesser becomes one with the greater. Impurity and imperfection is caused by separation of lesser from greater, that in turn causes sin, sickness, poverty, and death. Purity in the union as one consciousness is being whole. Separation from unity is the descent on the 'Ladder of Consciousness.' Return to unity is ascent. The great work for each Soul is to lift the personal viewpoint to such heights in consciousness that it becomes one with the whole—that all things visible and invisible have origin in Source. This is called the 'Mount of Transfiguration.' When the Holy Spirit fills the consciousness, the sense of delusion of sin, sickness, poverty, and death become no more. This is the great purpose of the silence."*

---

*From *Life and Teaching of the Masters of the Far East*

THE ELOQUENCE
OF THE ETHEREAL

*The most beautiful thing we can experience is the mystical.
It is the source of all true art and science. He to whom this
emotion is a stranger, who can no longer wonder and
stand rapt in awe, is as good as dead; his eyes are closed . . .
to know that what is impenetrable to us really exists,
manifesting itself as the highest Wisdom and the most
radiant beauty which our dull faculties can comprehend
only in the most primitive forms—this Knowledge, this
feeling, is at the center of true religiousness. In this sense,
and in this sense only, I belong to the ranks of devoutly
religious men.*

ALBERT EINSTEIN

THE HOLOGRAPHIC PRINCIPLE

Recent scientific discoveries have dramatically impacted our lives
through a better understanding of the holographic nature of the
Universe. A living holograph is formed by the twin lights of creation
that are pulsated while spinning and passing through each other, forming infinite nodal points of energy. As the nodal points intersect, they
create standing wave forms in time, which in turn creates a collection of

particle/wave nodal points within the atom that both appear and disappear within the life force structure of the being. This process is directed by the electromagnetic resonance of the Divine Law of Similitude—a frequency of geometries that determines conscious awareness.

The essence of all creation is Light. There are different levels of light: visible spectrum, common light; the invisible spectra Light, infrared and ultraviolet; and Superlight, multidimensional spectra Light that is universal. Superlight is the eternal Light of the Soul, the Universal Mind of Creation. A hologram is an electromagnetic signature of light. Holograms demonstrate a unique principal of common light in nature that may be symbolically applied to the world of cellular biology. The holographic model provides us with an understanding of how each fragment of an electromagnetic signature or pattern contains the whole energetic or vibratory blueprint of a being. This exact blueprint attracts to itself the emanation, or mirror image, of what it is giving off. In book three of *Life and Teaching of the Masters of the Far East*, it was recorded that Jesus said of the crucifixion, "Had they burned my body, I could have reassembled it from the same particles that were released in the seeming destruction. Had they divided every particle of the body, it could have been reassembled instantly; there would have been no change. Thus you see that the whole scene of the crucifixion was a symbol of Humanity's heritage."

THE HOLOGRAPHIC MIND

The freshest scientific information regarding the interactions and connections between mind, matter, and spirit actually aligns with the same current as the great mystical traditions of the world. Mysticism and science have united in the exploration of the "Holographic Paradigm." This encompasses the mathematic interplay of the brain, constructing reality by interpreting frequencies from other dimensions that transcend time and space. In the book *Earthway*, Mary Summer Rain relates that the Native American visionary named No-Eyes explained that the brain functions as a hologram, interpreting a holographic universe.

Prominent scientists and thinkers have uncovered new interpretations of the holographic paradigm through Dr. Karl Pribram's studies in brain memory and function and David Bohm's work in subatomic physics. The sciences of relativity and quantum physics also play a role in exploring how experience becomes processed and how perception plays into what is being experienced. Our biological brains sense modalities and are partitioned into compartments within which the principle sensory systems interact. Neurons act as channels, or resonating receptive fields, that resonate the information. The layers of the network of information operate within the multidimensionality of geometry and mathematics. The holographic paradigm leads to a plethora of dimensions and enlarged perception.

Because each cell communicates via electromagnetic signatures of Light, it has been established that thought and the process of thinking occur in the fourth dimension. Thought then has its own dimension and environment and is a fluid tool imbued with the ability to transcend the physical realm of the third dimension. There are varying degrees of consciousness, and when we are in the third-dimensional brain state of consciousness we are utilizing only about 10 percent of the brain's capacity. The remaining 90 percent of the brain's capacity operates within the realm of a universal hologram; in fact the brain operates as a galactic hologram.

It is this holographic functioning that allows us to transcend the physical realm and have mystical experiences and attune to psychic phenomena. Out-of-body experiences, astral travel, and other psychic phenomenon assist us to evolve spiritually through experiences within various dimensions beyond the body. As mentioned previously, many artists, creative people, scientists, inventors, and others have developed a high degree of focus and ability to build the bridge that allows them to take impressions out of this ethereal holographic mental realm and actualize them into a three-dimensional physical expression. Whether thought forms are high or low, they integrate themselves as light codes into the universal holographic mind: a mind within Mind.

The human brain is like a radio receiver that is capable of tuning in to the flow of Universal Knowledge ever present in the creative holographic flow. The magnetic fields surrounding each body function like antennas. Our acquired belief systems may cause us to unplug from the universal station and instead plug into the three-dimensional environ of the five senses, the interior brain, and intellect. The spiritual aspect of guidance and a fuller self-empowerment is diminished in this way. It is frequency and not the size of the brain or a higher IQ that determines one's capacity for higher conscious awareness. Frequency is a wave form, a thought matrix of geometries that glow within the auric field, attracting others who have similar geometric thought forms.

Each person is unique and will not access higher Intelligence while operating from a relative position of polarized thinking. However, through choosing to consciously breathe into the Soul of Universal Intelligence, the overall frequency shift will create harmonious holographic geometries. Therefore, ascension has always been possible through harmonizing the frequency of the bodies of Light and radiating with the original breath of the frequency of love.

There is a crucial difference between an electronically produced hologram and a biologically produced hologram. An electronically programmed synthetic hologram can be produced through a series of lenses, as may be observed in 3-D movies and holographic cameras. Light projected electronically through a series of lenses casts the illusion of being a real place or a solid being, when these are merely translucent holograms. A living biological hologram is produced through the breath of frequency. Part of our work in the various planes of being is to discern what is real and what is illusion.

The combination of gravity and electromagnets in space causes light to turn in upon itself, creating a finite dormancy of energy. This forms the space/time continuum—a kind of suspended holographic animation temporarily trapped in matter. It is gravity that produces the so-called curves of space that Einstein contemplated. A hologram is a pattern of interacting microscopic curves or rings that store information containing the whole holographic blueprint, or image.

If the hologram is divided into a multitude of pieces and they all retain the same information, then we can perceive the essence of physical

Laws as being informational blueprints. One interesting example of this is the Akashic Records that are stored as holographic cosmic archives. The surface mind expresses in third-dimensional reality, and the inner life of the mind expresses in holograms in fourth-dimensional reality. Within a holographic framework all is interactive and dimensional in the context of vibratory variation. Words prove to be somewhat inadequate to fully explain how a living holographic form can simultaneously exist in similar but different dimensional variations.

For example, the human body itself may be described as a fluid puzzle. It can function at multilevels of dimensional experience. The gift of experience within a real holographic body is an adventure to be greatly honored and appreciated. Moving beyond the body and into a larger universal "holomovement," it would be observed that the pieces of the puzzle are not firm and do not necessarily come together in a fully recognizable stable picture. Rather, the pieces are of a gelatinous nature and are moving in a dynamically flowing, changing pattern that pulsates with the vibrancy and colors of life.

It is as though many breathing movements are gently bouncing to and fro within a broth of light, each one nudging up against the other. If one can imagine this process, it is then possible to conceive that thought can also cause the ebb and flow to form a rigid damlike structure restricting the freedom of the natural holographic flow. If the restriction is maintained, it causes the end of the experience, as life must continue to express in a free-flowing fashion or it is withdrawn. This is also true within a larger group context of the human family and the Earth as a whole.

When we process and encompass the elementary concept of Mind expressing as the very essence of creation, then we can see how the restriction of this flow of expansion and progress causes chaos. The flow of this expression can move all around the restriction and leave it behind, or if the consistency of the restriction can be softened or dissolved, all may again rejoin the flow.

Within the flow of creation, the Universal Knowledge that is lived into wisdom moves through stages of Truth within the vibratory, dimensional realms of experience. As Knowledge becomes Wisdom, the restrictions are surpassed and the old concepts become outdated and no longer applicable. If the restrictive belief systems of the mass consciousness of Earth can be transmuted, then the expansive flow of creation will be restored. This requires a literal rebirth within each individual as the conscious awareness is released and expands into a greater sphere of Light. A deeper understanding of how multiple layers of energy are operating simultaneously with multiple agendas is a leap toward understanding and entering higher dimensions of life. The choice to transmute chaos into the Light of Wisdom is always available, but it must be accompanied by a shift in attitude and deed. Surely, humankind has had enough of the same old repackaged repetition that has produced both physical suffering and spiritual stagnation.

Within the holographic process of change is the important element of maintaining focus. Genuine focus of our intentions will enable a manifested pattern of Light to complete its cycle and come into fruition. One way that the focus of thought is maintained for long periods of time is by the vibratory oscillations and emanations of sound. There is a harmonious living presence within each spiral galaxy, a continuous melody of bell-like sounds, which is described by the masters as the music of the spheres. In a pure sense, the music of the spheres can be grasped as being of a crystalline bell-like quality that can reverberate beyond that which the ear can hear. The ethereal music of the Universal spheres may be duplicated, although in a cruder form with musical instruments and toning with the vocal cords.

At this moment, would we perceive life upon the Earth as harmonious or quite out of tune? Imagine hearing the pure crystalline resonance of the music of the spheres and then compare it to the acid, nonsensical impression of punk rock, a frequency very similar to the resonant sound of chaos. Perfect resonance is attained through balance. This is the reason that discordant music is so destructive to the resonant harmony of young people. It is designed to be unbalanced and disorderly in its basic construction and enhances chaotic tendencies within the psyche of those listening to it by slowing down the natural human frequency. Some of these lower frequencies can even stop the heart from beating.

HOLONOMIC RESONANCE

Interestingly, the I Ching is considered to be the code form of a science based on holonomic resonance rather than atomic physics; the system of Mayan science is also one of holonomic resonance. Mayan science bases itself on Mind as the foundation of the Universe, a universality of consciousness or intelligent energy. Knowledge or information is transmitted through the principle of harmonic resonance. This principle helps to clarify how the potential of the whole is connected to the individual within the energetic processes of life. As each person is a focused, self-aware component of the whole, the potential of that whole belongs to each individual. We could call this the Souls of Spirit, or minds within Mind.

We are unique individuals with the entirety of the whole of Creation underlying and supporting the immortal journey of eternity. Cooperation with the Universal Laws that underlie creation is the important keynote toward progress. The more playful the attitude and the greater the sense of humor that is brought into the process, the easier the passage through becomes.

Focused thought really does create reality. The question is, Does the mind follow the natural flow of Spirit, or is the mind entrenched within the dispirited ego? Thoughts also instantaneously shape the reality of the astral planes. Ascension from the astral planes requires self-mastery . . . a change of mind. On a physical level, over one hundred controlled experiments on the aspects of prayer have proven that prayer can influence plant growth, positively affect health conditions, increase enzyme activity, control bacteria growth, and stimulate healing rates and seed germination.

Prayer can function at any distance to change physical processes in a variety of organisms from bacteria to humans. When objects are placed in a lead-lined room or in a cage shielded from all forms of electromagnetic energy, the effects of prayer are not neutralized. The thoughtful prayer need only contain a pure and holy qualitative consciousness that is sustained as genuinely spiritual healing in the direction of what is best for higher purpose. Since we do not always know what is best for ourselves, others, and the world, we can direct our energies to harmonize with higher knowledge. Sometimes, what is best for a physical body may be death, such as for a person suffering from intense pain. We do well to pray only for what is best, rather than what we want.

Interestingly, a holographic record of disease and trauma can be plainly seen by reading the blood. After injuring my ankle, I began to seek possible alternative solutions for healing, and I had a hemobiographic consultation. A drop of my living blood was placed under a special microscope, then projected onto a large screen. It was stunning to see the activity and light patterns in living blood and a ghostly white holographic image of the shattered anklebone floating as a record in the blood. Looking through a book depicting the variety of images taken from this process, it was fascinating to see the blood register a red flame like wildfire burning in the lungs of a smoker and the tiny translucent image of a fetus in a pregnant woman, as well as many other images regarding the unique health issues of individuals. Holograms are living ethereal images recorded as history in our blood! This begs the question as to what one actually receives during a blood transfusion.

EARTH'S ASTRAL FIELD AND THE HOLOMOVEMENT

Human actions and thoughts coagulate, are preserved, and are transmuted in Earth's astral field, which parallels the physical world. The astral field reflects every vibratory nuance of thought that creates the aura, or what is sometimes referred to as the holographic Soul of the world. Traditional science has avoided investigating many experiential phenomena that do not fit within its narrow, intellectual framework of reality. However, many people experience paranormal and mystical experiences that can be explained by the holographic model. The holographic model explains the inexplicable, such as telepathy and precognition; mystics describe it as the unity of everything. The holographic principle can explain the near-death, out-of-body, and lucid-dreaming experiences—all of which are part of the path of the multidimensional Soul of Spirit.

The astral realms may be thought of as being in the fourth

dimension of time, and this is usually where our minds operate during the sleep cycle. It is here that each thought form instantly creates a reality, and that reality instantly changes as the thought form changes. What we experience during sleep may be determined by the last thought form held in the mind before slipping through the veils of consciousness. Holding a frequency of Light as we expand into sleep will open higher passageways of intelligence in the fourth dimension. One who has attained the highest beatitude of self-mastery bypasses the fourth dimension and ascends to the fifth dimension—pure universal awareness, Absolute Truth, and a return to one's totality of Being—a total state of supreme enlightenment. Once in the fifth dimension all of the bodily sheaths are released and dissolved, and the Soul no longer returns to the lower realms of the third and fourth dimensions.

Both reality and illusion are coddled into form through a giant hologram where past, present, and futures become fixed to a certain point. The future destiny of any given holographic universe is predetermined. When a person has a precognitive glimpse of the future, then he or she is looking into the future destiny of that particular hologram. Nothing in life is stagnant. Every quark, atom, and molecule is pulsating with thought and movement, even what appears to be a lifeless rock retains a modicum of movement. When the holographic process is expanded through the added fourth dimension, which is thinking, the evolving thought processes can be mastered, and various challenges are lived into Wisdom.

Parapsychologists have searched in vain to explain the energy that transmits telepathy, clairvoyance, spontaneous healing, and the like. If these experiences emerge from a Universal frequency of Mind transcending time and space, they don't have to be transmitted. They are simultaneous and everywhere.

Neuroscientist Karl Pribram of Stanford University and theoretical physicist David Bohm of the University of London have proposed theories that, in tandem, appear to account for all transcendental experience, paranormal events, and even normal perceptual oddities. They agree that there are intriguing implications in a paradigm that posits that the brain employs a holographic process to abstract from a holographic domain. Both Pribram and Bohm describe the holographic paradigm as a system from which arise explanations for the various flows of energies and activities that we associate with life and consciousness—for example, dreams, ideas, paranormal experiences, and spiritual phenomena. They agree that every aspect of the Universe exists as various degrees of energetic vibratory expression. The holographic paradigm is considered to be the biggest revolution in brain research. The unity of science and religion may now commence as we begin to unravel the true nature of existence.

David Bohm prefers to use the term *holomovement* to describe the holonomic and dynamic nature of reality. Holograms are defined primarily as ways of storing information in terms of a network of interference patterns that represent the interaction of frequencies, such as light waves. These interference patterns are recorded in the hologram as light waves that do not literally resemble the objects they represent; rather they make up a "holographic blur" that has no recognizable form, but which contains the whole pattern.

Some scientists venture so far as to claim that the whole universe is a giant holomovement. However, the advanced masters teach that thought is the most potent agency in the Universe. It is the perfect thought of Love and Divine Knowledge cooperating with poise and power that maintains the balance of life in all of its forms. One cannot adapt the Divine Mind Principle to his or her own thought; rather one must adapt to the movement of Divine Mind Principle, and thought evolves from this unity of Mind. Divine Intelligence, life, and holographic substance are one and the same. The ultimate union of religion and science will also be recognized as one and the same thing. We would be wise to contemplate the omnipresence of all forces that exist, whether they are visible or invisible, if we are to develop self-mastery.

BIOPHYSICS

The emerging science of biophysics is devoted to the study of the realm of the living energy of life—from the mineral and the plant kingdom, to animals and humans. The emphasis in biophysics is on how energy creates matter. In the year 1984, the Swiss atomic physicist Carlos Rubbia was honored with the Nobel Prize for a revolutionary discovery demonstrating that every form of matter is subject to higher energetic interactions. Rubbia discovered a natural constant with which he could calculate the ratio of mass particles (matter) in relation to navigating energy particles. He found that the ratio of matter to the energy that forms matter requires one billion energy units to create one single unit of matter in a tangible form. It is here that we begin to appreciate the monumental spiritual energies required to create material worlds.

Rubbia's discovery clearly indicates that the immense underpinning of the invisible energy required to actualize life has been overlooked in science and medicine. This brings us to the question: What manner of inextinguishable energy is required to form and create matter? Biophysics has emerged from the fringes of science to study and examine this very question: Where can the cause of life be found?

SOUL BREATHING PRANA

The Light of the energy referred to as prana can be defined as the cosmic life force that stimulates all cell growth and is essentially the sustaining element of all life. Prana is the Universal Substance referred to as the Spirit of God in the scriptures because it is the reality sustaining all lesser forces. The pranic Light is much finer than air; it interpenetrates every atom and can be drawn into our bodies through breathing, yet prana is not oxygen. Prana is that which gives life to oxygen, consciousness to mind, and force to electricity. All of the moving elements of Creation are mediums through which prana works. Little could survive without the impact of prana on life. Prana is a unity of electromagnetic force and cosmic radiation working to sustain life.

The essence of Universal Substance in its original state is energy. Energy and substance are the two polarities of a single primal energy, and this primal energy is prana, or Spirit. Prana is one of the elements of Spirit, for Spirit is not only energy, it is also intelligence and substance—God in action. Receiving this Universal Substance into one's whole being requires that it be breathed more deeply into one's nature through quietness and stillness; with attention to the surrounding spiritual ethers and complete confidence in the workings of the pranic Light that underlies the holographic structures of life. When prana disappears, the plant or animal's biological body dies.

Forgetting one's sense of physical limitation and completely relaxing the body and mind is necessary in order to maximize the inner breath of prana, or Soul Breath. The soothing, elegant, and melodic voice of the magnetic personality vibrates with luxurious pranic energy. Learning to wield the powerful, yet subtle currents of pranic energy in the mind is the key to overcoming fear and attaining self-mastery. The most magnetic, talented, intelligent, creative, sensual, and memorable people wield their pranic power unconsciously; it is an innate, naturally occurring form of inner radiance that is earned by simply aligning with the natural energy of the breath of the Soul of Life. Although prana is the breath of life that is undetectable with scientific instruments, it passes through space to support the Soul like a wireless phone connection.

Soul Breathing expands the cells and tissues, thereby giving greater oxidation to the body and mind. Soul Breathing may be likened to a spiritual airing that is an invigorating method of keeping young and vibrant. The advanced masters teach that if prana were constantly breathed into the whole being, the body and mind would be eternally renewed and old age, and even death, would be overcome. When the mind is tense, it lacks fluidity and compresses so that it does not function freely. Soul Breathing has the same effect as loosening the bearings on the mechanism of the brain and allowing a lubricating oil to penetrate through it. This lubricating airing awakens the flow of intuition as the Inner Teacher, as well as opening the way for more intelligent activities.

Prana is not ether; ether is prana coming into manifestation. When the physical body disintegrates it reverts back into prana, or life force. Intelligence, or knowledge, is the primal attribute of consciousness, and consciousness is built through the influence of pranic energy. The frequency of prana vibrates far beyond the psychic forces. Therefore, mediumship and the development of the psychic forces are not necessarily stepping stones toward cultivating a fuller attainment of direct pranic Light.

Substance is the aspect that has the capacity of form. This intelligence moves to direct and determine the created physical forms. Just as a ray of pure white light reveals the seven colors of the rainbow, the emanations of the pranic ray reveal nine creative energies. Creation recycles, divides, and recombines the various energies emanating from prana. Substance and prana working together as a Primal Force is the nearest we can come to understanding the Mother/Father aspects of Creation in action. If Creation were just attributed to being an expression of God the Father, it would only be a partial and incomplete equation. For the pranic Light to expand within one's own life it must be called upon to overcome any degrading forces that oppose it. Just as Light dispels darkness, we are awakened when the consciousness merges into the realization that the two expressions of Mother and Father, of Life and Substance are equal.

SOUL BREATHING AFFIRMATION

The following affirmation from the advanced masters honors the one action of Pranic Force throughout Creation and may be voiced from the silence within, as the highest embodiment in cultivating harmony and unity in one's life:

> *I Am the force of Pranic Light, and I project it forth as all powerful*
> *in dissolving all conflicting conditions.*

LIFE = ENERGY = INFORMATION

When the energy content of matter is analyzed, it reveals the pure vibrating energy of the atom. The atom has a nucleus at its core that is encircled by electrons, like a miniature universe with a central sun. This vibrating energy creates a frequency or wavelength that is a signature, a spiritual blueprint for a particular type of information. Each unique form of matter is characterized as a specific frequency spectrum even though at this point it is intangible. Electricity, for example, will illuminate a lightbulb, yet we do not see the electric current itself. This same energy of life flows through a biological body and can be measured. A healthy individual has enough electrical current flowing through the body to run a 100-watt lightbulb. Individuals that have mastered the understanding of their personal energies appear to be lit from within, and a radiating glow will emanate from them. The ability to manifest form from the formless is the ultimate co-creation between the frequencies that are available for intelligent life to use.

Every form of biological energy strives to manifest itself according to a precisely defined Spiritual, energetic blueprint that follows the impulses of a higher order. The science of mathematics reveals the components of matter. The field of geometry reveals how energy and information are determined by the geometry of shapes. For example, an artist draws by using geometrical shapes to form a picture. It is here that we begin to gain a better understanding of the holographic universe and the mystery of the metaphysical science of the cosmos. The Greek word *cosmos* means "order" and indicates that nothing is coincidental. The ancient Egyptians as well as other high cultures understood the indwelling forces of energy, information, and consciousness as being represented through the pyramid.

Today the pyramidal structures in Egypt remain as reminders of how past cultures utilized the electromagnetic frequency of patterns through geometric shapes to enhance conscious living. These higher cultures understood that healing is a process of conscious living, and illness is a sign of the energy deficit of unconscious living. Healing requires uncovering the source of the deficit, rather than suppressing the symptoms of the deficit. Consider the information and the energy in the diet, the environment, and the frequency of words, thoughts, and deeds that all carry a vibratory wavelength. When two or more people get along and are able to live together in harmony, they share a common wavelength. We see that there are both powerful and subtle energies that Creation employs to form all planes of existence and manifestation. Life is a sacred extension of Divine Creation that encompasses the Universal Law of Action and Reaction in both its negative and positive vibratory patterns.

THE POWER OF DREAMS

A great deal of growth, healing, and protection is communicated through our dreams. The Native American tribe of the Iroquois, traditionally a matriarchal society, taught their children that reading the riddles of dreams is the most important source of personal guidance and authentic power: power that comes looking for those that dream strongly. When the Soul is allowed to communicate strongly through the mind of the individual, the dream life will be strong. And sharing dreams was the first business of the day for the Iroquois. In ancient Greece healers called *Therapeuti* formulated treatments for those who were ill based on the patient's dream life.

When we do not live life through the Wisdom of the Soul, our lives lose both vitality and the magic of the unseen realms. When we seek to align with our Spiritual consciousness and ask for a clearer sense of direction in life, our dreams become a medium through which we can recognize the consequences of our actions. In sleep the subconscious mind that connects to the Soul and the superconscious (God/ Mind) can link to one's personal condition, exposing both the positive and negative aspects of one's life. When sufficient credence is given to dreams, they will serve as practical guidance in all areas of existence. The signs, messages, symbols, and images in dreams have the potential to inspire, warn, and guide the individual to greater degrees of awareness, inventive ideas, creativity, and safety.

The superconscious is our link to the Universal Mind Principle as well as our source of inspiration and creativity. In the waking hours of daytime, the superconscious flows through the subconscious mind to the conscious mind in the form of intuition, knowledge (real Intelligence), patience, love, talent, and genius. This is the natural way in which the step-down process of energy and information is meant to flow. When our intuition is cultivated to a high level, it is easy to interpret dreams more precisely than depending solely on the capacity to reason. Symbolism and imagery in dreams are similar to what shorthand is to words. We dream in pictures because we tend to think in images rather than script. The messages in dreams are as unique as the life of the individual, and this is why it is impossible to compile a universal list of dream symbols that apply to all people.

However, dreams operate according to Spiritual Laws and can be categorized into four main types: physical, represented by Earth; mental, represented by air; emotional, represented by fire; and spiritual, represented by water. Dreams may relate to the likes and dislikes of the individual, loved ones, world events, levels of the subconscious, the subconscious of another, the superconscious, relationships to others, and all phases of one's nature, including past lives and experiences in the astral realm. Two mental categories of dreams account for most dream activity in all people. Psychological dreams account for the majority of dream activity and reflect hidden emotion—fear, rage, anger, and themes of sorting through unclear emotions. Psychic dreams impart messages of guidance and instruction regarding issues such as health, diet, relationships, hidden danger, and future events.

Dreams attempt to direct us toward higher, more balanced accomplishments regarding our physical, mental, emotional, and spiritual life. Superficial dreams may reflect the problems and stresses of the workday, family life, and the somewhat pointless obsessions of the personal mind. At a deeper level we may receive warning dreams from the subconscious related to physical well-being. The subconscious has charge of bodily assimilation, elimination, and the rebuilding of tissue. These dreams take stock of the possibilities of the Law of Cause and Effect before becoming a reality. The corrective dreams are often advanced warnings of emotional tensions that may soon get out of control. These dreams may involve family, friends, coworkers, business partners, and even unknown people. Lucid dreaming is the process by which the dreamer maintains full consciousness during the dream and can control the events taking place in the dream. Precognitive dreams can be explained using the example of the holographic model. The internal hologram warns of an accident that may never occur because the individual is given the opportunity to alter the future event via precognitive dreams. The precognitive consciousness also operates while we are in the hypnogogic state, the lucid period of time between sleep and waking.

The precognitive, telepathic, and clairvoyant dreams emanate from the superconscious and are rarely forgotten. The protective subconscious and the all-knowing superconscious never sleep. I had the unusual experience of opening my eyes and being fully awake at about 4:00 a.m. one morning, and I wondered why I was so keenly awake. After a short period of time, I heard a rather odd sound of squeaky brakes near my home. Then, to my utter horror, I heard the sound of a stranger attempting to break in through the back door, as I lay in bed. Fortunately, a new dead bolt had been installed a few days earlier, and the intruder was unsuccessful in the illegal attempt to enter my home. It happened very quickly, and I was frozen with fear. There was no time to call for help; however, it appeared I had all the help that I needed at that moment. I was awakened and aware of the crisis, I stayed calm and soon heard the person drive away in the direction of the home of a trouble-making teenage boy that lived down the road. We all come into the world with protection. The question is, are we educated, disciplined, and open enough to accept and receive the messages and the feelings of our own intuition, dreams, and Spiritual guidance?

The truth is we cannot fully access our greater potential without the guidance of dreams. Exquisitely inventive ideas are presented in dreams. The mechanization of the Singer sewing machine was conceived through a dream during a time when Mr. Singer was seeking a solution to the perplexity of creating a machine that sews. The author Robert Louis Stevenson received the entire outline of *Dr. Jekyll and Mr. Hyde* through a series of dreams. The modern author J. K. Rowling stated that she received the inspiration for the wildly popular Harry Potter books through her dreams with help from her deceased mother. The well-known composers Mozart and Handel received inspiring melodies in the semiconscious state of the higher dimensions of dreams. Niels Bohr, the famous Danish atomic physicist, conceived of the planetary system of our galaxy as the microcosm of the atomic nucleus surrounded by circling electrons through a dream. The answers to our focused perplexities may indeed be revealed in dreamtime.

The dreams, visions, and experiences that emanate from the highest sources always leave a brilliant impression of creativity and inspiration relating to our interrelationship with life and Creation. Dreaming is a safe means of communication with the various dimensions of consciousness. Regardless of whether we fail to remember our dreams, most people dream from four to seven times per night, with each dream lasting from five minutes to one hour. The sleep state appears to shadow the state called death, but we actually function at a higher frequency during sleep than when we are awake. Sleep recharges the physical body with life-giving pranic energy, and without sleep the body would quickly perish. When the body is asleep it appears to be unaware. Yet in sleep we may actually be more aware, as the higher senses that are independent of the physical brain centers continue to work. Some people have a difficult time remembering their dreams. Interestingly, the herb mugwort (*Artemesia vulgaris*) is a plant that helps to promote lucid dreaming. A cup of mugwort and peppermint tea before bedtime is helpful for those with difficulty remembering dreams (see the recipe on page 247).

The entire sympathetic system governed by the subconscious forms our sixth sense and is part of the Spiritual Self, or superconscious, ever on guard and in communion with the Soul. This is the higher Self that experiences at all levels of consciousness. The sixth sense may be trained or submerged and left uncultivated, which results in disease, anger, and depression unless the warnings in dreams are heeded and the person gets the message. A Spiritually minded person knows that dreams are not merely disconnected groups of images but present definite patterns relating to the background of the dreamer. Take time to translate dream symbols; put the pieces of the puzzle together; and decode and interpret the words, sounds, imagery, physical sensations, and feelings in dreams to the best of your ability. Dreams offer very personal information that may only be understood by the dreamer. Messages that seem unusual may actually be reduced to simple, common terms that explain one's relationship to people, places, and oneself in order to better understand life. Persistence is required to learn the language of dream symbols and imagery. When this forgotten language of the subconscious is properly implemented, much pain, suffering, and illness can be avoided. The advanced masters teach that suffering begins when we forget our connection to the Divine, and Divine messages are found in dreams.

Honesty in the analysis of one's dreams is essential for growth, and this is where the difficulty lies. We tend to project blame on others because we can't admit to negative qualities in ourselves. If higher levels of consciousness did not guide us, we would indeed struggle in a state of ignorance. Dreams give us information in small doses as needed because time is needed to fully assimilate what we learn. When we allow the higher forces to light the way to truth through dream interpretation, wonderful gifts come through our efforts.

In sleep the consciousness has the ability to become universal and knowing, with all divine attributes of the mind alert. Yet we are not always conscious of what is taking place. In dreams we must strive to be just as conscious as in our so-called waking condition. Although sleep allows our complete consciousness to surface—dreams are also mixtures of Earthly and higher cosmic experiences. Dreams oftentimes resemble a clairvoyant state of a very low order unless one trains the mind to resonate in a higher condition.

The difference between a dream and a nightmare is that the nightmare is the result of one's outer activity producing a fear, or mesmeric influence, of the lower mind that dominates the psyche. Releasing the mind from a nightmare requires raising the consciousness by declaring that you are one with perfection. When the nightmare involves others, focus your energies to hold Light for those in peril. This mental exercise actually strengthens the energetic auras of all those held within the higher frequency that you create for them—including you. It is a way of benefiting yourself while benefiting others.

When the body is at rest, the Soul resides in the supersensory astral world, and this is why the interpretation of dreams has always been acknowledged as a sacred and valued art in all cultures of the world. The polar opposite of dreaming is nondreaming. In a state of nondreaming, one's Spirit finds rest from disturbing dreams that alarm the Soul with the many dangers of the world. The value of cultivating a deeper understanding of dream life as a resource for human nourishment has been particularly prevalent in modern Egyptian, African, Native American, and Aboriginal cultures. In times past, the third eye and sixth sense were a fully functioning way of life. Therefore, people were more spiritually aware, and their frequencies were higher, less dense, and consequently, there was a beautiful love vibration among the people. The common practice was to discuss dreams together in the morning, so they could help one another warn of impending change. In Egypt the pyramids were also used to rebuild and enhance energy fields in people. The process of meditating and fasting for three days and three nights in the pyramids allowed them to go out of body to higher realms where they would be taught. The Atlanteans and the Lemurians had the ability to transform energy into matter and matter into energy through opening the Christ Center within the heart.

We are all working on the evolution of ourselves, our world, and the Universe as well. Therefore, we all have a responsibility to develop and to strengthen our understanding of dreams and to respect the true value of these telepathic creative communications. Dreams serve as portals of Wisdom between the mind and the Soul and contain spiritual and moral language that is important for the well-being of the dreamer. Our role is to keep the greater good alive within ourselves and to live it into being. Dreams help us to achieve this goal.

ORACULAR DREAMING

Oracular (noun): 1. A Divine utterance by an agency of Divine communication that delivers authoritative, wise, or highly regarded and influential pronouncements. 2. Giving forth utterances or decisions as if by special inspiration. 3. Ambiguous or obscure. 4. Prophetic.

Oracular dreams are the language of the Soul. The wishes of the Soul invite us to align with the Soul's purpose. If the mind is the medium that serves the higher Spiritual energies—then oracular dreams are invaluable guides for transformation. Oracular dreams perform an important service as a bridge between the physical reality and the nonphysical reality by offering the greatest benefit for one's potential growth. Important work is achieved in the sleep cycle; as the energy body is rejuvenated, certain access codes can open higher pathways of intelligence in the various dimensions.

When the body and the mind are at rest there is an expanded capacity for the reception of important keys that release and unlock the struggle between the false ego and the God/Mind. The individual must interpret the dream in relation to current life circumstances. The energy in dreams is meant to feed, seed, and nurture consciousness. Dreams can tell us what to eat and what not to eat, warn us of danger and the hidden character of individuals that we may be involved with. Some dreams tell us something about our lives that we are missing or that we need to change or look out for. We may receive messages through animal totems in dreams, and this symbolic imagery may be abundant in dreams. Each Soul is gifted with one or more guides that work with us during the sleep cycle. Yet progress with our guides may be frustrating and painfully slow because so much is lost between the conscious and the subconscious modalities. Consciously choosing to rise to our true potentials through a deep desire for higher truth creates a chemical shift and increases the voltaic charge in the tissues of the brain and body.

Oracular dreams are very important and make a powerful and unforgettable impact. Some oracular dreams must be repeated until we take notice. Not all dreams are oracular. Many dreams are the continuous outworking of the mind—discordant, vibratory thoughts or emotions, and overactive mental processes. Just as everything that we see and do does not hold a symbolic or sacred meaning, so too, not every dream is oracular in nature. Oracular dreams are the master dreams that must be decoded and respected as a gift of invaluable Love.

Oracular dreams offer wisdom and guidance when we are off track, in harm's way, or in crisis or have a message that is not accessible through the rational mind. If we honor our dream images as a special Spiritual Language, then self-mastery is strengthened and we learn more of the realms of darkness and Light.

There are guidelines, but there is no textbook explanation for all of our dream images. These images are as unique in meaning as each life story. Our dreams change as our lives change and our path and purpose evolve. Dreams are part of the voice that every person needs to hear, part of the inner voice that supports our work on Earth and beyond. The subconscious—the mind of the Soul—will direct the conscious self to seek a fuller understanding of life through symbols, some of which are listed below.

- Dreams with spiritual implications will depict vivid and beautiful colors.

- Past-life experiences are seen in bright colors and in the clothing or costume of that period.
- Muddy, dark colors in dreams often have negative connotations.
- Tired expressions on faces in dreams denote debility and excessive burden.
- Bloated appearance of the body signifies ill health and egotism.
- Distortion of eyes, ears, mouth, nose, face warns of distortion in these areas.
- Head turned backward refers to prejudices that stand in the way of progress.
- Loose teeth warn of loose and careless speech; false, crooked, falling teeth refer to false words; wearing braces in dreams may be a warning to control your words.
- Clothing often reflects a certain state of consciousness.
- Babies represent a new birth, new consciousness, rebirth of the self to higher ideals.
- A high mountain represents the development of the mind to a higher understanding.
- Dreams with water and fish depict spiritual progress.
- Anxiety in life produces frightening mental images in dreams.
- A sore or infection may symbolize the dangers of being sexually promiscuous.
- Dreams of animals may reveal the animal totem of the individual as being a protective ally in facing challenging life situations and revealing things that need to be seen but may not be noticed without the powerful senses of the animal.

DREAM CATCHER

Everyone has a higher purpose in life that must be discovered in time and with patience and dedication. People often commit their lives to relationships before they are ready, be it through impatience, conditioning, or social pressures. Consequently, opportunities for important relationships with higher purpose are missed. In order to keep sight of the best move on the chessboard of life it is useful to keep a dream journal.

Noting particularly memorable or powerful dreams in written form is very helpful for interpreting dreams, especially if they seem confusing. Note the date and time frame along with feelings or emotions that arise in the dream. Does the dream repeat itself? What is it that is trying to get your attention? As time passes, the dream journal begins to reflect the growth patterns of the individual. A dream journal connects us with a life that makes itself known through impressions and imagery.

Oftentimes we are good at receiving images and impressions but have difficulty understanding or expressing them. Describing dream impressions through keeping a written record helps to clarify the experience and releases the energy of the dream. This assists the individual in filtering through the information for insights relating to past, present, or future circumstances that require new courses of action or understanding. This is why it is important to keep a chronological record of your important impressions and dreams through writing and drawing. Keep a small Dream Catcher journal and pen near your bed, and take it with you when you travel.

It is especially important to record powerful oracular dreams. Like a diary, a dream journal is a useful tool for growth and for understanding the deeper aspects of one's physical, mental, and spiritual life. It is also essential to review and interpret the meaning of dreams. Taking the time to make a record of what you remember is not only of great value, but it is a fascinating way to achieve deeper insight into how Spirit communicates.

OBSTACLES TO ORACULAR DREAMING

Perhaps the more we understand how the mind serves as the vehicle for the Soul and Spirit, the more the denigration of the mental faculties will be clearly recognized as the danger that it really is. When addiction to any substance—be it alcohol, drugs, nicotine, exitotoxins, caffeine, artificial sweeteners, and the like—becomes the ruling factor in one's life, then dreams will reflect this distortion in proportion to the damage.

If you think you do not dream, examine and reflect on why this may be. What could be fogging the true function of the personal mind in perceiving one's dreams in relation to the journey of the Soul? A lack of interest, physical exhaustion, EMF pollution in your sleep space, and impurities in the body may cause difficulty in remembering dreams. Help yourself remember dreams by drinking a cup of mugwort tea before bed or saying each night before falling asleep, "I will remember my dreams." Dreams are of value for guidance, inspiration, healing; to face the self, stimulate creativity, expand consciousness, experience other dimensions; for out-of-body travel, past life memories; and to establish communication with your higher Self and Creation. All of these assist us in developing our spiritual nature, establishing inner peace, and increasing service to humanity as a whole.

✳ *Medicinal-Strength Mugwort and Peppermint Dream Tea Recipe*

A simple recipe for a medicinal-strength cup of mugwort tea to better promote lucid dreaming is made with two and half cups of purified water that has been boiled for ten minutes; turn off the heat and add two tablespoons of dried mugwort herb and one tablespoon dried peppermint leaf herb (double if fresh); cover and steep for twenty to thirty minutes. Strain the tea and drink one cup before bedtime. Chill the leftover tea. This may be repeated as needed for up to three months. The rotation for all herbal usage is three months on and three months off of any herbal formula. The flavor of mugwort is pleasant: slightly sweet and slightly bitter and mild. Other flavorful herbs such as sage, rosemary, lemon balm, or lemon verbena may be added along with the mugwort for variety if desired.

BEYOND THE VEIL

Oftentimes when our dear ones pass beyond the veil, we realize how utterly unprepared we are for what may be a difficult and challenging event: the death of a loved one. It has too often been stated that we do not know what happens when we pass from the temporal world into the realm of Spirit upon the death of the body. However, there is ample evidence that clearly points toward a more expanded understanding of one of life's most profound mysteries.

By opening to historical and esoteric records as well as our own experiences regarding the enigma of death, we see there is a great body of work that supports the transition or continuing existence of the individual Soul force beyond the physical body. It has also been established within the treatises of many religions that transitioning through the veil between physical and nonphysical reality is not the end of experience, but rather a further step toward the continuum of experiencing life's infinite processes.

Those who find positive meaning and a greater understanding in these experiences are less likely to remain depressed for a long period of time after the passing of a loved one. With the death of a loved one, it is very important to overcome our grief and replace it with supportive loving prayer on behalf of the transitioning Soul. Our extended sorrow over the death of a loved one has the effect of holding the loved one back from a new spiritual journey. After the passing of Souls, it is especially important to release vengeance in the heart and avoid selfish pleasure in seeing another meet disaster. People with positive and flexible minds have the ability to transmute change and misfortune into opportunities, learning to grow from challenges. Prolonged negative thinking is merely a bad habit. Resiliency and gratitude can be cultivated. The reality of Spirit is a form of Grace that represents the good and miraculous aspects that sustain life. The work of Souls is to learn to follow the path of our divine destiny in harmony with the Universal Intelligence of Creation.

Empirical spiritual science has described five stages of the Soul's evolution to and from the body. Stage one begins with a small beam of Light that is pulsed into the Soul's Light on the mental and causal plane of existence. In stage two the astral body (emotional vehicle) forms a heavier vibration. During stage three the Light body begins to assume a physical shape. In stage four the electric or ethereal body develops. As the physical body develops in the final stage, it vibrates at its lowest level and takes on the densest shape of form and frequency. In so-called death, this whole process is reversed. The Soul sheds the physical body, ethereal body, astral body, and mental body, moving back through the frequencies of manifestation toward Light. People have described this process repeatedly in near-death experiences and out-of-body experiences. Animals go through the same process when they pass as humans do.

The Soul has been equated with consciousness resonating through a course of evolutionary change. Until the Soul achieves self-mastery, the death of the body is an act of mercy and reprieve from the false ego, which is at the root of great suffering and misery. Misery is further exacerbated by a world that is governed by manipulation, extortion, and usury. Between embodiments, the Soul will ideally partake of the Light and Wisdom of higher realms. It is reasonable to say it is a rare Soul, if any, that achieves self-mastery in one temporal lifetime. Although we reenter third-dimensional existence with certain talents, preferences, and personality traits, in reincarnation the entity for the most part forfeits memories of previous lives to begin a new study in the incomparable mystery of one's own being in relationship to the nature of Creation. Sometimes young children will remember and talk about past-life memories that are so precise that coroners' reports and other documentation confirm the details the children recall. To help identify an individual returning from a past life, to find them in their new body, look for the same eyes as your departed loved ones. As early as two years of age, memories of former family members, or violent deaths, may surface. After the Soul has completed its evolution, it merges more fully with its Source of Creation as a co-creator in a higher realm of existence.

In death as in life, our deep desires and wants create a magnetic attraction to the frequency where the wants and desires exist. At death we magnetically gravitate and are drawn toward the dimensional frequency that is compatible with our own frequency. Thoughts, attitudes, actions, and beliefs all work to raise or to lower the frequency of the astral body, which may take a very long time to move through the various planes of existence. The astral plane is linked with the body, mind, and emotions that in tandem create distinct holographic energy fields of shapes, colors, and characteristics. Therefore, the astral realm is a plane where our thoughts can hold us at certain levels when we resonate with a separate identity apart from the higher Self. Ultimately, the Soul would resonate at a high enough frequency to bypass the third and fourth dimensions and ascend directly to the fifth dimension, the causal plane of deeper Spiritual Truths and the closest plane to the higher Self. The causal plane is the essence of wholeness and creativity.

Communication between Souls on the astral plane occurs naturally through mental telepathy—as spiritual beings do not have larynxes, mouths, or physical bodies in general. The Soul forms its frequency according to its state of mind. It is always the state of mind that is both one's own judge and executioner. Lower thought forms that radiate with gloom and doom, cruelty, deception, and conceited egotism draw the Soul into a dense lower astral plane. Our thoughts and emotions create highly magnetic, nonphysical frequencies as aspects of consciousness. Magnetism attracts frequencies in harmony with it and repels frequencies not in harmony with it.

LOWER VIBRATORY ENTITIES

A lower astral entity is an invisible, discarnate being with slower, denser vibratory frequencies than Spiritual beings. The entity world has been largely denied and ignored by religion and society out of fear. However, the entity world requires healing to abolish the detrimental influences that entities project into the astral, mental, and physical realms. Certain Souls with dense auras are not magnetically able to propel toward the Divine Light after death and become trapped in a lower astral prison of their own making. A living person weakened by fear, depression, ignorance, mischievous intentions, senility, maliciousness, victim consciousness, substance abuse, or mental illness may attract a parasitic mental form from the lower astral plane or a loved one who has passed. It is possible for large numbers of incarnate people to be possessed by discarnate lower astral entities that feed off people's vibrations—keeping them in fear, doubt, worry, addiction, violence, and misuse of sexual energy. The individual attached to the presence of a lower astral entity may feel drained and depleted and have insomnia, headaches, and bodily illness. The personal habits of unsuspecting people may become unusual and bizarre as their own thought and living patterns are unduly influenced by lower astral thought forms. A living individual may actually protect and assist the lower astral entity, which drains energy. Samuel Sagan, MD, author of *Entity Possession*, claims that entities are not generally evil, though some of them may be. Some of his clients believe entities have attracted accidents and forms of physical violence to them, such as making them black out while driving. We can protect ourselves from lower astral energies from becoming attached by requesting protection from our Spiritual Guides and mentally forming a cocoon of white Light around our energy fields or silently saying a prayer such as, "As God is my witness—I Am strong and protected. I Am Light and Love, cleansed, whole, and free of any dark energies from the astral realm." We may also increase our pranic energy by raising our quality of life by seeking out our connection to the higher vistas of consciousness and cultivate our link to Spirit as our rightful inheritance. Sagan warns that people who claim to be in constant touch with spirit guides may actually be connecting with discarnate astral entities. To discover and clear deeply embedded lower astral entities is serious work and must be done by a professional (see the resources section for some suggestions). There is also a quick affirmation for discouraging dark astral energies that must be said forcefully:

All healed and forgiven!

This affirmation may be repeated as often as needed.

In the astral realm and on the Earth, the higher spiritual planes radiate positive thoughts to the lower thought forms so that these Souls may awaken and turn toward the Light. In third-dimensional existence mental energy works in a similar manner to the astral plane, with the exception that what we think will manifest instantly on the astral plane. Those on Earth whose lives resonate with peace, love, and harmony accomplish much for the plane of Light. We practice operating in the astral realm in dreams when we are asleep. When we have a strong desire to connect with a loved one that has passed, the intention in the form of a prayer before sleep will seed the field of experience.

JAMES AND JERRY

When my father, James, passed beyond the veil, I was very worried about him because he suffered greatly in the hospital for a year before he passed. I prayed for him often after he passed and honored him in a Native American sweat-lodge ceremony. And then one night I saw him in the realm of his subtle body when I was asleep. In death the subtle elements of the body do not change. The Soul moves into a higher realm of existence accompanied by prana, the mind, the senses, and the seeds of a new body. When Souls are reborn they wear the same subtle body that has persisted through all cycles of incarnation. Here my father was young and handsome, and he was with his beloved brother Jerry, who had passed before him. James and Jerry did not see me observing them in their subtle bodies. It was as though I was only allowed peace of mind in knowing that they were together and happy.

When my mother described her wonderment at the joyous smile on my father's face when he passed—his blue eyes still sparkling—I felt that this was because Jerry's Soul had come to meet the Soul of his brother James. A smile on the face at the time of death also expresses the Soul's return to the force of superconsciousness through the subconscious mind.

In his Earth life, my father oftentimes smoked a pipe filled with fragrant cherry tobacco. I loved the aroma of the heady smoke, and I always equated the smell of cherry pipe tobacco with my father. When my mother informed me of my father's passing, I rode my scooter to the oldest church in San Francisco—Mission Dolores. While stopped at the intersection of 16th and Dolores, I smelled the unmistakable aroma of cherry tobacco wafting through the air. This was shocking, because I had not smelled this scent in many, many, years. I looked around and saw no one in sight, not even another car next to me on the road.

It is possible for the Spirit of those passing through the veil to communicate and send signs to loved ones. They can convey something familiar and recognizable about themselves—a scent, a sound, or a signal—to let us know that they are near. Brief spiritual communications are possible through the supersenses—either olfactory, of the inner ear, or the optics. Many people have had similar experiences when the bond of love is strong between Souls. It is the force of Love that makes this communication possible, for Love permeates the dimensions of time and space.

WHERE DO WE GO WHEN WE DIE?

Where do we go when we die? The truth is—we do not die, we are multidimensional; the Soul changes dimensions upon the death of the body. The death of the body is a birth into the spiritual plane. When called away from the Earthly life, one's spiritual fruits must be in order and readiness to undergo the process of shedding one's vibratory layers. The full spectrum of all of our energy bodies can only exist in the fifth dimension. As long as we resonate with the third and fourth dimensions, we remain in the astral plane and fourth dimension in separation or as a partial equation of light.

A discarnate spirit communicates with the same resonance as incarnated in life, and the Soul holds a record of an exact measure of an individual in the form of a quantum holographic shape. This ethereal body is a self-organizing holographic energy template that reflects how much Light has entered the atoms of the individual in a physical lifetime. The more Light that has entered the atoms, the higher the number of hydrogen atom rings within the life form. Souls that are heavier are restricted to resonating closer to the edges of the atom where the force is greatest, and Souls that are lighter are free to gravitate toward the center of the space resonating with a lesser force. When spiritually and cosmically advanced beings die, they are guided through the dimensions via their personal seraphic guardians. Others may be detained until a review of their affairs has been completed, after which they may proceed to what is referred to as the "many mansion worlds." Some Souls are assigned to the ranks of the sleeping survivors who wish to wait for the end of the current planetary cycle.

The main work of humanity is to cultivate a resonant Light body while in the flesh—not after the death of the body. It is through repetitive incarnations tempered by trial and error that the individual develops a Light body that is sufficient to result in power over death. When all five dimensions of mind are activated and harmonized, the need for energy from food is gradually eliminated until one is mainly sustained by absorbing prana, or Super light. The Super light of creation must be converted, or stepped down in frequency, to create material worlds. This conversion is accomplished through the double pyramidal energy construct and double spirals of codified energy.

Upon the death of the body, the step-down process is reversed. The biomagnetic field in living matter is produced by the iron in the blood circulating in a spiral that keeps the stream of energy locked in place where the atoms are just about to touch. Upon the death of the body the heart stops beating, the circulation of blood ceases, the biomagnetic field is canceled, and the stream of life withdraws along with the Soul to the spaces in between the atoms to find its natural point, or dimension of resonance. There is nothing to fear in this process. Several days before passing, the energies of Spiritual guides are present 24/7 to help create a calm, peaceful state that prevents the Soul from being trapped in the Vortex between dimensions during transition. Twenty-four hours before transition the individual who is passing begins to see flashes of white Light as the veil between worlds becomes thinner. At birth, a Spiritual lifeline in the form of an invisible silver cord accompanies the Soul upon slipping into the body. This cord is linked to the seven major chakras of the body; it energetically attaches the Soul to its biological parents and ties one to the Earth plane of existence as a human being. The silver cord dissipates and breaks free during the Soul's passing, allowing the Soul to enter various vibratory realms of existence.

MASTER SLEEP AFFIRMATIONS

We both transmit and receive energy from thought forms. Words and thoughts seed the field of intention; where your thoughts and actions are focused is where you are focused. The following affirmations may be used to align yourself each day with the gift of your greater intention. Turning your thoughts toward these simple yet powerful affirmations before sleep will help you to shift your focus toward a higher frequency in your experience. Take notice of any resistance, results, or reception of new energies that may occur as you go forward. Remember to take time to write down your most important insights and dreams in a small notebook, keeping track of the dates so that you can clarify your progress.

Before sleep, the advanced masters suggest silently contemplating the following:

> *I Am Light's purest intention; I have a beautiful spiritual body, a beautiful spiritual mind, eyes, nose, mouth, and skin. It is the body of a Divine infant, which now is perfect. I invite my guides to teach me through dreaming, and I will do my best to retain what I am learning.*

Upon arising, make this affirmation to yourself:

> *I Am the Light of Love, there is a Divine alchemist within.*

By the spiritual power of these simple daily affirmations, a subtle daily transmutation takes place and the unfolding from within begins as the Spirit strengthens and rebuilds the body and mind.

Upon rising, the inner alchemist has caused dead, worn-out cells to fall and the gold of new skin to appear with perfect health and vigor. In the morning, learn to smile and breath deeply from the strength of the Soul and maintain this spiritual relaxation for the day. A real smile is a thing of true beauty, the artistic expression of the Inner Teacher. Think a healing thought for the world, and offer a loving prayer. As you encounter challenges in your work, the following affirmation is useful:

> *Within me is a perfect Divine form; Infinite Harmonious Love.*

ATTRIBUTES AND FAILURES OF LEADERSHIP

In our work, no matter how simple or complex, progress is made when we cultivate the true attributes of leadership by example and avoid the qualities that lead to failure of leadership.

Attributes of Leadership

To encourage development of the attributes of leadership, tap into the resource of self-mastery as a form of self-education; understand the difference between work relationships and nonwork relationships; support the body with seasonal foods and periodic detoxifying diets; balance time indoors with time outdoors in nature; and enjoy exercise and purposeful meditation. The following list of leadership attributes may be of help in reminding oneself of qualities to foster.

Able to delegate to people's strengths rather than weaknesses	Able to focus on tasks
Attentive to detail	Cooperative with others
Courageous	Decisive
Honest	Just
Leads self and others through encouragement rather than fear	Personally aligned with the spirit of harmony, compassion, play, and love
Self-controlled in balancing technology and nature	Understanding
Willing to accept full responsibility for own actions	

Failure in Leadership

The following list of attributes of failed leadership may be of help in reminding oneself of the qualities to avoid, both in the work environment and in all aspects of one's life.

Addictive, particularly to drugs, alcohol, and gambling	Careless
Coldly manipulative	Criminal tendencies

Deceptive	Deficient in mental power
Depressive, irritable, and insomniac from tech overdose	Disharmonious in marriage or mate selection
Disharmonious in work environment and associate selection	Disloyal
Evasive	Fearful of competition
Fearful of failure	Heartless
Hungry for media attention	Hyperactive
Lack of ambition to aim above mediocrity	Lack of compassion
Lack of imagination	Lack of persistence
Lack of self-discipline	Lack of sexual control
Lack of well-defined purpose in life	Negative personality
Operating from the false ego	Procrastinator
Self-interested	Self-serving attitude
Unable to admit error	Unable to organize details
Unhealthy	Unwilling to render humble service

THE NEW COSMOLOGY

The Dilemma

To laugh is to risk appearing a fool.
To weep is to risk appearing sentimental.
To reach out for another is to risk involvement.
To expose feelings is to risk rejection.
To place your dreams before the crowd is to risk ridicule.
To love is to risk not being loved in return.
To go forward in the face of overwhelming odds is to risk failure.
But risks must be taken,
Because the greatest hazard in life is to risk nothing.
The person who risks nothing does nothing; has nothing, is
  nothing.
She or he may avoid suffering and sorrow, but will not learn,
  feel change, grow, or love fully.
Chained by certitudes, one becomes a slave and forfeits freedom.
Only a person who takes risks is free.

AUTHOR UNKNOWN

Cosmology (noun): The understanding of humanity's relationship to the Universe and a fundamental knowledge of Natural Law; the study of how the individual fits into the plan of the galaxy and universe; a holistic system in which the totality of our experience may be encompassed.

The most recent explorations and observations in space have revealed upwards of two hundred billion stars in the galaxy of our Milky Way. The Milky Way is situated within a universe of roughly one hundred billion other galaxies. The planets and the life forms that may inhabit space are staggering to the imagination. And the human family has barely begun to perceive the ramifications of exploring the possibilities for responsible cosmic citizenship within what we now know is an ever-expanding arena of life.

At present we have come to a threshold that requires a new understanding of the Universe and our place within it. Many people in the world do not consider the importance of becoming educated in respect to humanity's position in the galaxy and the value of the biologically abundant and vibrantly beautiful planet on which we exist. The various races of intelligent beings that may inhabit and explore space are rarely a mainstream topic of conversation. However, as we know, many cultures throughout history have upheld the great importance of understanding the influences of the galactic communities as well as the cycles of the Universe.

The Native American and Australian Aboriginal cultures have spoken of the "Great Star Nations" from whence they came, and to which they will return. In these societies, the "Sacred Spiral" of the Milky Way has been revered as the universal sphere in which human DNA harmonizes life with Earth's cycles within the evolutionary processes of space and time. The ancient races of the Anasazi and the Maya also possessed great knowledge of the rhythmic movements of the heavenly cycles that were integrated into their lives in ceremonies. It is recorded that Earth has been visited by otherworldly races in spaceships at various times, for various reasons, throughout history from historical Celtic and Egyptian records, as well as the Bible.

UOLOGY

One night I had a dream that depicted a beautiful vine of green on a background of soft yellow. At the top of the vine was a violet cluster of what looked like tiny grapes. The vine was delineated with short lines that represented the various epochs of time—the various ages of human development. The stages of life on Earth and the advancing epochs of time and humanity's place in it were symbolized by the vine. The grapelike cluster at the top represented both the flowering of Consciousness and the fruits of our labors. It was very beautiful and simple. At the top of the vine the word *uology* (pronounced you-ology) was written, and I was showing it to a few others in the dream. Then someone said, "This is your best idea yet!"

In recognizing that this vine represents the evolutionary process for the human race and uology is at the top, it appears to be symbolic of the threshold of humanity's emergence into higher consciousness as stewards

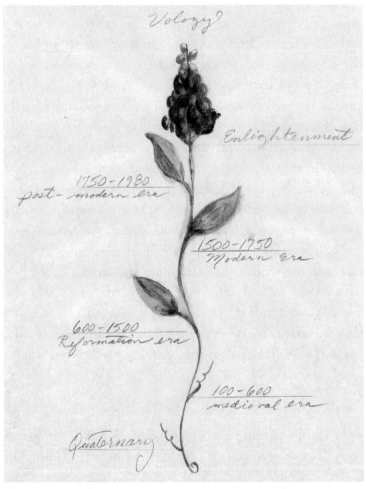

Figure 7.1. Author's drawing of Uology Vine

of the Earth. The question is . . . will we enter this new phase as genuinely enlightened human beings or as hypnotized technological zombies? Will the truth emerge so that the human family can break down the wall of fear that exists in people's minds regarding the subject of other intelligent life forms apart from our own? Will we wake up in time to avoid another Dark Age for human experience and create an age of Light instead? Will we experience the Spiritual flowering of the human race, or will we become technological slaves unfit to steward our own existence?

CROP CIRCLE SIGNS

There is no subtle way to approach the subject of the fascinating crop circles that have appeared all over the world for the last few centuries. Those who have visited these sites claim there is a measurable amount of electromagnetic, microwave frequency emanating from these geometrically

Figure 7.2. Two examples of crop circles

precise and unearthly designs. We know that high intensity microwave beams can cause severe headaches, nausea, vomiting, diarrhea, body pains, burns, hair loss, swelling, cancer, and numbness. An article on crop circles in the journal *Nature* implies that crop circles have been appearing on Earth since at least the eighteenth century and that high-frequency electromagnetic radiation forms the geometric shapes. Since antigravity technology requires thinking in four dimensions rather than three, crop circles are beyond human invention and there has been little truthful forthcoming information to explain them. We must consider crop circles to be a show of technological prowess on Earth. The question is, by whom? Secondly, for this technological prowess to be demonstrated in the crop fields of Earth, it stands to reason that those demonstrating this technological prowess must be present on the planet.

Some people claim that crop circles are a hoax; some claim that they move a band of frequency around the planet that helps to activate the Earth's magnetic grid work. Yet we know the grid work is already activated. Others claim that these intelligent geometric shapes are designed and constructed by ascended masters and can be created by a wave of frequency from afar, rather than a spacecraft. Yet many people have seen spacecrafts on Earth. Still, there are others who claim that in times of great stress for the Earth, energy in the form of crop circles is focused into the various grid systems by spaceships that maintain the orbit, spin velocities, and other physical maintenances of Earth. This sounds like an absurd statement considering that the forces of Natural Laws holding the Earth in balance are absent from this equation. It has also been claimed that crop circles are dynamic energy codes that are made visible as an attempt to awaken humanity to the truth that outside help is maintaining the balance, rather than Natural Law. Others warn that crop circles and the energies behind crop circles are interfering with the natural course of life on Earth. What is really happening?

The Hubble and the Kepler space telescopes have ushered in the golden age of space exploration, providing science with undeniable proof that there are billions of universes and certainly infinite forms of life that exist within these material universes. However, these facts do not appear to alter the beliefs of many people who reject the reality that we are not the only race presently inhabiting our galaxy. Some people fear the idea of alien races, and they will withdraw completely from the subject. Some people know what is really happening, and they choose to hide the truth. And there are many people who have had very sobering and surreal experiences that leave no doubt that alien races are occupying the territory of Earth along with humanity. Then there are those who have a very whimsical, nonchalant attitude regarding inexplicable signs like crop circles and other alien sightings. They claim that "space brothers" are here to save the human race from itself.

By now, we must know enough about ourselves to recognize that there are no shortcuts to spiritual maturity and redemption. Anyone who has witnessed alien technology in action can see that we are now surrounded by digitized alien technology. It is right in front of our eyes, close to our bodies, and under our noses. This leaves no doubt that we have visitors. Regardless of whether those visiting our planet are here to help or to hinder the evolution of humanity, it would be wise to demand transparency as to what is really happening and to establish some important codes of conduct. After all—would any one of us be comfortable with having an uninvited stranger rummaging around in our kitchen cupboards, dresser drawers, and wallets?

If the current visitation of our world were really for the good of humankind, no hidden agenda of secrecy would be necessary. Since there has been little transparency until recently, it may be that there has been a wish not to be discovered as a threat to our species, which would jeopardize alien interests. Perhaps the visitors and the people helping them have determined that alien technology is worth paying any price for. If the visitors perceive that the human race is weak and incapable of being responsible stewards of our valuable and beautiful planet, the possible consequences dealt by artificial intelligence and deceptive alien probes could have enormous consequences.

For thousands of years, the various systems of managing and governing humanity have come and gone, one after the other. These systems have all been implemented with one single goal in mind: to suppress the Inner Teacher and wise Creator within the human Spirit and attempt to transform individuals into soulless slaves. It is true that currently a very dangerous form of usury is being implemented through government, the military, and technology in a potent attempt to fully manage the human race. However, in the Universe it is common knowledge that planetary difficulties and obstacles must be encountered and overcome as a part of the progressive experience and training provided for Soul development and evolvement.

ANTIGRAVITY TECHNOLOGY

People that have witnessed the antigravity technology used in alien spacecraft have no choice but to accept what they have seen with their own eyes and proceed with caution. Proceeding with caution is very prudent and highly recommended. The truth is that humanity has very little to no experience with "space brothers." Let us remember that these are material beings with material needs that may be different or similar to our own needs. We must also consider the fact that as the integrity of all people on Earth will vary, so too must alien races possess varying degrees of integrity—regardless of technological prowess. By now we are recognizing that the dissonant energies of alien technologies do not raise the physical, mental, and spiritual strength of human beings.

We know that antigravity technology has been on the modern human radar since at least the 1950s when George Adamski wrote the book *Flying Saucers Have Landed,* asserting the existence of other races on Earth beside our own. Since then thousands of sightings have been recorded and scores of books, articles, and societies have blossomed to explore the facts of this unexplained phenomenon. There are to date over 7,500 in-air pilot encounters with UFOs cataloged all over the world. However extraordinary these encounters may be, the pilots were grounded, fined, and imprisoned if they spoke out. Consequently many sightings are not reported. The media and governmental authorities have also suppressed dissemination of this important data.

Since the 1940s, seamen have observed UFOs appearing out of or disappearing into bodies of water. In 1998 a radar operator named Harry Jordan testified before a U.S. Senate UFO hearing that the UFO he observed while aboard the USS *FDR* in 1962 and 1965 was traveling at about 3,600 miles per hour at an altitude of 30,000 feet. Yet this ever-growing body of evidence has yielded little progress for the general public. Observing the labyrinthine edifice of technology that now surrounds us, it seems out of order that the space brothers are really here to help humanity and to balance the planet. If this were true, why then do we seemingly teeter on the threshold of destruction?

The science behind alien antigravity technology—subquantum kinetics—boasts a thrust-to-power ratio thousands of times greater than a jet engine and is unexplainable by using conventional physics or relativity theory. Antigravity technology is perceived as being capable of revolutionizing air travel and energy production. Human knowledge of antigravity technology dates back to the 1940s, and vehicles based on microwaves as a means of propulsion have been developed for the military and are being tested; yet this technology has been a closely guarded secret undisclosed to the general public until recently. Certain documents regarding alien contact with Earth are now in the public domain, and these have been made available with the intention of slowly acclimating the public. These documents prove that many of our so-called technological leaps have resulted from what we have learned from alien technology. Antigravity aircraft is supported and propelled by downward-directed microwave beams that are capable of exerting or repelling force on solid objects.

This would explain how crop circles are created and observed on underlying vegetation. The craft emit no engine noise or sonic boom. However, microwaves do cause severe headaches, nausea, vomiting, diarrhea, body pains, burns, cancer, hair loss, swelling, and numbness. The military has not yet been able to safely duplicate the performance of alien antigravity aircraft because the minerals used for this technology are not found on Earth.

However, the military has duplicated fiber optic technology first brought to us by aliens. It is a well-known fact that the first fiber optic wire was discovered in the wreckage of an alien spacecraft. This technology was developed by the American military and used to transform its communication systems. This technology allowed the military to be the first to implement the use of Internet and e-mail. It is important that people understand that the military is greatly influenced by bioincompatible alien technology without being fully aware of its ramifications. However, we are beginning to recognize that the delicacy of our evolutionary position hangs in the balance and depends on our ability to steward life on our home planet Earth.

WHERE DO WE STAND?

A great deal of information exists concerning the next phase of human development and awakening. This awakening must certainly include humanity's acknowledgment that it does not claim sole survivorship in the vastness of existence of intelligent life. We are at the embryonic stage of establishing where we stand and how we will sustain life upon our home planet within the context of acknowledging the multitude of worlds, galaxies, and universes as well as what they may contain.

The human Spirit is programmed to resonate with balance, and it has been subliminally known in the hearts and the minds of people that a great imbalance has been perpetrated by outside forces. And Earth indeed has both outsiders and insiders contributing to this current era of experience. The time span of influence and involvement by extraterrestrial interests on Earth may actually be measured in the thousands of years. However, the current era is unique in that it poses challenges like no other.

Now we have Echelon satellites that can eavesdrop on our phone conversations, e-mail, and faxes. And Tempest looks through walls to see what is on our computers and televisions; there are biochips, data mining, nanotechnologies, and street-cams to name just a few strange, new, so-called advances. It is very important for us to recognize that it is possible for beings to become adept at manipulating material existence without understanding spiritual connections. We know that people have made this particular mistake in regard to understanding both animal and plant life, and alien forces are not exempt from misunderstanding life forces.

We know that it is possible for things to possess intelligence and not be spiritually endowed with a Soul. It is entirely possible that certain alien entities may function with digital brains and have computer clocks for heartbeats. This renders them incapable of operating on a frequency of Light, Love, empathy, and feeling. Thought on an organic scale is a phenomenon; thought thinks as a self-perpetuating action. Thought on a technological scale is programmed and limited and will never advance beyond material existence. Here we discern that a technological overlord would present quite a dilemma for the human family. Nevertheless, approaching this dilemma by retreating into victim consciousness will not serve our evolving consciousness. Victim consciousness resonates at the lowest rate of human existence, which is below the possibility of conscious evolvement. It is incumbent upon humanity to empower itself, transcend the current and approaching events through education, and transmute them into a higher level of understanding.

When we apply the Universal Laws that balance and harmonize existence, a middle ground of experience can be achieved. It is learning to discern where in the process our experience is leading us that will allow us to attain wisdom. If there are no victims and only a group of spiritually mature aggressors to interact with, there can be no deceitful game. The transition of humanity from victim consciousness into self-mastery (self-empowerment) will result in a rise in the vibratory emanation of the planet and its inhabitants. The understanding and the application of simple Natural Laws will provide the passageway that leads to a new and sustainable future. If we pay attention and improve upon the present situation, what comes later will also be more hopeful as consciousness masters its domain, leading to the artistic and creative flowering of humanity, rather than the artificial intelligence of a technoculture and barren worlds.

Have I lost you? I hope not. This chapter would be impossible to share without being backed up by the actual experiences of the writer. People may not comprehend the urgency and the importance of the new cosmology that is upon us until they encounter a life-altering experience of their own. There is a big difference between believing and not believing in alien contact. Seeing for oneself—life as one knows it is altered forever, and those who have "seen" become members of a very different kind of club.

THE ALTERED PERSPECTIVE

Over the course of about twenty years' time, a series of inexplicable and interrelated events took place in my life; when these events were slowly unfolding, I did not understand them. By the fourth encounter the bigger picture began to emerge and become comprehensible. The first time that I witnessed what could only be described as something not of this Earth, I sadly realized from other stories concerning similar events that calling the local authorities would be pointless.

Of greater concern, though, was the reaction of those whom I trusted and attempted to confide in. Having inexplicable encounters with unexplained phenomenon greatly altered my perspective of life. It set me upon a more awakened path—at first I was afraid; then I had to contemplate these experiences and share them with those close to me. It was disappointing to discover that a wall of ignorance, fear, and denial discouraged a reasonable dialogue with most people. It was shocking to discover the various ways that people shield and shelter their psyches from the truth.

One day at a conference, I met a woman who was curious about UFOs. I shared with her a bit of my experience, and her response was interesting. She proclaimed that she felt she was protected from aliens because of her faith in Jesus. Does she really believe that she is guided by her faith and religion, while the rest of life has been spiritually denied? This type of human ignorance inhibits the ability of people to respond to the present, and the future, due to fixed ideas and beliefs. One of the best-documented cases of an ET encounter happened in 1967 to the Andreasson family in Massachusetts, a family "secure" in their Christian faith. Life will move forward whether people are open to learning or not. Theology represents the will and the work of the Divine in life. To recognize our work with the Divine we must be realistic in facing the issues as they really are; redemption is fueled by accomplishment. It is both apparent and concerning that very few people are able to go beyond fear. However, our work is to receive the messages of Creation, not bury our heads in the sands of illusion. It is necessary to summon the courage to understand the age in which we are living and contribute in a conscious way toward the solution of the world's problems and dilemmas.

SIX ENCOUNTERS

Until more people become aware of what is in their own backyards, allow me to share the following six encounters that I have experienced. Some people have discouraged me from telling these true stories. However, I feel that silence betokens consent. It would be a disservice to those who are able to accept what others cannot, or will not, accept. Perhaps this is not what people want to learn, but it is what people must learn if we are not to become biochipped slaves, subservient to alien technology.

Encounter Number One: A Strange Light

In October of the year 1995 I was one of a four-person crew embarking on a three-month sailing trip that left from the port of San Francisco. We steered left after sailing under the Golden Gate Bridge and began a trip that eventually took us through the Panama Canal and into the Caribbean. The *TeTahua,* a beautiful sixty-seven-foot wooden ketch, sailed far out into the Pacific, about four days from land. All sailors take up their watch throughout the day and night to guide the boat away from danger. The watch is especially important at night, when all but one of the crew is asleep. It was during one of my watches between 2:00 and 4:00 a.m. that all seemed clear on deck.

A glittering, star-filled night above—and below—the bioluminescent, phosphorescent sea critters glowed beneath the surface of the darkened waters of the ocean like sparkling stars in the night sky. The star-filled ocean and the star-filled sky bled into each other, and when the dolphins swam close to the boat at night, their swirling figure-eight movements were traced against the black water with illuminated agitation. These magical patterns had the look of milk, like the Milky Way. It was a stunning and inspiring example of the old adage, "As above, so below."

Yes—all was clear above deck, not another boat in sight. It was time to check the radar below deck for objects that may be far away. At the very moment that I had gone below and reached the inner cabin, the entire interior of the boat lit up in a potent flash of hot white light. It was as though a bomb went off nearby, and yet it did so without making a sound . . . then it was dark again, and our boat sailed onward as if nothing had happened. I quickly scrambled above deck to scan the horizon and saw nothing within sight—I looked to the bow . . . to the stern . . . portside and starboard, skyward and seaward. Nothing. I was struggling to absorb this inexplicable episode that happened so quickly that it was beyond my immediate understanding. The thought occurred to me that if had I not gone below deck a few seconds before the explosive flash, I might have been blinded by the potent flash and lost my eyesight; in fact my eyesight was affected after we returned.

Strangely, I did not understand what really happened until years later when I learned that there are alien bases submerged deep within the seas. These are underground bases that have also crept onto land and may be found in certain mountainous and desert areas. Although I experienced a very strange event that occurred only once on the trip far from landfall, I had no idea that one day it would become imperative to understand the reason for this experience.

Encounter Number Two: Whoosh!

It was August 11, 1999, and a very big astrological event in the night sky—the alignment of certain planets would form a grand cross, according to the astrologers and the stargazers. This night would yield yet another very strange and unusual event. I had fallen in love with a special piece of land and decided to camp out under the stars to become more acquainted with it. I drove a rental car into a semiremote area, not far from where a friend lived that I was visiting in Northern California. The beauty and wonder of the night sky was fully absorbed, and when it was time to sleep, I curled up in the backseat of the car, locked all of the doors, and fell fast asleep.

At some point around 3:00 or 4:00 a.m., I was awakened by an abrupt motion and realized that the whole car was shaking and it seemed to be turning. Oddly—I was not able to open my eyes . . . or move my body, and yet I was fully conscious and awake. It was as though my eyelids were glued shut and I was rendered helpless to operate my body at will during an experience that I was sure was going to destroy the rental car. I rationalized that it may be a bear attempting to break into the car—and then I heard a sound that was like a strong burst of air . . . Whoosh!

This was unlike any sound that I had ever heard. However, if you form the letter *O* with your lips and blow out hard, like you're blowing out trick birthday candles, you will get the idea. This episode did not last very long. I believe it all happened rather quickly. After the car stopped moving . . . and because it was dark, I decided to wait until morning to assess the damage. It was not long until the day dawned anew, and I timidly peered out of the back window of the car. I was surprised and delighted to see a dozen or so deer grazing nearby. After the deer moved on, I got out of the car, and to my utter disbelief and relief there was no damage, not so much as a dent on the car. Was it all a dream in the night? I know that it was not a dream; rather, it was more like a nightmare.

After I described this encounter to a friend, he said, "Gosh, weren't you scared?" I did not know how to answer him. Yes, I was afraid, and no, I was not afraid, because I did not know what to be afraid of. It was yet another inexplicable experience. Although I was unable to move my body or open my eyes, my mind remained acutely alert to every detail of this encounter. This was very strange and had never happened to me before. Has it happened to you? It was an unforgettable and very perplexing event—thankfully, I did not appear to be harmed in the process.

Encounter Number Three: No Blood

People that live in the countryside practicing animal husbandry have had times when their chickens are stolen and eaten by a bobcat, or a rancher may have a sheep or a goat disappear due to a pack of wolves. The animals are taken to satisfy the hunger of the wild, and though heartbreaking, this is nature's way.

One day this same scenario happened to a fine reddish-colored chicken of mine named Copper. She was grabbed right off our front porch by a bobcat, never to be seen again. It was later, in the same year that Copper disappeared, that after a brief absence we returned to our cabin the day after a full moon. The night before had been cold and bright with a slight sprinkling of snow. What greeted us that day was a strange occurrence that would mark the end of keeping chickens in the garden. There were six chickens left in the pen after Copper had been taken, along with a warrior rooster named Helmut. This rooster was a toughie, and if you came too close to the hens, Helmut made it risky business to do so. The hens were safe when Helmut was around, and we were always able to travel for a few days as long as the birds had enough food and water.

However, upon our return on this particular day, only one black hen was moving about in the pen. All of the other birds including Helmut were lifeless. Upon closer inspection, it became evident that something very bizarre had happened to the birds. All of them had been precisely and cleanly slashed with a razor-sharp instrument across the chest area, near the heart. The bodies of the chickens looked deflated as though all of the fluids had been carefully drained out of them. Their lifeless bodies were fully intact except for the fact that there was no blood or fluids at all. Anywhere.

The emotional trauma of this experience blurred the most important details of this event at the time. The razor-sharp single cut was to each bird's chest—between the neck and the heart. And why the complete lack of blood? Details such as these are so strange that they tend to be brushed aside when emotions become overwhelming and shock sets in. In time, however, all of these inexplicable events would become interrelated and the explanation would shed light on understanding a new challenge that faces life on planet Earth.

Encounter Number Four: Three Ships

It was on a chilly winter night with a full moon in 2009 that my questions to these perplexities were finally answered and my perception of life as I thought it to be was forever altered. I was in the country, relaxing in a small rustic cabin with only one candle alight. The moon shone brightly through the window near the bed I rested in, as I quietly watched a movie. Suddenly, out of the corner of my eye, there was an unusual movement combined with patterns of light that caused me to focus my eyes on a tall pine tree on the property. If I had looked away for only a second, I would not have witnessed a very shocking event. There—in close proximity to the cabin and the tall pine—were two smallish, circular spaceships dodging around the pine tree, moving like two hummingbirds jockeying for position . . . up . . . down . . . sideways . . . backward and forward, all in a quick flash. Then they disappeared in the direction of the open range of the foothills.

I was both stunned and energized at once. I grabbed the binoculars and ran down to the lookout point to observe where these spaceships had gone. To my utter amazement, the two had joined a third spaceship! The three spaceships had landed in a clearing over the ridge but could be seen within range of normal eyesight. The crafts were positioned in a small triangular clearing the shape of a perfect pyramid. With the aid of binoculars I was able to observe the undulating illumination of red, green, and yellow lights. The lights were clearly visible and alternately surrounded the circumference of each spacecraft. The crafts were not large, perhaps between fifteen and twenty feet in diameter. The design was the classic flying-saucer shape depicted many times in the various sources of media: a round disc with a smaller circular mound in the middle, then raised up gradually from the edges of the craft. The outer edges sported a series of alternating circular red, green, and yellow headlights spaced evenly apart, and these surrounded the entire circumference of the vehicle.

One could only guess that the beings inside these ships would also be somewhat smallish in stature; they could be no more than about three feet tall to fit in the center dome. However, the extraordinary feature that set these craft apart and made them unlike anything that people have ever seen is the antigravity propulsion that allows these crafts to move in any direction effortlessly in seconds flat, without making much more sound than a "whoosh!"

In the morning, two of the three craft remained in the clearing that was now visible in the forest. After a day, the craft had all left. It was distressing to conclude that there was really no county authority to report this to and no safe way to proceed with getting help in coming to mental and emotional terms with this event. The multitude of stories that have been altered, denigrated, and suppressed by governments, the military, and the media in relation to other forms of intelligent life are legendary. Unfortunately, this has paralyzed our understanding, acceptance, and much needed progress in the area of sighting and reporting unidentified flying objects.

As mentioned earlier, it quickly became clear that people do not welcome this kind of information. The range of emotions after sharing my experiences with friends and neighbors was once again disappointing. People that I confided in resorted to fear, denial, disbelief, arrogance, or the belief that all extraterrestrial life is beneficial and has our best interests at heart. In light of my experiences it would be ignorant and dangerous for anyone to believe that the intentions of these forces can be fully understood without a greater striving for knowledge and experience in this area.

Interestingly, as a child I often pondered that if Earthly tribes, states, and countries are subject to takeovers by forces of power, greed, and control by others—why then would Earth as a planet not be subject to larger outside forces seeking the same? Yet another example of "As above, so below."

We know that Earth has a long history of visitation; many of these stories have been documented in cultural world lore, and yet there are too many strange things that are happening now that do not bode well for humanity at this particular time in history. Hiding our heads in the sands of denial will not alter the reality or diminish the responsibility that humanity has to become consciously aware of the next phase that we will be required to not only understand but to act upon with integrity and Wisdom.

It is nature's way of saying, Wake up, humanity! Set down your weapons, forget your petty differences, and respect yourselves, respect your environment, and respect your inherent gifts! Unite as brothers and sisters, and go deeper, especially because the influences of these uninvited guests may be formidable.

Encounter Number Five: Skywatchers

In the autumn of 2010 a call came out of the blue from a friend whom I had not seen for several years. We spent the autumn equinox together in

San Francisco, and it was evident that the purpose of our reunion held more importance than a casual social call.

Greg was not feeling well, and he felt the urgent need to retreat to the country to focus on the greater needs of his health. Greg was fascinated when I pointed out the sight of the undulating colored lights looming high up in the night sky. They were unlike anything that he had ever seen before. Few people ever take notice of them, perhaps because the delicately flickering lights attempt to mimic stars. They are usually seen lower on the horizon in the northeast skies; however I have also seen them in the western skies while I am in San Francisco. These flickering stars reveal themselves as reddish-yellow undulating lights when observed through a good pair of binoculars. Once you actually witness the stunning technology of an alien craft you can spot their technology easily, and there is no question that these objects in the night sky are highly unusual. They exhibit the habit of moving closer to the Earth in the early morning hours between 2:00 and 4:00 a.m. when they can be observed to greater effect. These objects are stationary for weeks at a time but occasionally move away from the areas where they are most often seen.

It had been over a year since I had seen the two smaller craft dodge their way around the tall pine tree. This warm summer night, however, Greg and I gazed for hours at the stars, when he suddenly pointed to what he thought were two airplanes flying in tandem low in the northern sky. Quickly, and upon further inspection, we looked at each other and realized that it was two huge round soft amber-colored lights floating silently through the air in a slow, forward motion. The craft then began to gently drop straight down into the ground. It happened very quickly, and we were both in awe, realizing that this was a huge spacecraft, very different from the smaller craft that I spotted early in 2009. These sightings are very rare, and it was a first for both of us. We scrambled to the lookout point with the binoculars and did our best to locate where the craft had gone. We determined that the craft had disappeared below the hill where there is most likely an underground base.

When people have not had this particular experience, they are inclined not to give it much credence. After a while, Greg admitted that he would not have believed my stories of seeing spacecraft if he had not been witness to that night's event with his own eyes. It altered his perception of life, just as it had altered mine. We are now astute members of a club of "Skywatchers."

Encounter Number Six: Witnesses Abound

There was a special concert in our small town on the evening of this last encounter in 2011 . . . a night out to enjoy a wonderful musical performance by Ritchie Havens, an iconic and legendary folk singer from the 1960s. As he stood outside of his dressing room, I was blessed with a rare chance to chat with Mr. Havens, who had just performed in Alaska and was impressed by the environmental movement there. The intimate theater was a perfect backdrop for listening to the inspiring music and lyrics of Mr. Haven's songs.

It was about 11:00 p.m. as I drove the last stretch of winding road homeward after the concert. There were five or six cars following behind me when I saw something moving perhaps 150 feet above my car. I looked up and saw a small spaceship following along the same road that we were all driving on, but the spaceship was moving in the opposite direction of the flow of traffic. It was incredible that this sight was so obvious for all to see, and I almost drove off the road! I slowed down and looked behind me to see if the other cars had stopped. It was apparent that they had not seen what was traveling along above us. It was too late to pull over, stop the cars, and ask if they had seen what was already gone. It was interesting to note that no one seemed to notice what was happening, although it did happen very quickly.

A neighbor, who has seen the lights of these craft hovering far off in the night sky after I showed them to her, confided that she closes the window curtains and does not want to think about them. Another person said that she had enough problems in her life and that she could not be bothered with more difficulties involving UFOs. Others have advised me that this is a subject that should not be discussed. So there is a reason that people will not see, address, or confront what is important. It is imperative that this reality be accepted as a truth, shared, and better understood. Alien contact is a fascinating and very important subject. Why are people afraid rather than interested in the further study of the vast array of life that traverses our galaxy? What could be more pressing than accepting the responsibility that we have to unite as a race of people in order to sustain life on our planet and remain sovereign stewards? There has never been a greater challenge and a greater reason for unity in history. The New Cosmology must not be a taboo subject; cosmology is *you*-ology! Every day that passes without people putting cosmology on the front burner—to lobby congress and demand a planetary protocol for contact and submission of a bill of rights for planet Earth—brings extraterrestrials closer to subjugating and dominating the human race.

THE PHOENIX LIGHTS

The most documented modern mass sighting of otherworldly spaceships happened in the skies over Phoenix, Arizona, on March 13, 1995. An estimated ten thousand people witnessed the event that is referred to as "The Phoenix Lights." This sobering event was documented in the film called *The Phoenix Lights,* by Steve Lantz and Lynne Kitei, MD. The credible and courageous Dr. Lynne Kitei witnessed the event, filmed it, and wrote a book describing the experience. The book, *The Phoenix Lights: A Skeptic's Discovery That We Are Not Alone,* and the film revealed the intelligent, physical presence of huge black space vessels hovering in front of South Mountain in Phoenix, Arizona. The spaceships over Phoenix were massive, estimated at a mile long and wide, triangular in shape with amber-colored orbs that were attached to the ships. The amber orbs being three to six feet large and oval in shape, uniform and soothing looking, were described as mesmerizing and dimming on and off. The ships floated silently in a *V* formation close to the ground, floating effortlessly and cutting slowly through the sky.

For a short time, there was a media frenzy focused on this event that attracted international attention. Imagine the shock of the people when the mayor of Phoenix, Arizona, refuted the information and publicly denied the existence of the very spaceships seen by thousands of local citizens as well as captured on film! This must have been very frustrating and disheartening for the people of the city of Phoenix.

Two years later on January 22, 1997, there was a second sighting over Phoenix, this time with fewer spaceships. Anything that is not understood must be investigated and presented for public disclosure regarding the subject of unexplained phenomenon. When this posture is not forthcoming by the body of government, then the people must take action to learn about the next pivotal step in uncovering the truth, uncovering what is really happening at this time on Earth. Due to my own experiences with unexplained phenomenon, I have researched this subject extensively. Interestingly, encounters with alien beings or craft are most common near places with high electromagnetic fields such as military bases and power stations. These fields can be disturbed by alien craft, which in turn can cause widespread power outages.

PLANET SERPO

Perhaps the most stunning and mind-blowing case of human and alien contact is recorded in Len Kasten's *Secret Journey to Planet Serpo,* a book that describes a planned exchange between the U.S. government and other world officials with an alien race called Ebens. Based on actual government documents now available on the Internet, Kasten confirms that alien technology is used for conquest to enslave galactic citizens via a dictatorial, fascist Council of Governors that controls each action on the planet. The tenet of fascism binds all citizens into one organism, and the state becomes supreme while the individual amounts to little or nothing. The populace is molded into robotic, enslaved beings whose lives are structured with little leisure time and allowed no artistic and creative works. The current alien agenda to achieve the goals of the intervention on Earth extends to the year 5000 CE.

Government documents confirm that alien intelligent life does indeed exist and that their craft are infiltrating Earth's environment conducting various missions and that the abduction phenomenon is very real and crossbreeding has occurred. President Kennedy, who detested government secrecy, planned to make the true story of the mission to planet Serpo public, but he was assassinated five months before the first officially sanctioned landing at a Nevada military test site north of Las Vegas. On July 16, 1965, the alien visitors known as Ebens welcomed twelve human trained military personnel aboard a massive spacecraft for a ten-month journey to the alien home planet of Serpo. And only seven of the twelve aboard would return to Earth thirteen years later. Government officials from around the world were there to meet the returning alien craft, including officials from the Vatican, the United Nations, China, and Russia, as well as U.S. intelligence officers, a linguist, five U.S. military representatives, and four special guests—eighteen people in total. This group of people denied all members of the human race their fundamental rights regarding contact with alien nations.

THE ALLIES OF HUMANITY

We pray to God for little things, but God gives the great things.
THE ALLIES OF HUMANITY, BOOK TWO

There is a great deal of information on this subject. The most hopeful and useful body of work to prepare humanity for this new epoch in time is the previously mentioned work: *The Allies of Humanity* by Marshall Vian Summers. This body of work offers the most important and complete information available on Earth to help humanity remain a free race. It is an invaluable resource that must not be ignored if we are to become stronger and not weaker in meeting the challenges to come.

For centuries civilization has wondered what life in the Universe is like, with a mixture of hope and fear. And rightly so, because in the times to come we will learn that we have friends in the Universe and we have foes in the Universe as well. This is a reality that is not so different from our friends and foes on Earth. We align with our friends, and we protect ourselves from our foes. Just as the red flag of protection is waved in warning of earthly dangers, so too must we apply this ability when we are inexperienced and unprepared for encounters with the various races of other worlds.

There has been no other time in the history of the human race that has posed such a challenge, yet such a great opportunity. The challenge is that we are the vulnerable and blundering natives of a beautiful world that is rich in resources and positioned in a galaxy of barren worlds. Our explorations reveal that there are few worlds that support the evolution of intelligent life, or any life at all, such as the life on Earth. Yet here we are—destroying the environment that sustains us as quickly as possible without considering the delicacy of our evolutionary position.

It stands to reason that we could actually live in a very competitive universal environment considering the competition for resources occurring on our own planet. Competition for resources throughout a barren universe could very well be beyond our imagination. Those who have not experienced extraterrestrial phenomena would do well to leave these questions unanswered rather than projecting their own untried theories into the mix. The idea that a new experience is on the horizon makes people feel vulnerable and challenges their position. The truth is that the extraterrestrial intervention is upon us largely due to humanity's abuse of the Earth, which began with the advent and improper use of the atomic bomb—a bomb so destructive that the plumes and devastation from the force of it was visible from space. To further exacerbate the problem, we are broadcasting endless human conflicts, issues, and vulnerabilities out into space via satellites, which also assists the intervention to gain an advantage in manipulating our human struggles.

The Allies of Humanity have been acting as skywatchers for Earth, and because of their own experiences with certain alien races, they lovingly—and through great effort and risk—have offered humanity a very important perspective that we do not have.

Through the messages from the Allies of Humanity, we learn that it is humanity's present destiny to emerge into and to engage with a greater community of intelligent life in the Universe—and that this contact represents the greatest threshold that humanity has ever faced. The Allies of Humanity define what is really happening presently on Earth as an "extraterrestrial intervention." They claim that there are four arenas that the intervention is influencing: those in positions of power, a pacification program, manipulation of religious values, and the creation of new leadership.

The Allies of Humanity warn us that the "potentially beneficial" star races have all retreated from Earth in the face of this alien intervention, so it is the responsibility of the human race to either progress or regress in this serious situation. There is much to learn about this subject because we are woefully unprepared for the divisiveness of these clever alien visitors that are here in conquest for resources.

It is humanity's destiny to evolve into sovereign citizenship within the galaxy, the Universe, and the greater community of worlds by choosing responsible cosmic citizenship and applying the Universal Laws in daily experience both individually and collectively as a group. When the Law of Polarity draws together a group intention, it also repels those who choose otherwise. We are mainly empowered by applying the Natural Laws that allow for protection from the actions of the other groups that do not have our best interests at heart. The proper use of mental reasoning in relationship to Natural Law will allow humanity the freedom to steward its native home as we are surely destined to do.

It is painfully evident that there is a clandestine foreign presence on Earth and that the sightings all over the world signify our emergence into a greater community of worlds that will require the establishment of boundaries, or rules of engagement. In books two and three, the Allies of Humanity have given many insights as to why and how this must be achieved. And although all of the information cannot be given in this book, a brief outline will be useful until further study of the finer details may be achieved.

GALACTIC COMMERCE

Space travel encompasses a great deal of trade, both legal and illegal. The barter races involved with the intervention are intelligent, but they are not spiritual beings. Their power lies in mental persuasion and in technology. However, advanced technology cannot compare with the spiritual morality and ethics of the Soul. These intervening races have the ability to take over our world without firing a shot if humanity cannot unite and recognize that it must become self-sufficient and discrete if it is to maintain sovereignty of its native home. So far we have not met these criteria, and we have attracted a collective of galactic scavengers who require a great deal of resources to maintain their technology. In many cases, their worlds have been stripped bare. They view humanity as a resource, much like we view our domestic animals as resources. To gain a foothold and control, this collective of barterers need human assistance and cooperation because they cannot survive in our environment unless they interbreed.

The power of spiritual knowledge that lives in the Soul is what makes humanity valuable to the highly spiritual races in the Universe. The highly spiritual races are not the races that we are encountering at this time. The current intervention taking place on Earth is designed by technologically advanced races that do not possess Souls and do not acknowledge this inner spiritual trait in humanity; although they will cleverly claim that their religion is our religion and that they are our saviors. To prove this, they can project digital holograms to simulate the saviors that humanity expects.

Although there are many levels of advancement and beings represented in the billions of galaxies, the higher races will not become interlopers on Earth because they recognize that a fledgling humanity has the propensity to misuse and abuse power. They are enlightened Beings that do not need our resources. They have achieved peace, unity, and self-sufficiency. What more spiritually advanced races can do is send wisdom from afar with the hope that it will be received wisely, which is what they have done, as represented in the website based on the work of Marshall Vian Summers (www.alliesofhumanity.org).

There are angelic forces that oversee the affairs of evolution, and they have sent a preparation that is like no other that exists on Earth. This preparation will restore hope and is designed to help humanity to gain the advantage in the challenging times to come. If enough people educate themselves with the information that has been given us regarding life in the Universe, these interlopers will exert little power over the human race. If the majority refuses them, they must withdraw. There are rules of conduct in the Universe. What is happening here is not allowed unless the presence of these foreign races is accepted and welcomed. Some people are being seduced with power and riches and desire contact with alien races, mistakenly believing that the human race will be rescued from itself.

The intervention is no casual matter; it is the most serious threshold in human history. The alien collectives are resource scavengers but will present themselves as noble emancipators and peacemakers. Yet this is not the benevolent and charming ET that thoughtfully "phones home." While we are at war destroying each other, they wait to intervene with promises of peace and advanced technology, with the hope that a weakened human race will become dependent upon their technology. As we struggle with greater environmental and political instability, this technology will become more seductive. We must resist this exploitation. Interventions are always carried out for self-interest. What we know about these visitors so far is that they are probes sent out to explore the Universe for resources. They are programmed to a high degree of intelligence, yet have no free will to act independently outside of the program.

In his book *Grey Aliens and the Harvesting of Souls,* author Nigel Kerner claims that the alien visitors that we are encountering are assembled out of an unidentified biological tissue, interspersed with an amalgam of mercury and the finest gold wires. Because they have no nervous system, they have black eyes with no iris or dilating pupil. They have been described as resembling foul-smelling insects. The biotissue they are made of can hold and modulate our own DNA. However, because they are soulless, they are unable to reproduce, produce conscious feelings or intuition, or think beyond a limited digital program, so they are cloned. These robotlike creatures think digitally and function binomially, until remanufacture is required. They are programmed to act in clinically expedient ways to abduct and reshape natural indigenous life forms and obtain DNA. Their secret effort encompasses the hegemony and total control of entire planets. Currently, they are using tactics such as working toward erasing the capacity for memory in human beings, which means that the current technology adversely affects the brain's prefrontal cortex region associated with memory and higher function. They use light to move, intercept, and induce all kinds of experimental and scientific procedures, including digitally produced and projected holograms of illusion.

According to Nigel Kerner's book, a scientist from the Soviet Union has revealed a deeply covert cooperation between the United States, Russia, and China to supply new DNA for the visitor's ongoing clone and hybridization program. This could very well be possible, considering that each year millions of people are reported missing or are imprisoned. Only about one-third are ever accounted for, and now we observe that full planeloads of people are disappearing without a trace. China is well known for its abuse of Spiritual practitioners of Falun Gong, imprisoning them and harvesting organs while people are still alive. This does not seem so far-fetched considering that controlling people through mental manipulation is the brand of alien warfare. This also sheds light on the United Nations Agenda 21, which calls for designing all cities as controlled "human islands" and allowing only the elite to live in the countryside. In addition, the recent concern over the secret—and controversial—Trans Pacific Trade Agreement does not bode well for the people. The alien agenda functions with ruthlessness and has no conscience in following the master command: protect your individuality at all costs so that you may protect your creators at all costs.

The alien collectives have powerful command of the mental environment and will not hesitate to use it against people in unethical ways. The Allies of Humanity have warned of the darker side of the intervention. It involves the mental projection of messages to some religious communities—that all enemies of Christ must be eradicated if they cannot be saved. The propaganda will be spread far and wide that the Second Coming will require the cleansing of the human family. This would result in another deplorable inquisition and holocaust for humanity. The intervention does not care which religion they use, so long as they achieve the intended results.

Obviously, the human family must resist attacking people of various faiths, cultures, or nations if we are to achieve unity and peace. There is a great strength in unity, a unity that begins with becoming informed and aware.

THE CASE OF SINGAPORE

The darker side of the intervention is already visible on Earth for those who know what to look for. A case in point was documented in the January 2010 issue of *National Geographic* magazine in the small country of Singapore. In a few words, the article stated that Singapore's government-enforced model for its people is one of tightly controlled personal liberties. Technology, economic empowerment, and the idea that humanity can be trained and disciplined—but not improved—are additional tenets of Singapore's new ideology. They begin by tracking students into test-based groups at age ten. "Special" and "express" are the top tiers; "normal" is the path for those headed for factory and service work. Today, Singaporeans are not reproducing, so the country must depend on immigrants to keep the population growing. As one local put it, "Singapore is like a warm bath. You sink in, slit your wrists, your life blood floats away, but hey, it's warm." The highlight in life for Singaporeans is eating, and eating is the true national pastime and refuge. But even here, the food is tightly controlled and distributed in uniform food courts.

This description fits what the Allies of Humanity call the pacification program. It is part of a methodical process of enslavement used by the alien intervention. The yoke of the pacification program is necessary for the development of technology to be used to control people (the workforce) and keep them compliant. The pacification program will ultimately result in a nightmare scenario of slavery played out until dehumanization sets in. Yet the victim consciousness of enslavement and humanity's emergence into cosmic citizenship are two opposite poles of experience to be deliberately chosen and understood.

FLYING ROBOTS

Humanity will have to place limits on technology for obvious reasons and make it more biocompatible with Earth's environment. In the winter of 2012, I was tending to chores on a mildly misty day in San Francisco when a flying robot appeared over my head from the garden next door. It was small and moved like a hummingbird in all directions. I immediately recognized it as alien technology even though it was the first time I had seen such a tiny dronelike flying robot. A neighbor was responsible for flying the menacing thing via remote control and claimed that he had developed the software for it.

A short time later I was sent a chilling article from the Sunday, March 11, 2012, issue of the *Tampa Bay Times*. The article, called "Flying Robots Will Take Over the World," seemed to imply that soon human beings may have little control over the future of technology. The full-page article, complete with a large photograph of an insectlike drone, informs us that a new federal law has legalized the flight of these irritating invaders.

The Stanford University political scientist Francis Fukuyama gives us a forecast for where this technology is headed. Fukuyama claims, "Down the road are insect-sized drones that could be mistaken for a housefly or spider, which could slip in under a doorsill to record conversations, take photos, or even inject a lethal toxin into an unsuspecting victim. Systems such as these are under development by the Army's Micro Autonomous Systems and Technology (MAST) program, in partnership with a variety of corporations and university labs. Further into the future are nanobots, particle-sized robots that could enter people's bloodstreams or lungs."

As the technology gets easier to manufacture by amateurs, every country's criminals and drug cartels will more easily achieve unethical acts with drones. There could also be anonymity to their use that doesn't exist now with other technologies.

Although the article stated that the drones have raised privacy alarms, this will only be the tip of the iceberg. It will be just a matter of time before freedom itself will become a privilege of the past considering that the two key features of nanodrones are extreme agility and instant swarming. People that support, influence, and aid this technology may benefit financially for a short period of time for selling the human family down the river; but if some lose freedom, it is just a matter of time before we all lose our freedom.

A PASSION FOR FREEDOM

Each person possesses an intrinsic human dignity, an inner majesty, and a passion for freedom. The privilege to remain free is the basis of what the human race has fought and died for over eons of time. For humanity to continue on the intended path of its evolutionary destiny, the banner of freedom must be held high. Yet we can no longer afford to labor in the darkness of war's desolation. Rather, a great spiritual renaissance can better accomplish more tangible results.

Humanity shares a common spiritual sympathy that supports higher consciousness, authentic power, real knowledge, and spiritual presence in the world. Following it requires refinement and preparation. When religion is used to separate people and to incite war and hatred, then we must go beyond religion to the genuine guidance and power of spiritual knowledge, which is the real foundation for reality. It is the nucleus of God within each of us that patiently awaits the open and uncluttered mind to receive its great value. Having allies who support us, are on our side, and understand what is happening because they have been through it themselves is tremendously valuable. Anyone who is blessed with the support of a true ally knows only too well that it makes all the difference in the world.

Our problems are man-made—therefore, they can be solved by man.

JOHN F. KENNEDY, THIRTY-FIFTH PRESIDENT
OF THE UNITED STATES OF AMERICA

Declaration of Human Sovereignty

Regarding Contact with Extraterrestrial Nations and Forces

WE, THE PEOPLE OF EARTH, extend greetings to all races in the Greater Community of the Universe. We acknowledge our common heritage before the Creator of the Universe, both visible and invisible. We declare the planet Earth as Humanity's Planet of Genesis, our Home World, and our sacred inheritance. We pledge henceforth to sustain and preserve the Earth for all generations to come. We call upon all humanity to treat all races everywhere with wisdom and justice, here on Earth and throughout the Universe.

Fundamental Rights

We, the People of Earth, regard the need for freedom to be universal. Therefore, we hold that all individuals in all worlds are created equal and are endowed by the Creator with sacred and inalienable rights. Fundamental among these are the right to live as a free race on their Planet of Genesis, their Homeworld; the right of self-determination, self-sufficiency, and creative expression; the right to life without oppression; and the right to pursue in life a higher purpose and a higher calling that the Creator has provided to all.

Before the Greater Community of the Universe, we, the People of Earth, do now invoke these fundamental rights for ourselves and for our Homeworld, along with certain rights that naturally derive from them, including:

- The right of sovereignty. The people of Earth shall be self-governed and independent, neither subject to nor dependent upon any other authority. No extraterrestrial force shall contravene or abrogate the human sovereignty of this planet.
- The right of planetary sanctity. As our planet of Genesis, the Earth shall be free from extraterrestrial intervention, intrusion, interference, or exploitation, both mental and physical. No extraterrestrial force shall make close approach, or assume close orbit, or make any landing, or engage in trade, except openly and with the

expressed consent of the People of Earth achieved through a democratic means.

- The right of sanctity of biological and genetic material. No extraterrestrial power shall take, possess, or manipulate human biological or genetic material for any purpose whatsoever.
- The right of occupation. As the native people of the one known inhabited planet of this Solar System, we claim this Solar System as our sphere of influence. No extraterrestrial bases may be established on bodies or stations orbiting the Earth, or on other planets or bodies of this Solar System, except with the expressed consent of the People of Earth.
- The right of peaceful navigation. We claim the right to travel and explore within our Solar System without interference or restraint from extraterrestrial forces, and maintain the right to deny access to this Solar System by any extraterrestrial forces.

We, the People of Earth, consider it our rightful responsibility to assert and defend these fundamental rights, and to give and receive aid consistent with these rights. In the case of any dispute with extraterrestrial forces, the burden of proof of innocence shall fall on those who are not native to Earth.

The Assessment

When in the course of their evolution it becomes necessary for the native people of a planet to unite, to transcend the conflicts and differences that have separated them from one another, and to assume among the powers of the Universe a separate and equal sovereignty, a respectful consideration of that sovereignty requires that they declare the causes which impel them to this present course of action.

Although the Earth has undergone a long history of extraterrestrial visitation, the current situation is that the People of Earth are now suffering the effects of a global extraterrestrial intervention into human affairs. This intervention employs a strategy of deception, manipulation, and exploitation, the goal of which is control over humanity, which will result in the loss of human freedom and self-determination. It is now the sacred right and duty of the People of Earth to oppose, resist, and repel this extraterrestrial intervention, to declare and defend our sovereignty, our freedom, and our independence from all extraterrestrial forces.

Let these violations be considered by those supporting the cause of freedom throughout the Greater Community:

- Intervening extraterrestrial forces have refused to openly disclose and reveal the nature and intent of their activities on and around Earth. This extraterrestrial presence is clandestine, covert, uninvited, and unapproved by the People of Earth. These extraterrestrial forces have concealed their own identity, their political or economic alliances and allegiances, as well as the authorities and powers that they serve.

- As is becoming increasingly apparent from their actions, extraterrestrial forces intend to exploit the Earth, its resources, and its people, and are engaged in a systematic program of colonizing humanity into a subservient client state to be ruled by agents of these extraterrestrial forces. The extraterrestrial intervention and occupation seeks commercial gain, economic power, and the strategic advantage offered by this world in relation to other worlds.

- Extraterrestrial forces have repeatedly and with impunity violated national and international laws of the Earth's people. These offences, which still continue today, have included violation of restricted airspace; abduction and transportation of humans without their consent; murder, rape, torture, sexual abuse, interbreeding with humans, and cruel experimentation; theft and trade of human biological and genetic materials; theft and trade of Earth's natural resources; covert mental and psychological influence; mutilation of humans and animals; tampering with and disabling of military defense systems; and clandestine infiltration into human society.

- Extraterrestrial forces have secretly negotiated treaties and agreements with human individuals and groups, without the informed consent of the People of Earth.

- Extraterrestrial forces have systematically attempted to persuade and mislead humans through extending false hopes and promises of wealth, power, and protection; rescue from planetary catastrophe;

membership in a "galactic federation"; and spiritual salvation and enlightenment.

- Extraterrestrial forces have exploited and exacerbated human conflicts to serve their own ends.
- Extraterrestrial forces have been disempowering humanity by leading us to believe that we can only survive with their help and their advanced technology, thus fostering our complete dependence upon them and denying our ability to ensure our own survival.

Demands and Declarations

ACCORDINGLY, WE, THE PEOPLE OF EARTH, do hereby declare all previously existing agreements and treaties between any human government, group, or individual and any extraterrestrials to be forthwith null, void, and permanently suspended. We demand that any such previously existing treaties be fully and publicly disclosed. Any future agreements or treaties between human governments, groups, or individuals and extraterrestrials must be negotiated only with the full consent of the People of Earth, publicly and openly expressed by an international democratic body representing the nations and peoples of Earth.

We demand that all extraterrestrials now cease all operations and activities and immediately vacate and depart from the Earth and its surroundings including the Sun, Earth's Moon, and all planets of this Solar System. This includes vacating any natural or artificial satellites, as well as all space within the Solar System.

We demand that all extraterrestrial organizations that have established or operated bases on Earth, its Moon, or anywhere else within this Solar System, dismantle these bases and fully disclose their nature.

We further demand that all living humans who are now in custody of extraterrestrials be returned immediately in good health; further, we demand a full accounting of all humans who have been taken or held by extraterrestrials, including those who have died in captivity. In addition, we demand that all human biological or genetic materials taken from any individuals be accounted for and destroyed, and their intended use be identified. Any devices implanted in living individuals must be identified so that they may be safely removed.

We demand full public disclosure of the purpose and details of the extra-terrestrial hybridization program, including the location, identity, and activities of all living human-extraterrestrial hybrids, whether on Earth or elsewhere.

Be it known throughout the Universe that from this time forward, extraterrestrials may only enter our Solar System, approach our Earth, fly in our skies, set foot on our soil, or enter our waters with explicit consent of the People of Earth.

We, therefore, do solemnly declare that the People of Earth are and should be a free and independent people; that all humans are hereby absolved from all allegiance to extraterrestrial powers, and that all political and economic connections between them and the People of Earth are totally dissolved; that as a free and sovereign race in the Greater Community of the Universe, we assume full power within this Solar System to conclude peace, levy war, contract alliances, establish commerce, and to undertake all other actions which a sovereign planetary race might rightfully and ethically do.

Concluding Statement

LET IT BE UNDERSTOOD that in making this Declaration of Human Sovereignty, we, the People of Earth, affirm our future and destiny as a free race within a Greater Community of intelligent life. We recognize that we are part of this Greater Community and that we are destined over time to encounter many different races from beyond our world.

To them and to all others, we hereby declare that our intention is not conquest or domination in space. We declare that the rights and privileges that we affirm here for ourselves, we also affirm for all races of beings whom we might encounter.

In making our Declaration of Human Sovereignty & Freedom, we proclaim our rights, responsibilities, and privileges as a free race in order that we may pursue greater unity, peace, and cooperation within the human family without unwanted or unwarranted intrusion and interference by any outside nation or force from the Greater Community. We make this proclamation as an expression of our divine right and honorable intent for the human family and for all races in the Universe who seek to be free.

BIBLIOGRAPHY

Ambrose, Kala. *The Awakened Aura: Experiencing the Evolution of Your Energy Body*. St. Paul, Minn.: Llewellyn, 2011.

Anderson, Christopher. *The Day Diana Died*. New York: Dell, 1998.

Argüelles, José. *The Mayan Factor: Path Beyond Technology*. Rochester, Vt.: Bear and Co., 1987.

Babbitt, S. Edwin. *Principles of Light and Color*. New York: Citadel Press, 1980.

Banynes, C. F., and Richard Wilhelm, trans. *The I Ching: The Book of Changes*. Princeton, N.J.: Princeton University Press, 1950.

Baylock, Russell L. *Exitotoxins: The Taste That Kills*. Santa Fe, N. Mex.: Health Press, 1997.

Bohm, David. *Causality and Chance in Modern Physics*. Philadelphia: University of Pennsylvania Press, 1971.

Braden, Greg. *Awakening to Zero Point: The Collective Initiation*. Bellevue, Wash.: Radio Bookstore Press, 1993.

Capra, Fritjof. *The Tao of Physics: An Exploration of the Parallels between Modern Physics and Eastern Mysticism*. Boulder, Colo.: Shambhala, 1975.

Cerminara, Gina. *The World Within*. Virginia Beach, Va.: A.R.E. Press, 1985.

Cole, Natalie, and David Ritz. *Love Brought Me Back: A Journey of Loss and Gain*. New York: Simon and Schuster, 2010.

Cusack, Margaret F. *The Black Pope: History of the Jesuits, What Rome Teaches*. 1896.

———. *The Nun of Kenmare*. 1888.

Dossey, Larry. *Healing Words: The Power of Prayer and the Practice of Medicine*. New York: Harper, 1993.

Embracing the Rainbow. Carson City, Nev.: Bridger House Publishing, 1999.

Falone, John J. *Genius Frequency*. Virginia Beach, Va.: Global Light Network, 2000.

Fowler, Raymond E. *The Andreasson Affair, Phase Two: The Continuing Investigation of a Woman's Abduction by Alien Beings*. Newberg, Oreg.: Wildflower Press, 1994.

———. *The Andreasson Affair: The True Story of a Close Encounter of the Fourth Kind*. Pompton Plains, N.J.: Career Press, 2015.

Gerber, Richard. *Vibrational Medicine: The #1 Handbook of Subtle Energy Therapies*. Rochester, Vt.: Bear and Co., 2001.

Goodman, Amy. *Breaking the Sound Barrier*. Chicago: Haymarket Books, 2010.

Hirsh, James S. *Willie Mays: The Life, the Legend*. New York: Simon and Schuster, 2010.

Hurtak, J. J. *The Book of Knowledge: The Keys to Enoch*. Los Gatos, Calif.: Academy for Future Science, 1977.

Ivereigh, Austin. *The Great Reformer: Francis and the Making of a Radical Pope*. New York: Henry Holt and Co., 2014.

Jensen, Bernard. *Iridology: The Science and Practice in the Healing Arts*. Vol. 2. San Marcos, Calif.: Bernard Jensen Intl., 1982.

Karim, Ibrahim. *Back to a Future for Mankind: BioGeometry*. Egypt: BioGeometry Consulting Ltd., 2010.

Kasten, Len. *Secret Journey to Planet Serpo: A True Story of Interplanetary Travel*. Rochester, Vt.: Bear & Co., 2013.

Kerner, Nigel. *Grey Aliens and the Harvesting of Souls: The Conspiracy to Genetically Tamper with Humanity*. Rochester, Vt.: Bear and Co., 2010.

Kuthumi. *Studies of the Human Aura*. Colorado Springs, Colo.: Summit University Press, 1975.

Lange, Sente. *Enne: Please Continue to Write*. Book 1. West Germany: Senta Lange, 1984.

Langley, Noel. *Edgar Cayce on Reincarnation*. Virginia Beach, Va.: A.R.E. Press, 1967.

LaViolette, Paul. *Secrets of Antigravity Propulsion: Tesla, UFOs, and Classified Aerospace Technology*. Rochester, Vt.: Bear and Co., 2008.

Leir, Roger. *Alien Implants: Whitley Strieber's Hidden Agenda*. New York: Dell, 2000.

L'Esperance, Carrie. *The Ancient Cookfire: How to Rejuvenate Body and Spirit through Seasonal Foods and Fasting*. Rochester, Vt.: Bear and Co., 1998.

———. *The Seasonal Detox Diet: Remedies from the Ancient Cookfire*. Rochester, Vt., Healing Arts Press, 2002.

Letcher Lyle, Katie. *The Complete Guide to Edible Wild Plants, Mushrooms, Fruits, and Nuts: How to Identify and Cook Them.* Guildford, Conn.: Falcon Press, 2010.

Manjoo, Farhad. "Flying Robots Will Take Over the World." *Tampa Bay Times*, March 10, 2012. www.tampabay.com/news/perspective/flying-robots-will-take-over-the-world/1218987

Marciniack, Barbara. *Bringers of the Dawn: Teachings from the Pleiadians.* Rochester, Vt.: Bear and Co., 1992.

Martin, Joel, and Patricia Romanowski. *We Don't Die: George Anderson's Conversations with the Other Side.* New York: Berkley Publishing Group, 1988.

Martino, Regina. *Shungite: Protection, Healing, and Detoxification.* Rochester, Vt.: Healing Arts Press, 2014.

Montgomery, Ruth. *A Gift of Prophecy: The Phenomenal Jeane Dixon.* New York: William Morrow, 1965.

Moss, Robert. *Dreamways of the Iroquois: Honoring the Secret Wishes of the Soul.* Rochester, Vt.: Destiny Books, 2005.

Newton, Michael. *Destiny of Souls: New Case Studies of Life between Life.* St. Paul, Minn.: Llewellyn, 2000.

———. *Journey of Souls: Case Studies of Life between Lives.* St. Paul, Minn.: Llewellyn, 1996.

Orloff, Judith. *Second Sight: An Intuitive Psychiatrist Tells Her Extraordinary Story and Shows You How to Tap Your Own Inner Wisdom.* New York: Three Rivers Press, 2010.

Pert, Candace. *Molecules of Emotion: Why You Feel the Way You Feel.* New York: Simon & Schuster, 1998.

Phelps, Eric Jon. *Vatican Assassins: "Wounded in the House of My Friends."* Tehachapi, Calif.: Halcyon Unified Services, 2001.

Rain, Mary Summer. *Earthway: A Native American Visionary's Path to Total Mind, Body, and Spirit Health.* New York: Pocket Books, 1990.

Rich, Mark. *Energetic Anatomy: An Illustrated Guide to Understanding and Using the Human Energy System.* Dallas, Tex.: Life Align, 2004.

Richards, Keith. *Life.* New York: Little Brown and Company, 2010.

Sagan, Samuel. *Entity Possession: Freeing the Energy Body of Negative Influences.* Rochester, Vt.: Destiny Books, 1997.

Sams, Jamie, and David Carson. *Medicine Cards: The Discovery of Power through the Ways of Animals.* Rochester, Vt.: Bear and Co., 1999.

Sechrist, Elsie. *Dreams: Your Magic Mirror.* Virginia Beach, Va.: A.R.E. Press, 1995.

Shumsky, Susan G. *Exploring Auras: Cleansing and Strengthening Your Energy Field*. Pompton Plains, N.J.: New Page Books, 2006.

Siblerud, Robert. *The Science of the Soul: Explaining the Spiritual Universe*. Vol. 3, *Sacred Science Chronicles*. Wellington, Colo.: Sacred Science Publications, 2000.

Smith, Patti. *Just Kids*. New York: HarperCollins, 2010.

Spalding, Baird T. *Life and Teaching of the Masters of the Far East*. Vol. 1–5. San Francisco: California Press, 1924. Marina del Rey, Ca.: DeVorss and Co., 1955.

Stearn, Jess. *Edgar Cayce on the Millennium*. New York: Warner Books, 1998.

Stone, Kevin, R. "Sex and the Olympics: Why Gender Shouldn't Matter to Sports Medics." The Stone Clinic, January 26, 2014. www.stoneclinic.com/blog/2014/1/27/sex-and-olympics.

Summers, Marshall Vian. *The Allies of Humanity*. Books 1, 2, and 3. Boulder, Colo.: New Knowledge Library, 2001, 2005, and 2012.

Sweet, Victoria. *God's Hotel: A Doctor, a Hospital, and a Pilgrimage to the Heart of Medicine*. New York: Riverhead Books, 2012.

Talbot, David. *Brothers: The Hidden History of the Kennedy Years*. New York: Simon and Shuster, 2007.

———. *The Season of the Witch: Enchantment, Terror, and Deliverance in the City of Love*. New York: Simon and Shuster, 2012.

Tucker, Jim B. *Return To Life: Extraordinary Cases of Children Who Remember Past Lives*. New York: St. Martin's Press, 2013.

The Urantia Book: Revealing the Mysteries of God, the Universe, Jesus, and Ourselves. Chicago: Urantia Foundation, 1955.

van Gelder Kunz, Dora. *The Personal Aura*. Wheaton, Ill.: Quest Books, 1991.

Walker, Dael. *The Crystal Book*. Sunol, Ca.: The Crystal Co., 1983.

Webster, Richard. *Aura Reading for Beginners: Develop Your Psychic Awareness for Health and Success*. St. Paul, Minn.: Llewellyn, 1998.

Wetzl, Joseph. *The Bridge over the River: After Death Communications of a Young Artist Who Died in World War I*. London: Anthroposophic Press, 1974.

Wilber, Ken, ed. *The Holographic Paradigm and Other Paradoxes: Exploring the Leading Edge of Science*. Boulder, Colo.: Shambhala, 1982.

Williams, Lisa. *The Survival of the Soul*. Carlsbad, Calif.: Hay House, 2011.

Winternitz, Helen. *A Season of Stone: Living in a Palestinian Village*. New York: Atlantic Monthly Press, 1991.

RESOURCES

For retreat and workshop information you can visit the author's website **www.carrielesperance.com.**

The following are resources and websites that can support further study of human development. They are meant to prepare and inspire you to pursue further education.

ANIMAL ADVOCACY AND EDUCATION

- **ASPCA, www.ASPCA.org**
  This organization collects donations for food, shelter, and love in support of homeless animals.

- **BlueVoice, www.bluevoice.org**
  This is another organization working to save whales and dolphins and protect the oceans. They also provide information on persistent organic poisons (POPS) affecting dolphins and humans.

- **Sea Shepherd, www.seashepherd.org**
  Learn about environmental activism to save whales and other sea creatures and to defend ocean sanctuaries.

BIOSIGNATURES AND EMF FREQUENCIES

- **BioGeometry, www.BioGeometry.com**
  Dr. Ibrahim Karim offers information about the science of BioGeometry, as well as products and services to bring the benefits of the energy-balancing principles of BioGeometry into your home and life.

- **Brane Power, www.brane-power.com**
  Source for Spiritcare amulets of quantum crystal radio frequency tuned to the Shumann harmonic. These amulets help the brain to access the alpha and theta ranges of frequency and enhance dream recall and meditation.

- **Crystal Way, www.crystalway.com, and Karizma, Karizma1@att.com**
  Two shops based in San Francisco that carry high quality shungite products. This stone can be used to balance EMF radiation among other qualities. Crystal Way also has a Healing Center with a variety of healing modalities.

- **Dr. Royal Rife, www.rife.org**
  This site provides information on Dr. Royal Rife's research and work history including information on wave frequency technology.

- **Lotus Guide Directory for Healthy Living, www.YouTube.com/ LotusGuide**
  The "Earthcalm Interview" with Jean Gallick discusses the effects of EMF waves (there are also many other useful interviews on this site on various relevant subject matters).

- **Research Center for Wireless Technology, www.EMFnews.org**
  Here you can find current research and information on EMF waves.

- **Shungite Protection and Healing, www.shungite-protection-and -healing.com**
  The best selection and most reliable source for shungite products from author Regina Martino's shop in Paris. This stone can be used to balance EMF radiation among other qualities.

- **Vesica Institute for Holistic Studies, www.Vesica.org**
  This institute offers trainings on BioGeometry, holistic health, and more, as well as offering biosignatures for use on cell phones and computers and providing current information on Dr. Karim's work.

ENVIRONMENTAL AND SUSTAINABILITY ADVOCACY AND EDUCATION

- **350, www.350.org**
  This organization, cofounded by author Bill McKibben and a group of university students, is a global grassroots movement working to hold world leaders accountable for climate change and solutions.

- **Center for Biological Diversity, www.biologicaldiversity.org**
This organization has a plethora of programs from protecting endangered species to studying population growth to create a more sustainable lifestyle. They are also undertaking nonviolent, direct action against climate change, oil drilling, and tar sands development.

- **Earthship Biotecture, www.earthship.com**
This company uses alternative methods of building with recycled resources to create more sustainable homes—Earthships—and has an academy for learning the trade.

- **Environmental Cleanup Coalition, www.gyrecleanup.org**
Learn about the Pacific Ocean Gyre garbage patch and how you can help clean it up. This organization is working toward promoting solutions to remove plastic and chemicals from the oceans without damaging marine life, as well as teaching water stewardship. The current engineering challenge and educational campaign is focused on crowd sourcing the best ideas worldwide. It will take a world of people to make a difference, and everyone can do something to shift the tides of destruction on the oceans of Earth.

- **GeoEngineering Watch, www.geoengineeringwatch.org**
This website provides education on the dangers of geoengineered climate change as well as ways to get involved in the cause.

- **Hempstead Project H.E.A.R.T., www.hempsteadprojectheart.org**
This project promotes awareness of industrial hemp as a green resource and alternative to cutting down forests.

- **Peaceful Uprising, www.peacefuluprising.org**
This is another organization that supports nonviolent, direct action against climate change, oil drilling, and tar sands development.

- **The Primary Water Institute, www.primarywaterinstitute.org**
U.S. Geological Survey maps and education regarding how water is made deep within the Earth. They will come to properties to locate water resources.

- **Water.org, www.water.org**
This website provides education on and opportunities to get involved with safe water and sanitation solutions.

- **Quest, www.questscience.org**
  Biosolutions and eco-alternatives for our Earthly needs.

EXTRATERRESTIALS AND OTHER OCCULT FORCES

- **Allies of Humanity, www.alliesofhumanity.org**
  The most important source for accessing information and books regarding alien contact. *The Allies of Humanity,* books 2 and 3, are currently among the most important books on the planet for understanding what is really happening.

- **Declaration of Human Sovereignty, humansovereignty.org**
  Here you can find the Declaration of Human Sovereignty Regarding Contact with Extraterrestrial Nations and Forces and join the call to action.

- **MUFON, www.mufon.com**
  Report a UFO and UFO activity. Order the latest books regarding contact. Support MUFON by donating to their dedicated work involving alien contact.

- **Phoenix Lights Network, www.thephoenixlights.net**
  This site is a companion to the *Phoenix Lights* book and documentary, which follows Dr. Lynne Kitei's journey from skeptic to believer while investigating extraterrestrial and UFO history.

- **Serpo, www.serpo.org**
  This is Len Kasten's website on government documents released to the public regarding interplanetary travel and alien contact.

FOOD AND HEALTH PRODUCT RESOURCES AND EDUCATION

- **Campaign for Safe Cosmetics, www.safecosmetics.org**
  A personal care product and safety guide with in-depth ingredient information on toxic cosmetics, lotions, toothpaste, soap, shampoo, and others, and offers safe alternatives.

- **Center for Food Safety, www.centerforfoodsafety.org**
  Here you can find a wealth of information on food safety including a "Shoppers Guide to Avoiding Genetically Engineered Foods."

- **Dr. Schulze's, www.herbdoc.com**
  Dr. Schultz's herbal tea blends are outstanding, not treated with pesticides and delicious.

- **Futurebiotics, www.futurebiotics.com**
  This company is a great source for natural supplements, beauty products, and cleansing products.

- **Global Culture, www.globalculture.us**
  This agency certifies organic farms based on USDA National Organic Program Regulations and helps promote sustainable practices in agriculture and food production.

- **Guide to Less Toxic Products, www.lesstoxicguide.ca**
  This is a great source for safe alternative formulas for most home and personal care products.

- **Native Seeds, www.nativeseeds.org**
  This company provides heritage seeds and nutrient rich forms of corn to grow, as well as information and educational opportunities to learn more about the food we grow and eat.

- **Purium Health Products, www.puriumcorp.com**
  Among the products this company provides are high quality green powders based on Ann Wigmore's philosophy for supporting health. The Apothe-Cherry contains melatonin to help promote sleep, and the company has excellent quality spirulina, chorella, and kamut. If you go to **www.mypuriumgift.com** and enter the code yellowood, you can save up to $50.00 on your purchase.

HEALTH CARE RESOURCES

- **Agency for Toxic Substances and Disease Registry, www.atsdr.cdc.gov**
  The Agency for Toxic Substances and Disease Registry responds to and educates on public health concerns regarding harmful exposures and diseases related to toxic substances.

- **Doctor Yourself, www.doctoryourself.com**
  Here Andrew Saul provides an alternative to Western health care, explaining the ins and outs of health homesteading, taking care of your own health.

- **National Kidney Foundation, www.kidney.org**
  The National Kidney Foundation offers free screenings all around the country. There are more than 50,000 different chemical processes for manufacturing plastics alone, and the kidneys are one of the important filtering organs of the blood to be tested for toxins.

- **Paul Craig Roberts Institute for Political Economy, www.paulcraig roberts.org**

  Here you can read several of Roberts's articles on Obamacare (and myriad other topics).

- **Registry for a Cause, www.RegistryForACause.org**

  This registry is founded by Suzanne Agasi, the originator of the ClothingSwap. It is for people with cancer and other life-changing health crises who need help with daily challenges. Register for help and donate services here.

NEWS, RADIO, AND MEDIA OUTLETS

- **Conversations with Michael Stone, www.arewelistening.net**

  Access critical documents and join a global people's movement respecting the rights of Mother Earth.

- **Democracy Now!, www.democracynow.org**

  This site provides free speech radio and news reporting of world events not covered in the mainstream media.

- **Independent Media Center, www.indymedia.org**

  This is a collective of independent media centers and journalists reporting unfiltered, real-time coverage from the people's perspectives.

- **Making Contact, www.radioProject.org**

  An alternative to mainstream media, this media outlet addresses social and environmental issues, as well as grassroots solutions and advocates for action.

- **Moyers & Company, www.billmoyers.com**

  This site reports on current affairs and discussions outside mainstream media.

SOCIAL JUSTICE

- **Brennan Center for Justice, www.BrennanCenter.org**

  Support prison reform. Join big city police chiefs, sheriffs, and prosecutors coast to coast pushing to reform our dysfunctional prison system.

- **Citizen Soldier Support Program, www.citizensoldiersupport.org**

  This organization provides behavioral and mental health support for Reserve and National Guard service members and veterans who have returned from active duty.

- **Democracy Is For People, www.democracyisforpeople.org**
  A people's movement to help fight big money politics. Learn about ways to challenge government policies.

- **Encore, www.encore.org**
  This organization invests in and provides opportunities for inventive, resourceful, doggedly resilient people age sixty-plus who are changing the world.

- **Equal Justice Initiative, www.eji.org**
  Brian Stevenson's website to free innocent people who have been incarcerated, many of whom suffer from mental illness.

- **Idle No More, www.idlenomore.com**
  This is a movement led by Native Americans in Canada to reclaim their sovereignty and protect the environment and the people who live in it.

- **Nuclear Age Peace Foundation, www.wagingpeace.org**
  This organization is working toward a world free of nuclear weapons.

- **Paul K. Chappell, paulkchappell.com**
  Chappell is an Iraq war veteran and author who now works as the peace leadership director for Nuclear Age Peace Foundation and is a strong advocate for peace. You can find his poignant books on his website.

- **The Post Sustainability Institute, www.postsustainabilityinstitute .org**
  This institution, created in tandem with Rosa Koire's *Behind The Green Mask*, reveals that the U.N. plan for Agenda 21 is backed by supposedly green nonprofits and corporations who are considered shareholders. The institute is working to stop the progress of Agenda 21.

- **United Nations Sustainable Development, sustainabledevelopment .un.org/content/documents/Agenda21.pdf**
  Here you can read the 350 pages of Agenda 21, of intended restrictions on land rights, water rights, and resources. The UN plans to concentrate people in populated cities (human islands) of high density where a community of unelected officials has rights over the individual. Learn about the transfer of power to megacities and megaregions with restrictions on rural areas.

- **Veterans for Peace, www.veteransforpeace.org**
  This is a global collaboration of military veterans and allies sharing their experiences and working toward a culture of peace.

- **Women Rising Radio, www.womenrisingradio.com**
  This radio program profiles women in leadership who are working for peace and human rights, advocating for the environment, and more.

SPIRITUAL EDUCATION

- **The Bible's Buried Secrets, www.pbs.org/wgbh/nova/ancient/bibles -buried-secrets.html**
  This PBS *Nova* follows a scientific journey to the origins of the Bible.

- **Clarevision School, www.clairvision.org**
  School for learning meditation at the highest level. Dr. Samuel Sagan's work also encompasses clearing lower astral entity energies.

- **The New Message from God, www.newmessage.org**
  Here Marshall Vian Summers delivers a new spiritual revelation for our time that encompasses how to best navigate the great waves of change sweeping planet Earth.

- **Secrets of the Vatican, www.pbs.org/video/2365187642**
  This is a PBS *Frontline* special on the Vatican and the Catholic Church.

OTHER USEFUL RESOURCES

- **The Indigo Children, www.Indigochild.com**
  This is a companion to the books *The Indigo Children*, *An Indigo Celebration*, and *The Indigo Children Ten Years Later*. It explores the fifth wave of societal change predicated on what happens within ourselves on a spiritual level through children with a new expanding consciousness.

- **Kala Ambrose, www.exploreyourspirit.com**
  This is Kala Ambrose's website for reading the Human Aura.

- **Meetup, www.meetup.com**
  This is a forum for starting or joining local groups for pretty much any activity or subject matter you're interested in.

- **Restorative Communication, www.restorativecommunication.org**
  Tools for heart-based communication skills rather than learned mental projection, avoidance, and creating enemies by blaming others or taking a defensive stance.

INDEX